THE GURUS, THE YOUNG MAN,

AND ELDER PAISIOS

Elder Paisios of Mount Athos, Greece (1924–1994).

The Gurus, the Young Man, and Elder Paisios

By Dionysios Farasiotis

Translated and adapted by Hieromonk Alexis (Trader),
Holy Monastery of Karakallou, Mount Athos

Edited by Philip Navarro

ST. HERMAN OF ALASKA BROTHERHOOD
2011

Originally published in Greek as *Oi gourou, o neos, kai o Gerontas
Paisios* (Thessaloniki: Athanasios Rakovalis, 2001). Inquiries regarding the Greek edition may addressed to rakovalis@fastmail.net.
Correspondence with the author may be addressed to
dionisiosfarasiotis@in.gr.

All other correspondence may be addressed to:

St. Herman of Alaska Brotherhood
P. O. Box 70, Platina, California 96076 USA

website: **www.sainthermanpress.com**
email: stherman@stherman.com

First English edition: November 2008.
Second printing: July 2009.
Third printing: November 2011.
Printed in the United States of America.

Front cover: Stavronikita Monastery, Mount Athos, Greece.
Photograph by the author, July 16, 2004.
Back cover: Mount Athos. Photograph by Evgeni Dinev.

Publishers Cataloging in Publication

Farasiotis, Dionysios.
    The gurus, the young man, and Elder Paisios / by Dionysios Farasiotis; trans-
lated and adapted by Hieromonk Alexis (Trader); edited by Philip Navarro.—1st
ed.— Platina, Calif.: St. Herman of Alaska Brotherhood, 2008.
    p. ; cm.
    ISBN: 978-1-887904-16-2
    Includes suggested readings.
    1. Spiritual formation. 2. Spiritual life—Christianity. 3. Christian life. 4.
Paisios, Gerōn, 1924–1994. 5. Orthodoxos Ekklēsia tēs Hellados. I. Trader, Alexis.
II. Navarro, Philip. III. Title.

BX382.F37 2008
248.4—dc22   2008938048

Elder Isaac of Mount Athos (1936–1998).
(See p. 302 below.)

The English edition of this book
is dedicated to Elder Isaac, spiritual child
of Elder Paisios and, in my life, the elder
after the Elder.

Elder Paisios.

Contents

CONTENTS

CONTENTS

CONTENTS

FOREWORD

by Monk Arsenios (Vliangoftis)

I am honored to write the foreword to this book, whose author is among the thousands helped by the blessed Elder Paisios the Athonite. But it was not mere "help" that he received—Christ, truly, saved him from the mouth of the wolf through the elder's prayers.

It has been my joy to know him for many years, and I testify unconditionally to the authenticity of his account.

The author, a man with profound spiritual yearning, wanted not simply to learn from books but to know the Truth empirically. Thus—wanting to "experiment"—he surrendered himself to non-Christian experiences, such as yoga, hypnotism, and witchcraft. Not believing, as he himself records, that a person would be willingly aligned with evil, he placed himself in deadly spiritual danger. The infinite goodness of God—much more than his curiosity—directed his steps to the Holy Mountain. There, his eyes were opened to a different spiritual world, to the truth of God our Father, Whose love for us cannot be expressed. There began the healing of his spiritual traumas.

Through the God-bearing Elder Paisios, the spiritual experiences he had there had endowed him with the truth of God. And still—what mystery the soul of man conceals!—in spite of this, he chose to give "the same opportunity" to Hindu yogis that he had given to the Orthodox monks he had met. He obsessed over the question of whether the yogis, with whom he was particularly fascinated, were "with God" or "with the devil."

In such a state, he found himself in India, where he would undertake a lengthy search among the communities of three famous gurus, one of whom was worshipped as a god.

He achieved his spiritual goals, but this very achievement was his spiritual death. Had it not been for the prayers of Elder Paisios on Mount Athos, he would have descended to the darkness of luciferic "deification." The nature and depth of one's intentions, the spiritual dangers one faces, and the other circumstances of one's life—all are part of God's judgment of man. And, at last, his heart denied the darkness that blocked the light of Christ.

The gentle, all-powerful grace of the Triune God, which ever respects man's hallowed personal freedom, healed him from the heavy spiritual and psychic wounds he carried back with him from India. This grace was drawn down, with sweat and blood, by the paternal and maternal love of the saintly Elder Paisios.

In presenting this poignant, powerful memoir, the author has actually composed an account of a soul encountering the great problem of contemporary interest in Hindu spirituality, in witchcraft and occult practice—which over the last thirty years has practically inundated Western counties, Greece included.

In the *Ladder of Divine Ascent*, the incomparable sixth-century spiritual guide bestowed on us by Saint John the Sinaite, we read that those who have once fallen to passions[1]

---

[1] The word "passion," in ancient Christian terminology, refers to an impulse or desire—fear, for example, or anger—that seizes control of one's being (thus making one *passionate*). Being passionless does not mean that one is without feeling or will, but only that one is no longer tyrannized by one's impulses. (Notes are the editor's or publisher's, unless otherwise indicated.)

may become, by "restoration to health" through repentance, "physicians, beacons, lamps, and pilots for all; teaching us the habits of every disease and from their own personal experience being able to rescue those who are about to fall."

We can benefit greatly from the author's arduous experience. He expresses the hope that others, learning his story, will be able to gain the same understanding he did, without having to undergo the same suffering. This we too desire for all the spiritual seekers of pure intention who will read this book.

Monk Arsenios
Holy Monastery of Saint Arsenios
Vatopedi, Halkidiki, Greece[1]
May 2008

[1] The Holy Monastery of Saint Arsenios, located near the village of Vatopedi in northern Greece, had close spiritual ties with Elder Paisios until the latter's repose in 1994. Father Arsenios (Vliangoftis), a monk of that monastery, holds a doctorate in theology from Aristotle University in Thessaloniki. He is the editor of the Orthodox journal *Parakatathiki* (Legacy) and the author of numerous books and articles on Orthodox Christianity and other religions.

See the testimonies about the present book from the abbot of the Holy Monastery of Saint Arsenios, as well as from other Greek Orthodox spiritual fathers, on pp. 299–302 below.

Elder Paisios at the Holy Monastery of the Evangelist John
the Theologian, Souroti, Greece, where he is now buried.

PREFACE

To the Reader

I consider myself fortunate to have met in the course of my life remarkable people such as Elder Paisios. They have been instrumental in helping me find my way. Through the wondrous experiences they graciously offered me, they provided answers to disquieting questions I had been grappling with for many years: Is there any meaning to the universe? Does God exist? How should I live? Who am I, and what is my inner nature? Will I cease to exist after death?

Consumed with such questions, I was moving and breathing deep in the heart of a mystery. Life and the world were an immense mystery, and the most immediate mystery I faced was my own self: my self, that unknown entity. I was simply unable to live without answers to these questions; for me, such a life was impossible.

The people around me, and society in general, lived without giving the slightest thought to problems of this kind. The values according to which the life of society is organized are economic. Our lives are planned out. My life, too, had been prearranged. Other people had done all my thinking for me, long before I was born. I would get my degree, find a good job, get married, have children, raise a family, take a few trips and vacations, retire, and then die. Everything was arranged. I thought: Very nice, but why should I do all of this? What is the meaning and purpose of life?

I realized that every morning you get up early to go to work at a usually joyless occupation that drains you of all your energy. Afterwards, you return home for some food, take a short afternoon nap,[1] and for relaxation watch a soccer match or a mindless television show, which is followed by the evening news, during which you are told what is interesting and what opinions you should form on various minor issues. After some sleep, the cycle repeats itself. Of course, from time to time, you might see some friends and go to a restaurant to exchange some pleasantries, but who has the energy or the intellectual stamina to entertain serious questions? "Come on, pal, we just want some small talk, so we can have a good time to get us comfortably through the day." And, ultimately, this is how you pass your entire life.

This was too painful for me to endure. The idea that I would spend my life in this way, not knowing what was happening to me, nearly drove me to the brink. Yet, to others, my questions about the meaning of life in the face of the reality of contemporary man seemed like foolishness. The entire weight of society fell on my shoulders, pressuring me to conform, to live as did the vast multitude of mankind, to forget my questions, and to give up trying to find answers, since there were no answers, just the absurdity that everyone recognized at the core of their being. I felt like Sisyphus, trapped in a futile effort, trying and trying again, but all in vain.[2] I was not very strong, and I felt as though I were at my wit's end when I met Elder Paisios. This is when those wonderful experiences of which I have written began, when I received spiritual gifts that dispelled my ignorance and provided me with the answers I was seeking.

For some time, I was quite happy to keep these gifts to myself. I would take them out of the treasure chamber of my soul,

[1] An afternoon nap is traditional in Greece.
[2] In Greek mythology, Sisyphus was the cunning king of Corinth who was punished in Hades by repeatedly having to roll a huge stone up a hill only to have it roll down again as soon as he had brought it to the summit.

admire them, and stand in awe before what God had granted me. But gradually I began to think about other people as well. Still, it took me some time to decide whether I should bring these spiritual gifts out into the open. After all, Christ said, *Give not that which is holy unto the dogs, neither cast ye your pearls before swine, lest they trample them under their feet, and turn again and rend you.*[1] I knew this by experience, having seen how some people reacted when I would speak to them about these subjects. There is always a danger of acquiring enemies when you speak about the Truth in an age that loves falsehood. Nevertheless, I felt the need to write and to speak out. If I had remained silent for self-centered reasons, I would have had pangs of conscience. These wondrous occurrences, I realized, were so exceptionally precious that they should not be lost in the dark abyss of oblivion. When I considered how much paper and ink is wasted on printing rubbish that ruins our minds—such as sensational tabloids, pornography, fashion magazines, sports journals, and the rest—I felt strongly that what I would be writing would be worth publishing as an offering to others.

I informed Elder Paisios about my intentions, since the matter concerned him directly, and he gave me his blessing to write a book. On several occasions, we had conversations about what I was writing. At one point, he told me to stop writing, and then, several months later, he gave me permission to return to my task.

On the one hand, I am writing for myself, in order to remember what happened, lest it slip from my memory at a later date, and in order to understand it better. For me, the events that took place are an inexhaustible wellspring of knowledge. On the other hand, there are people whom I care about and to whom I would like to offer what I have experienced as a token

---

[1] Matthew 7:6.

of friendship, so that we might know each other at a more profound and substantial level. I am also considering my children, believing that this book could be an important offering to them. Lastly, I feel compassion for kindred souls, whom I may not know personally, but who surely exist or will be born, and who will struggle with the same questions with which I struggled. My book may not offer the crucial help they need, but it is a testimony that points out the way. It says, as it were, "Here is someone who says that significant miracles really do occur. They are not just fairy tales, myths, and figments of the imagination." These miracles are a part of my life. I heard them with my ears, saw them with my eyes, and felt them with my hands. Perhaps this will encourage such kindred souls to continue on their path, seeking so that they will find, even as I sought and found. My hope is that this, my widow's mite, could be a small contribution towards the edification of mankind at large, the vast family of God.

I am not claiming that I was or am someone special. I simply wanted to find out who I was, where I was, and where I was going. I simply wanted to learn what was happening in this world, what happens after death, what is important, what is insignificant, and how I should live. And I did find the answers to these questions; or, rather, the answers were given to me as gifts, for which I am deeply grateful to those who gave their life, knowledge, and love to someone as unworthy as I am.

I am not a writer by trade, and I have neither literary pretensions nor literary skills. I am not speaking about intellectual theories I have developed or about new ideas I have concocted or even about interesting possibilities I have explored. I am not trying to "make a case." I am simply writing my story and recording the experiences that I have had, even though many of them will sound unbelievable to the average man—for I am still overwhelmed by some of the supernatural, strange, paradoxical, powerful, and wondrous phenomena that have been such a fountain of knowledge for me. My aim is simply to tell my story, and to leave it up to the reader to evaluate it. Many of these experiences stirred up a barrage of feelings that I have also recorded, as part and parcel of the experiences.

Modern man wants everything to fit within his own perspective and resents being awakened from his blissful stupor. This is why he mocks, slanders, distorts, attacks, rejects, and hates whatever lies beyond his own worldview. He does not want to think, because television has taught him to hate thinking. He does not want to ask himself questions, because it is too tiring to do so. He doesn't want to struggle to go beneath life's superficiality, because modern culture has made him comfortable as he lives the pampered life of a hungry consumer in a cage of materialism. In a state of spiritual death, his life is defined by the biological life of his body, and his interests are defined by his exclusive fixation on his bodily needs and desires, which only make his bonds to matter and material goods increasingly constricting. When man despises the immortal soul, the higher part of his being, and becomes deeply attached to his body, he becomes utterly carnal and condemns himself to a life that is degrading. And so *man, being in honor, did not understand; he is compared to mindless cattle, and is become like unto them.*[1] My prayer is that these poor people, so unfortunate in their wretchedness, come to know their misfortune and find help even as I found help.

There are, in fact, people who free their mind and soul from the mesmerizing charms of today's materialistic lifestyle, who are open to spiritual words, and who have the strength and the disposition to change what needs to be changed for their betterment. These people have the courage and humble yearning to take the leap so that they might reach the spiritual source of life in the Holy Spirit. They are the ones who, in our foolish and

---

[1] Psalm 48:12, 21. (Psalm numbering is according to the Septuagint.)

vulgar age, preserve in man what is most majestic. Before such people, I humbly bow my knee as their servant, asking in advance that they forgive me for my omissions and failings.

The events described took place over a period of approximately ten years, and I present them like a collection of photographs of important occasions, which I have tried to put in chronological order, loosely indicating the connection between them, so that readers will be able to have the overall picture in mind as they delve into each story.

The names of some private individuals, and—very occasionally—insignificant details regarding them, have been changed in order to protect their privacy.

To preserve my own privacy and that of my family, I have written this work under a pseudonym. Of course, I would not have dared to write what I have without the blessing of Elder Paisios. Even still, since it is typical for an Orthodox Christian believer to be far more circumspect than I have been in discussing his spiritual experiences, I know that some may be surprised at my boldness. I beg, therefore, that the reader will receive this offering, unusual as it is, in the spirit in which it is intended: as a memorial to my "father in Christ,"[1] the servant of God, Father Paisios; and, more importantly, as an encouragement to others, a report of the great and mysterious works of God performed for a struggling young man in our own days.

I am pleased to see this book appear in the English language. My English was not adequate to the task of producing a translation myself, but I have reviewed the work carefully, and I am very happy with it. Moreover, the production of this edition has given me the opportunity to add to my recollections in some places and give clearer explanations in others.

I would like to express my warm gratitude to all those who

---

[1] Cf. I Corinthians 4:15.

contributed to this book by making recommendations or suggestions, by offering their advice, by correcting my mistakes and blunders, or by putting their talents and knowledge at my disposal. I will not mention them by name, because they are the kind of people who prefer anonymity. May God grant them their reward.

Before beginning my story, which so frequently involves the Holy Mountain[1] and Elder Paisios, I should point out that not all monks on the Holy Mountain or elsewhere are of his spiritual stature. Some have only recently become monastics and have not yet purified their souls of the passions, so it is not surprising that they do not differ greatly in their outlook and behavior from those in the world. Others, few in number, have not only failed to advance, but have even gone backwards spiritually, because they did not struggle conscientiously. But the majority of monastics on the Holy Mountain, like other Orthodox monks and nuns the world over, struggle as much as they are able; and so they become spiritual flowers that beautify the "garden of the Most Holy Virgin."[2] Some struggle so conscientiously, with such self-sacrifice and humility, that they acquire thoroughly the grace of the Holy Spirit and spread the spiritual fragrance of Orthodox spirituality throughout the world. As the elder once said, "If someone is like a bee, he will seek out flowers in order to draw out their nectar to make some honey. If someone is like a fly, he will seek out and land on other things." It is up to the layman to seek what is in his best interest, the most rare and most precious of flowers called holiness.

---

[1] Mount Athos, also called the Holy Mountain, is a self-governing monastic republic over a thousand years old, situated on a peninsula in northern Greece. It is considered to be the most important center of Orthodox monasticism.

[2] This is a traditional way of referring to Mount Athos.

A Biographical Note about Elder Paisios

Elder Paisios, whose name before becoming an Orthodox monk was Arsenios Eznepides, was born on July 25, 1924, and was raised in a family whose roots were in Farasa of Cappadocia.[1] When Saint Arsenios of Cappadocia baptized him, he prophesied that he would "become a monk following in my own footsteps."[2] His family raised the elder within the profoundly spiritual tradition of Cappadocia, which has produced numerous men and women of great holiness.

Two years before the elder's birth, after the war between Greece and Turkey had ended, in order to avoid genocide his family had joined the nearly 1.5 million Greeks of Asia Minor who abandoned what had been their native land for 2,500 years. The elder's family ultimately settled in Konitsa of Epiros,[3] where he spent his childhood years.

From his youth he manifested a desire for the monastic life, and he finally became a monk at the age of thirty. He was a monk at the Sacred Monastery of Stomiou at Pindos, in the desert of Sinai in Egypt and, most significantly, on the Holy Mountain, where he spent the greater part of his life. His monastic life was comparable with that of the ancient ascetics. He lived a life of great poverty and solitude in a cell in the

[1] Cappadocia is an ancient region of central Asia Minor. It was a notable center of early Christianity.

[2] Saint Arsenios (1840–1924) was the spiritual guide of Elder Paisios's family. He reposed shortly after baptizing Elder Paisios in his infancy. See the book *Saint Arsenios of Cappadocia*, written by Elder Paisios (Souroti, Thessaloniki, Greece: Holy Monastery of the Evangelist John the Theologian, 1996).

[3] Epiros is a region of the Balkan peninsula in southeastern Europe. The town of Konitsa, located in Epiros, is on the border between Greece and Albania.

Elder Paisios at the hermitage of Saint Epistimi on Mount Sinai,
Egypt, ca. 1963 (see pp. 260, 280 below).

forest.[1] His demeanor was very simple and sweet, and there was nothing pretentious in his carriage or tone of voice. His heart overflowed with love for everyone, and multitudes responded to this by flocking to his cell to visit him and receive his advice.

When he would leave the Holy Mountain to travel, thousands would gather to receive his blessing, waiting in lines until dawn in order to speak with him for but a few minutes. And, in that short span of time, many would find the solution to their problems. Others would be helped later, through his prayers.

---

[1] "Cell" is the term used for a monastic's private quarters, whether a room in a larger building or a small independent structure. It may also be used to refer to the entire grounds of a hermitage.

The grave of Elder Paisios at the Holy Monastery of the Evangelist John the Theologian, Souroti, Greece.

Even during his own lifetime, without ever being mentioned by radio, television, or the press, he acquired a reputation for sanctity throughout the world. His reputation was spread by word of mouth, and hundreds of people bore witness in writing to how he had miraculously helped them. Books have now been written about his miracles. He was a spiritual father for many people from every walk of life, including the elderly and the young, the prominent and the insignificant. By his holy way of life and his miracles, he enabled people to see the light of Christ and the power of God, thereby urging them on towards spiritual progress. He was in truth a great elder. It has been rightly said that Father Paisios was a gift of God to the people of our age.

The elder died on July 12, 1994, and was buried in the convent of Saint John the Theologian, in the village of Souroti outside Thessaloniki, in northern Greece. His grave has become a place of pilgrimage and a fount of healing, for he continues to work miracles even after his repose.

CHAPTER ONE

Pushed towards Evil: Experiences in the World of Hypnotism, Witchcraft, and the Occult

Roots

I once asked Father Paisios about something I found quite perplexing: "Elder, why have all these miracles happened to me?"

"Because," he replied, "starting from when you were a child, you didn't get the help you needed. And not only that—you were actually being pushed towards evil. So you deserved some divine help, and God gave it to you all at once." And, saying this, he gave me a fatherly pat on the cheek.

*   *   *

My father was always bringing books home, even though he didn't always read them. From a young age I loved to read. I was in the first year of junior high school when I came across a book in our house, its pages still uncut, entitled *The Power of Concentration: Methods for Developing Memory and Logical Thinking,* by Paul-Clément Jagot. "This will help me remember my math equations," I thought. In fact, it would never help me with anything—but, in any event, I took the book down and started to read it. In addition to presenting a philosophy about man and his hidden powers, the book also contained a number of practical exercises for developing the memory and increasing one's power to concentrate on a single subject—exercises, that is, on how to control one's thoughts. I was highly impressed by this and began to do the exercises in the book. Years later, when I was a university student and began to get more heavily involved with yoga, I realized that those exercises from my childhood were a popularized version of yoga exercises. I felt certain that the author was a yogi.

As an adolescent I had many questions about the world around me and about myself. I remember that one summer—I must have been twelve or thirteen years old—I kept almost entirely to myself, pondering these things deeply. I steered clear of my friends, who were constantly playing soccer—there were only a couple of them I would talk to now and then. They had some of the same questions I did, though none of them seemed to feel them with the intensity that I did. Whenever I began to examine a topic, I found that behind every question lurked another question that had to be answered first. Behind that question, another one was hiding, and behind that question there was yet another one.

The fundamental question, the answer to which all the other answers in my chain of questions depended on, was whether God exists. No matter which of the numerous questions that troubled me I began to consider, I always ended up back at this underlying issue. I quickly became aware that my attitude towards the world, my way of dealing with things that befell me, and in fact my entire life were entirely dependent upon the answer I would give to this basic and fundamental question.

I spent a lot of time thinking, reading books, and talking about these issues with friends, but I was getting nowhere. Whenever friends ran into me while I was taking one of my solitary walks by a bridge or through the woods at noontime, they would start teasing me: "How's it going? Find the answer to your question yet? Does God exist?" A few of them understood my anguish and had respect for it, but the others were simply indifferent and were soon off to play ball. (If I hadn't been the one helping them with their homework, and tall and husky as well, I don't think I would have been able to put up with all their teasing so easily.)

My father noticed this constant questioning of mine and my love of reading. After all, I had left the bookshelves in our house in disarray. "Let's go and see a friend of mine," he suggested, "who can give you a few books. He's got a lot of good books." So, one afternoon we went to his house, and I got a number of books.

The one that would have the greatest effect on me was by Lord Bertrand Russell. Russell was a social democrat in his political convictions and a great believer in humanity. The name of the book was *What I Believe,* and the first chapter, which was about sixty pages long, bore the title "Why I Am Not a Christian."

That book changed the course of my life. Bertrand Russell was a self-declared atheist. His book was not able to convince me of the non-existence of God, but, on the other hand, I was unable to respond with certainty that God did exist. That question remained on the shelf, unanswered. But the book did succeed in making me reject the Christian Faith and its precepts. In truth, I could find no serious response to Russell on the part of Christianity. I had not yet come into contact with the profound wisdom of the patristic tradition—and all the Christian magazines and books that reached my hands seemed like children's stories in comparison with his book. Lord Russell's work was a success: from that time on I had nothing to do with Christianity.

Ares the Hypnotist

Years would pass before I would enter the university, where I was once again ready to take on the fundamental question of the existence of God. Many things came and went in my life: ideologies, theories, the social movement of May 1968,[1] the hippie movement, night-clubbing, rock music, trade unions, sit-ins, and everything else. I was searching fervently for the rest that comes with Truth.

At the time I met Ares, my friends and I were second- and third-year university students attending university in Thessaloniki. This was the time immediately after the fall of the military dictatorship, and there had been an enormous shift in power at the university away from the professors and towards the students. So, since our parents supported us financially, our life was basically carefree, and where our university studies ended was where our real interests began. I had studied Mao, Lenin, Marx, and Murray Bookchin with my friends, even though to do so remained politically dangerous; and now I began to read about psychology, beginning with Freud's disciple Wilhelm Reich (whose works served for me as a bridge from Marxism). After turning as well to Fromm, Jung, Freud, R. D. Laing, and David Cooper, I soon found myself drawn to Eastern mystics such as Vivekananda and Krishnamurti, to the Buddhist and Patanjali sutras, to the works of poets like Rabindranath Tagore and Khalil Gibran, and to the novels of Hermann Hesse.[2] I also read the writings of authors concerned

---

[1] In May 1968, student strikes erupted in France. The sequence of events that followed, which included a vast general strike, nearly toppled the government. The events drew worldwide attention to themes such as educational reform and sexual freedom, which were among the chief concerns of the generally left-wing or anarchist protesters. These events energized student protesters around the world, including in Greece.

[2] Hesse (1877–1962) was a German novelist whose works were often concerned with the conflict between the individual spirit seeking enlightenment and its environment. In the 1960s and 1970s, English translations of his works became best-sellers, read by droves of devoted youth who identified with their suffering, searching protagonists. His

with the sciences, such as Isaac Asimov, Carl Sagan, Fritjof Capra, Lyall Watson, and Timothy Leary, many of whom were trying to combine or draw parallels between Western science and Eastern mysticism, aspiring to arrive at a synthesis between logical thinking and intuitive experience.

How in the world the sixty-year-old Ares got involved with a bunch of twenty-year-olds is a puzzle that I have never satisfactorily solved. In any event, during one exam period we had all gone to our friend Nikos's apartment, supposedly to study, and Ares was there—thin, about five feet, nine inches tall, and with black hair on the sides of his head and a striking bald pate. He was from a working-class background and had not gone to college, and it showed. But from a young age he had had the same infatuation that we did: an interest in spiritualistic phenomena. He was knowledgeable in various areas of the subject, and, after a long discussion in which he showed himself to be extremely adept at presenting spiritualistic issues, he told us that he himself had ended up concentrating on hypnotism. He was open to everything, he said, but liked hypnotism best of all.

He then began to tell us about the world of spirits, about how beautiful it was there, how you heard very beautiful music, how after visiting it you felt tranquil and refreshed, how your consciousness could become expanded, and how you could acquire unusual abilities, such as the ability to transport yourself from Thessaloniki to America. What he said about

---

interest in Eastern spirituality inspired a trip to India, after which he wrote *Siddhartha,* the story of a man's search for the meaning of existence and self-realization. Set in a mythic India of days long-past, *Siddhartha* would influence many young people to seek their spiritual fortune in the East. Hesse, who had scores of psychoanalysis sessions with one of Jung's students and some with Jung himself, also explored psychoanalytic themes in his novels.

unusual abilities aroused my interest, because I had always believed that a human being was something more than just a cog in the machinery of society—that we all had cosmic dimensions and capabilities.

"There is the body," he said, "and then there is the astral body, which is finer—let's call it the soul, to simplify things—and during hypnotism this is released from the material body and can travel through space with unfathomable speed, now that it is no longer bound by the laws of the physical world—by gravity, time, and all the rest." He said that whoever agreed to be hypnotized by him would experience this kind of journey and, upon leaving this world and moving in the realm of the spiritual world, would have contact with spiritual beings.

I don't think Ares could have found a more receptive group than ours. The books we had read had infused us with beliefs of this kind; and, now, here was our opportunity to put them into practice. He conducted various tests to see whether we would make good subjects and if we had the aptitude for being mediums, and he found that all of us were of above-average receptivity, myself and one other person in our group especially. So the first step had been taken: we had become active participants. Nonetheless, there was something about him I didn't like. I had a vague sense of something—something in the way he moved, something in his manner—that troubled me and made me hesitant.

When Ares left, we bombarded Nikos with questions, but received only very general answers. He had met Ares through his brother, who had made the man's acquaintance first. Ares was a retired technician of some sort who had worked for the government. But Nikos did tell us something that left an impression on us. His brother had agreed to be hypnotized, and while he was under hypnosis and had his eyes closed, he had been able to "see" a number that Ares indicated with his fingers and to read the title of a book. Nikos then told us that he himself had been hypnotized and had found himself sixty miles outside of Thessaloniki, watching traffic on the road.

We didn't go to Nikos's house very often, but twenty days later we all found ourselves there again—all the same individuals, although we hadn't made any date or other kind of arrangement. We had another discussion about the same topics, addressing our doubts and questions to Ares, who presented us with his answers. At this meeting I agreed to be hypnotized; and, once I was actually under, I began to have an intense awareness of a certain presence. It was a face, luminous and golden, with indistinct features, and it kept coming between Ares and me. Ares told me to chase it away. I complied, but, although the face would leave, it kept returning and eventually woke me from my trance. Afterwards, I continued to sense its presence in the room at various moments.

I asked Ares what it was. He managed to calm me down, more or less, and the group returned to its discussion. My friend Matteos was now persuaded to let himself be hypnotized, and we all observed with interest the way he relaxed, sank into a trance, and obeyed the hypnotist. When Matteos had reached the state that Ares wanted, Ares tried to steer him in a certain direction, but once again that presence made its appearance. A luminous, golden face, said Matteos, had entered the place where we were sitting and was moving around. It had, he said, the eyes of a cat. He tried to chase it away, but it wouldn't leave, so he started telling us exactly where in the room he could feel its presence.

Strangely enough, I was sensing exactly what Matteos was sensing: my own inklings of where the presence was located in the room coincided exactly with what he was saying. The presence soon woke Matteos out of his trance as well, but our interest had been kindled. What was this presence? Was it a spirit? And if so, what kind of spirit was it? Was it a good spirit or an evil spirit? Until we parted for the evening—as Matteos and I later confided to each other—both of us continued to feel the spirit's presence in our midst.

Such matters now became the main subject of our conversations, and we began to read books about them with greater attentiveness, books about spirits materializing, books about white magic and witchcraft.

The Signs

As a rule, I don't frighten easily. Even at night, nothing scares me. I often used to take walks in the moonlight in the forest outside of Thessaloniki, and quite a few times I slept out in the woods. When in a romantic mood, I used to like taking solitary walks late at night, at around two or three in the morning, through the city's back streets. I was particularly fond of walking through districts whose old buildings preserved the atmosphere of a bygone era.

Following my experience with hypnosis, however, I began to feel a variety of strange things. I used to sense a strange presence, a feeling that would make my hair stand on end, and I would hear noises. It wasn't the sounds themselves that were frightening, but their apparent source—the feeling that they were produced by something preternatural. For example, although not a leaf on the trees would be stirring, without a hint of a breeze, a door inside a house would suddenly slam with such tremendous force that it would almost come off its hinges. Sometimes it was as if something exploded five inches in front of me; at other times I heard two, three, or four loud sounds in succession all around me, but there wasn't anything there. In fact, I didn't see anything at all. I became annoyed with myself. Why was I paying attention to such foolishness? But not only did the noises continue, I now started to hear them at other places and other times. Of course, I ignored them or, in any case, tried to ignore them.

Our interest had really been piqued. We had encountered a mystery. True, every now and then these strange figures appeared and frightened us, but we had begun to get used to them. We continued to meet at Nikos's apartment. Matteos was the first to notice, the fifth time it happened, that Ares would suddenly gather us together, so to speak, not letting anyone know beforehand. On a given afternoon, for no apparent reason, we would all get the idea to stop by Nikos's, and Ares was always there. At that time, we didn't even have much of a connection with Nikos and were not in the habit of going to see him. "No one hears a word from you," I once cornered Ares. "How do you manage to bring us all together?" "'Well,' I say to myself, 'since they don't have anything better to do, let them all come here.'" So, he admitted that he somehow drew us all together.

I did not care for this at all. By now, Ares had acquired some kind of control or power over us, and he wasn't the kind of person you could trust. Did he have the ability to influence our thoughts and desires? And if so, to what degree could he influence them? And what would happen if we resisted him? In the meantime, his cunning—call it diplomacy, if you like—slowly began to become apparent, and I started to distrust him and be more cautious. I didn't stop going to the gatherings, however, and he gave me his home address so that I could go see him there.

Interestingly, Ares used to say that he was a Christian, and he had icons and votive lamps in his house. However, he considered the priests of the Church to be inferior because they were "ignorant of spiritual reality." He had a relationship with the Church, but it was a relationship on his own terms; and he used to interpret the Gospels any way he liked, any way that was convenient and that he cared for. And I noticed that he left out passages that didn't suit his purposes.

Around that time, I was lying in my room one night with the door closed. Then strange noises began—a sudden inexplicable banging from the bookcase or on the windowpane. I had slept in that room for years and knew all its sounds, but this was different. In fact, it was so loud that I was at a loss to explain why my parents didn't hear it or why whatever was making these noises didn't break something. Moreover, I had the feeling that there was a presence in the room, and this frightened me. I got out of bed and opened the door to feel closer to my family, and then I got annoyed with myself and closed it. Each time I was about to fall asleep, the banging would start again, and I would wake up, terrified, and open the door. This happened three times. Finally, I got really angry. Firmly closing the door, in my heart I cursed whoever was harassing me like this. I made up my mind to treat him with disdain, and to give him a good trouncing if I ever laid hands on him. I fell back asleep, and this time I really slept.

Then I heard a crash, violent and loud. I got up in my bed with a start and found the room filled with an eerie pitch-darkness: the light from the street lamp, weirdly, was not illuminating the room as usual. The darkness was actually preventing the light from entering—as if it weren't just darkness, but some kind of conscious being. I was terrified by this dark presence, and I immediately cried out, "My Christ!"

As soon as I said this, there appeared in the corner of the room the luminous outline of a person. Its light was somehow white and transparent, and, peculiar though it was, I found it soothing. It gave me an immediate sense of security, and filled me with a gentle calm that drove out all my fears. I relaxed, sank back down in my bed, and fell asleep. The whole scene lasted only a few seconds.

The following morning, as I went over the events of the previous night in my mind, I was bewildered. I was unable to come up with any interpretation or explanation of the things that had occurred, because I had no criteria on which to base a judgment, no yardstick against which to measure what had happened. But, in any event, it was something I couldn't just dismiss.

The next time that I saw the hypnotist, I described what had happened, including what had happened when I called out the name of Christ. He replied, "Don't be frightened. I forgot to warn you. Now that you're entering the world of the spirits, they're trying to scare you in order to stop you. Call me and I'll come and help you. Don't be frightened."

He "forgot." What did he mean by "forgot"? I didn't believe him. He had simply concealed the dangers from us—other friends of mine had similarly frightening experiences. He had placed us at risk, and had been using us: he himself had never been hypnotized, nor did he involve his children in such things. What did he mean, moreover, when he said, "Call me and I'll help you"? Were we now in need of his help—would we become dependent on him? Why should I call him? Had it been a mistake to call on Christ for help instead? Even to have Christian sympathies was unfashionable in our group—was he saying I had something to be ashamed of? Or was he saying he was better than Christ?

After experiencing these kinds of phenomena, a number of the others didn't want to continue. But I was burning with curiosity to find out what lay hidden behind all of this—I wanted to discover the truth, so I plowed ahead. Nevertheless, matters worked out in such a way that in the end Ares no longer wanted anything to do with me.

A girl I knew had returned from abroad, where she had been studying. While there she had become addicted to heroin, and was now a real junkie. She had almost died a number of times from overdoses and had been expelled from her university. I wanted to help her, so I suggested that we go to Ares so he could hypnotize her to help her quit. (He used to claim that hypnosis could be used in beneficial ways like this.) I took her to his house and explained the situation. He hypnotized her, but it didn't do any good. In the end, Ares became frightened of getting entangled with the police, and as a result we never again had one of our "chance" gatherings.

(As for the girl, years later she was saved from her dependence on drugs when I asked Father Paisios to pray for her. No one who knew her then, myself included, believed that there was any way to save her, because her habit was at an advanced stage and she hadn't the slightest instinct for self-preservation—quite the opposite, in fact. But today she has completely changed.)

Alexandra

It was around this same time that I became acquainted with a girl named Alexandra, and the way it happened was extremely odd. We had met at the university, and she had given me her address. A few days later I went to find her house. I parked my car so that I could get out and look around for the right street, but it turned out that I had parked just thirty feet from her door. I was hardly out of the car when I saw her open her door and look up and down the street. She came over to me, dressed in a jogging suit.

"I've been expecting you to arrive at this very moment," she said. We were both surprised, and we had a feeling that "something" was going on. After that, strange things would occur to us on a number of occasions. I had started trying to see her aura, using techniques I had read about in books on yoga, though she strongly objected. Then we began to hear strange noises. She wasn't frightened, though, until one day a door inside the house suddenly slammed shut with a loud crash. All the windows were closed and there was no breeze—it was completely beyond the laws of nature. We were terrified, and she fell into my arms almost in tears.

Alexandra had a secret, and, when I spoke to her about hypnotism, yoga, and witchcraft, she told me her story. "I had a grandmother," she said, "who could free people from the evil eye.[1] Shortly before she died she taught me the incantation she used, which she told me she was only permitted to reveal to one person. I didn't give it much thought. Then, sometime later, we believed that a young cousin of mine had come under such an influence: his head hurt, and he was constantly drowsy and started to act like someone who wasn't exactly sane. And so I used the incantation, and, for the first time in my life, I drove away from someone the effects of this evil power. My cousin recovered immediately, but I was in pain for the next twenty-four hours.

"That was when I began to be aware of strange presences. It began one night when I was alone in my family's house in Athens. The lights started going on and off in our apartment, while the power in the rest of the building seemed unaffected. Unnerved, I went out onto the balcony. As I was about to go back into the house, I saw that the curtains had risen and were stretched out in mid-air, parallel with the floor. I froze—I was

---

[1] Many dismiss the evil eye because it is the subject of much superstition. The ancient Greeks and others believed that one's eye could have the power of injuring another through visual rays or emanations. As Fr. George R. A. Aquaro's study, *Death by Envy* (New York: iUniverse, Inc., 2004), demonstrates, both the Old and New Testaments and ancient Christian writings do not accept this idea. They do, however, speak of an "evil eye," associating it, not with a special power, but with envy on the part of the one who looks. An envious person's feelings, states St. Basil the Great, of themselves can cause no harm, but "the devils ... use for their own ends such free acts as they find congenial for their wishes. In this way, they make the eyes of envious persons serviceable to their purposes" (St. Basil, "Concerning Envy," in *The Fathers of the Church*, vol. 9 [Washington, D.C.: Catholic University of America, 1962], p. 470).

too terrified to dare go back in. Instead, I stayed out on the balcony all night, smoking cigarettes and listening to music. At dawn I left the house, and I only returned a few days later, after my parents had come home from their trip."

After that, though, Alexandra's fears gradually left her, and she continued to use the incantation every now and then—it was her special talent.

Strangely enough, we were all materialists. We had studied Marxism and dialectical materialism, and, having had no involvement with faith since childhood, I had become a Marxist by the time I was nineteen years old. Anything that was connected to "religion" we saw as deception and muddle-headedness. Nevertheless—though we believed neither in the devil nor in any spiritual interpretation of the world or world history—we accepted the idea of witchcraft, practiced yoga, and used Ouija boards and practiced other spiritualistic techniques.

Demetrios

Around the same time I was introduced to Ares, I met a man named Demetrios, a cousin of my friend Matteos's roommate, Kyriakos. Demetrios used to come from Athens two or three times a year to visit, staying with Kyriakos and Matteos for several days. Demetrios wasn't a student. He was two or three years older than we were and worked in a travel agency. He was also a Freemason, and his visits would initiate philosophical discussions about mankind, the world, God, techniques used in witchcraft, and so on. Matteos began talking to him, as did I, because he had firm opinions and knew many things, but that was as far as the relationship went. Kyriakos didn't trust him and thought there was something suspicious about Masonry—as he put it, he didn't like his cousin's "energy."

Once, when the three of them were discussing witchcraft, Matteos started to make fun of Demetrios. This angered him. He walked over to the window in Matteos's room, breathed on the glass to steam it up, drew some strange figures with his finger, and then whispered something incomprehensible under his breath. When he was finished, he returned to the conversation. Late that night, at about two or three in the morning, they all went to sleep, the two cousins together in one room and Matteos by himself in his room.

This is how Matteos described what he experienced next: "As soon as I fell asleep—bang!—I heard a knock on the window, and I sat up in bed with a start. 'Calm down,' I said to myself, and I fell back asleep. A little while later—bang!—a louder knock. I sat up in bed again, frightened and angry. I smoked a couple of cigarettes, thought for a little while, and decided I'd been affected by our earlier conversation. I calmed down and fell asleep again, after first opening the window and looking around to see if someone was playing a joke on me. This time I slept very well. Then there was another knock on the window, sharp and loud. The first thing I saw when I opened my eyes was the figure, the strange characters, and the symbols that Demetrios had drawn, illuminated by the light of the street lamp. The windowpane was cracked in exactly that spot.

"I became frightened, jumped out of bed, ran into the other bedroom, and woke Demetrios. He came into my room with Kyriakos. The minute he saw the window he turned pale with fright and erased the drawing as well as he could. I had the feeling that he was more frightened than anyone else. We spent the rest of the night with the lights on, the three of us smoking cigarettes together. No one dared to go to sleep."

After about a year, I visited the house where Kyriakos lived with his girlfriend, who was a medical student. They told me that they were studying "Solomonic" magical texts containing written invocations of demons. These texts list the demons by name and according to the special area of expertise that each one has, as it were, along with the method by which each can be summoned. Kyriakos and his girlfriend were somewhat frightened by this book, but they didn't throw it out, even though both Demetrios and I told them they should. Some months later, less than a year after this, they began to have severe problems in their relationship. The girl had to start seeing psychiatrists. She was not in her right mind, and led an astonishingly profligate life, almost like a prostitute, and encouraged others to do so as well. I heard the filthy language she would use in public, whether she was with people she knew or didn't know. She eventually lost her mind, or became demonically possessed. The last I heard was that her parents were hauling her to various monasteries, as they had lost faith in doctors.

Struck by an Invisible Entity

I had for some time been practicing yoga techniques, making occasional visits to a local ashram. The girl who had first brought me there was named Anna. Anna had herself been introduced to yoga by her former boyfriend, who had even visited India a number of times. I went over to her house one evening, and she made us dinner. As we ate, we discussed the occult: yoga, witchcraft, supernatural powers, and the like. Suddenly strange noises began, just as they had before in my bedroom.

We looked at each other. "Do you think my boyfriend is jealous?" she asked, laughing.

"Don't be silly," I replied.

We continued our conversation. Half an hour later, there was a crash. It sounded like someone had kicked the door: the whole inside of it reverberated, and I thought it had cracked.

The girl became frightened—this was not a natural event. I flew to the door and shouted, "Who's there? You don't frighten me!" I opened the door and then closed it with a scornful laugh. "If you're such a tough guy, come and take me on!" I taunted. Nothing happened.

"It's probably my boyfriend," she said.

"Come on. You mean we don't have the right to talk? Whoever is doing this has no right to. It's rude," I said, and laughed. "Let's forget about it and go back to what we were doing."

She lightened up, and soon we really did forget about it. The time passed quickly and pleasantly: we had a lot of interests in common—something we appreciated better the more we talked, and quite a few hours went by. Suddenly, I felt something strike me, hard, on my back, like I had been hit with a long, thick piece of wood. I screamed in pain and sprang from my seat, putting my hands to my back where it hurt.

"What happened?" she asked me, shocked.

"Someone hit me on the back," I replied. She looked at me in disbelief—we were completely alone, not only in the room but also in the entire apartment.

"Next time," she said, "don't be so defiant."

"Let's forget about that jealous boyfriend of yours," I answered, and I sat down beside her.

But my back continued to hurt for two or three days after that. Looking back on matters, I'm amazed at how lightly we took things back then—how easily we got over these sorts of incidents.

A Bizarre Dream

One night, during this same period, I dreamt that I was walking along a dirt road. At the edge of the road sat a strange, human-like creature, medium-to-tall in stature, solidly built, with strong arms and a long, powerful tail. Its head had both human and animal features. It was completely bald, had long, pointed ears and two little horns on its head, and all its skin was the color of copper. It was sitting on the edge of the road, looking at me.

I grew nervous, but, ashamed of my fear, I continued on my way with a youthful swagger. "What's it got to do with me?" I thought. "I don't even know what it is. I'll just walk by and pretend it doesn't exist." But when I was right beside it, it pounced on me and, easily knocking me over, it beat me, leaving me covered in filth. That was frightening, but what truly put me in a state of terror was that I had also become paralyzed—I couldn't even move my little finger. I was utterly at its mercy. But suddenly it vanished, and I slowly began to move my numbed limbs.

When I awoke the next morning, I felt pain where the creature had hit me in the dream—it was as though I had really been beaten up. A dream is only a dream of course, but what was I to make of this physical pain? I tried to find some sort of explanation, but it all remained incomprehensible. Nevertheless, I would have forgotten all about it if something even more unsettling hadn't occurred afterwards. A few days later, my girlfriend came to see me and said, "I had a strange dream about you that shook me up. Take care of yourself, because I'm afraid it was an omen. I saw a strange, beast-like man with a club at his side. He threw you on the ground and was beating you." I started to question her in detail, and I realized that we had both seen the same being. Neither one of us could explain this phenomenon, but we were soon distracted—we had romantic interests that consumed us.

Around then, the two of us met a woman with whom we began to spend a good deal of time. She flirted with me, although she never made any overt suggestions. Though there

were many times that something more could have happened—we had even slept in the same bed at her home—things
never went any further. My girlfriend was jealous, but I simply
wanted to be the woman's friend, and I didn't find her particularly attractive.

Then, one day, she initiated a very odd conversation. We
discussed many things, speaking in an enigmatic way but understanding each other thoroughly. During this conversation
full of subtle implications, I made it clear that I wasn't interested in her. She in turn let me know just how hurt she felt,
and then she made what seemed to be a veiled threat: "All
right. I'll wait for my turn in September." It was June at the
time, and I didn't take her words very seriously.

After this conversation, our relationship continued as before. She gradually became very close to my girlfriend, which
started to bother me, because she had an incredible amount of
influence on her. They started eyeing up other young men together, and I became jealous. Now this woman also dabbled in
the occult world, reading texts by Mihail Ivanov, Carlos
Castaneda, and G. I. Gurdjieff,[1] and putting her interests into
practice using a deck of Tarot cards. She became quite adept
with the cards and would frequently lay them out for us. She
knew another woman, her teacher, who she claimed had an
uncanny skill in reading the cards and foretelling the future.
Our common acquaintance would often praise this other
woman for this skill and for her other capabilities, and began
to take my girlfriend to this woman's home.

---

[1] Ivanov (1900–1986), some of whose writings discussed magic, was a
major figure in the esoteric "Universal White Brotherhood." (For further
information, see p. 98 below.) Castaneda (1925–1998) claimed to have been
initiated into magic and mysticism by an aged member of the Yaqui tribe
from Mexico. Gurdjieff (1877?–1949), who developed an obscure teaching
that drew from, among other sources, Sufism and the Kabbalah, was a
student of occult techniques from childhood.

I never quite learned what game they were playing—I can only piece together clues from the events that took place. At any rate, as September came, I remembered the veiled threat, "I'll wait for my turn in September." And in fact my girlfriend and I split up shortly after September, following an unbelievable series of misunderstandings. But that wasn't all—everything in my life started to go wrong, and I began to experience a state of profound anguish that made me feel I was losing my mind, and that even pushed me towards suicide. You'd have thought the sky had come crashing down on my head. I kept wondering what was happening to me—I felt as if someone were waging a hidden war against me, as if my downfall had become the ultimate object of someone's life.

I later learned from a common acquaintance that I had become a frequent topic of discussion at meetings between the woman and her teacher. Indeed, they had made me the object of their spiritualistic activities. These women's witchcraft may well explain the unlikely series of misunderstandings and mishaps, and the mental anguish and confusion that I suffered during that period—I see now that my careless way of life had granted the devil some claim on me. "They cast a spell on you," I was told by an old man who was fond of me, and who had experience of such things, but I just laughed.

CHAPTER TWO

Divine Help:
Elder Paisios Enters My Life

A Visit to the Holy Mountain

My friends and I had reached the last days of summer, and the end of our spending money. But our break was not quite finished, and we wanted to keep on enjoying it, going to the beach and taking trips. Then one of my friends suggested that we go to the Holy Mountain. Not knowing anything about it, I asked him, "And what are we going to do there?"

"We'll wander from monastery to monastery and sneak in a swim from time to time. There's free room and board."

"Okay," I said, "let's go."

If our friend hadn't been so insistent the day we were to depart, we would never have been able to wake up at five o'clock in the morning to catch the bus: we had just fallen asleep three hours earlier. But we did, and the bus trip from Thessaloniki to the small port town of Ouranoupolis took about three hours. There, we boarded the daily boat for Athos, and sailed around the peninsula for about an hour and a half. I felt an inner joy as I watched pass before my eyes imposing monasteries and small hermitages perched amidst vegetation, overlooking the sea. I saw open up before me my dream of a quiet way of life, intentionally far removed from the vanity of the world. I had often had discussions with my friends about moving far away from society and its dehumanizing mechanization in order to live outdoors in simplicity, according to our own rules, and now I had the joy of seeing that some people had managed to do just that.

Our itinerary upon reaching the Dafni harbor was to visit the monasteries of Koutloumousiou, Iviron, Stavronikita, and Grigoriou, and then return to Thessaloniki. We would have the opportunity to get to know some monks and have conversations with them.

I remember how surprised I was to find out what interesting characters the monks were. They were intelligent men, quick on the uptake and often quite educated, and no strangers to the social, ideological, political, and existential issues that were so important to me. We had profound and fruitful conversations that I enjoyed thoroughly. This was the first time I had encountered their perspective on these issues, and I needed time on my own to reflect on their views. But I realized their views were serious, not to be rejected offhand.

I was also impressed by how their life was regulated by the "coenobitic" way, in which there is no private property and all possessions are held in common. They all ate the same food at the same tables together with the guests. Every year, there would be a gathering at which each monk would be assigned his daily work for the community for that year, so that each one would have the opportunity to do every task performed in the monastery. One year, a monk might labor as a gardener; the next, he might work as a carpenter; and the following year he might set the tables. The abbot was elected by the brotherhood for life, unless he chose to step down.

Values and relationships were of a different order in the monasteries. All the fathers strived to serve each other in a spirit of self-sacrifice and brotherly love. In fact, they found a lot of joy in being able to offer a helping hand. Their way of life stood in such contrast to the self-centered and callous individualism displayed by so many who live in large cities. In the early Christian Church, no one was destitute, because rich and poor alike gave their property to the parish's common treasury, and it became the common property of all the members. In the monasteries, the ancient spirit of Christianity with its *agape* meals and common property was kept alive.

At a certain point, I noticed an enormous discrepancy between the image I had formed in my mind about Christians and Christian life and what I saw and experienced there. I had always thought that Christians were narrow-minded, devious wretches with psychological problems. I had thought the Christian Faith and the Church were dead, and I had always viewed the Christian tradition as a relic of the past, used by charlatans, swindlers, and other lowlifes. I was shocked to encounter a different reality.

Something else, however, was mysteriously taking place in my soul, which experienced profound joy and tranquility during my stay on the Holy Mountain. It was as though someone were guiding my footsteps, directing me to speak to and learn from the right people. I tried to record my experiences while I was on the boat leaving the Holy Mountain:

While I was on Mount Athos, it was as though I were at a seminar where my soul received intensive training, but now I feel as though I am ready to leave. The rapid changes in my spiritual state made me feel that there was a path marked out for my soul, and an inner necessity compelled me to remain on Mount Athos until my soul had reached the end of this path, from which I learned three truths.

First: In the cemetery at the Monastery of Stavronikita, the three of us spoke with the abbot. This was our first conversation with a monk. We were already touched by the entire monastic setting with its icons and order, its sights and sounds. When this man spoke, he would at first seem to be lost in thought as he closed

Stavronikita Monastery, Mount Athos.

his eyes, slowly nodded his head, and entered into another state. At first, his words seemed peculiar, but in
time they became more understandable. I learned from
him about the mysterious existence of the Church, that
"life-bearing river that flows continuously down the
ages." I began to get a grasp on what is meant by God,
"the One Who created time when there was no time
and place where there was no place." I couldn't take my
eyes off the abbot. There was something else that I
should mention. His words were spirit-bearing and resonated deeply in my heart, where I felt all their mystical weight. This is when I realized that there was
something going on beyond our conversation. There
was Someone Else besides the abbot teaching us
invisibly from on high.

Second: I experienced something different at the

Koutloumousiou Monastery, Mount Athos.

Monastery of Koutloumousiou. I felt rattled and frightened by an inner compulsion to leave, because the people in the monastery had touched my innermost thoughts. They were quite familiar with the problem of existence. Father Athanasios was my age, and he spoke to me about his life and how he had experienced demonic attacks. This was the first time that I heard that Satan was an entity close at hand, whose existence was as real as the existence of the sky, the earth, and man himself. This was not a matter of speculation, but a palpable reality that my soul felt and recoiled from in fear. It wasn't clear whether I had learned all that I was supposed to learn here or whether I should continue to explore some more. That evening, I had a conversation with my friends.

Grigoriou Monastery, Mount Athos.
Photograph by Patrick Barnes.

"What's this new angle? Is it just their take on reality or is it reality itself?"

"What frightens me," my friend responded, "isn't what they say, but the feeling that we're really not just dealing with another angle." This was a new experience, the magnitude of which frightened us.

Third: I arrived at the Monastery of Grigoriou in the afternoon. I walked by myself to the monastery, and on the way I had a premonition that I would have a meeting with someone that evening and then leave the next day. Everything took place so naturally, yet was mysteriously connected like the links in a chain. At the very moment that I felt ready, I met the very person I needed to meet. I didn't have to search through the crowd of visitors and monks or inform anyone, because Father Simos came up to me and we became acquainted. I felt as though I could speak to him freely and in my own way. He was a former hippie who had been around. From our conversation, I again acquired a sense of responsibility for my personal path in this world. "Nothing happens to us by chance," he said. "The way we choose to face life is of great importance."

My first visit to the Holy Mountain lasted only three or four days, but it was an overwhelming experience, and it filled me to the brim with new impressions. There was so much to think about that concerned my inner life that I had to leave in order to digest it all.

An Encounter with Elder Paisios

My visit had brought my entire worldview into question, so a few weeks later I returned in order to explore everything more thoroughly. I went to the Monastery of Koutloumousiou, because I wanted to speak with Father Athanasios again. I admired him because he was a good and intelligent man who was very knowledgeable about the occult. That afternoon, when he had finished his chores, we sat on the balcony and had a discussion.

"Look, Father, I can accept the existence of evil as an inclination in the human soul, but when you start talking to me about the devil as a person, I find it pretty farfetched."

"Farfetched or not, it's a reality, and I can only talk to you about reality."

"And how do you know it? Have you seen him personally?"

He laughed. "Only once, but I'm not the only father in the monastery who's seen him and fought with him."

"What do you mean that you've seen him?"

"Well, once he came and ruined all the vegetable gardens in the monastery."

"How did he ruin them?"

"By breaking the stakes, uprooting the plants, and putting everything in disarray." I looked at him incredulously, but he met my gaze with a smile and continued. "Once he came into my cell and struck me so hard that I still hurt the next day."

This made me recall the inexplicable thrashing I received when I was with that girl, and I asked him with renewed interest, "So, did you see him with your own eyes?"

"Sometimes you can see him, sometimes you can't. Once I saw three demons that were trying to play a joke on me."

"And what did you do?"

"I laughed—what else was I supposed to do? After all, they were pretty funny."

I continued to look at him in disbelief, but also with a lot of interest, because I was reflecting upon my own experiences. Perhaps this explained the banging, the slamming of doors, and that thrashing.

"Do they also make noise?" I asked.

"Do they ever! Around this time last year, one of the novices was going to be made a monk. At three o'clock in the morning, we were supposed to gather in the monastery church before daybreak for his tonsure, but that night all hell broke loose. They didn't leave a cell untouched. They banged on the doors, knocked on the windows, and howled and barked like beasts. We all met in the main church around midnight for mutual support—we younger monks were especially frightened."

I continued to listen, but I made it clear that I found all of this astonishing and hard to believe.

"Look," he said, "the devil doesn't want people to know that he exists, because it's easier for him to fight them if they're unaware of his existence. You don't protect yourself from an enemy unless you realize he exists. But once you've detected him, there's no reason for him to hide, so he then fights you out in the open."

He recounted other similar incidents to me. We discussed

yoga and man's hidden potential. We thrashed out these issues in detail, exploring whether all of these phenomena could be explained in terms of self-suggestion or psychoanalytic theories. Perhaps, I said, they were but a figment of the imagination, or maybe this was a matter of the subconscious, as Jung suggests.

The next day we had another conversation. I had told him that I had the ability to see people's auras, so he told me to try to see his aura while he was praying with his prayer rope.[1] I tried, but without success. Then he spoke to me about Father Paisios.

"Not far from here, there's a dear old monk named Father Paisios, who's a miracle worker."

I wasn't the least bit impressed. In fact, I couldn't have cared less. "So what?" I thought to myself. "The yogis have powers like that, and I have some experience in this area myself."

He asked me to give him a demonstration of some of the spiritual exercises I did when practicing yoga, so I made an effort to concentrate and enter a contemplative state in order to clearly and vividly perceive his aura. Suddenly, I felt an abrupt and sinister change in my soul. I was so alarmed by what was happening to my soul and mind that I stopped. I asked Father Athanasios, "Did you notice or sense anything?" He looked very uneasy, and I felt very odd. Unconsciously, I picked up a pen and began to draw, even though I had never practiced drawing and didn't know what I was going to draw. But my pen seemed to move on its own, producing hideous, ghastly faces with a single stroke. These faces, with disproportionate noses, ears, and teeth, conveyed an intense malice. They resembled the faces of demons in frescoes portraying hell. At a loss, I looked up at Father Athanasios and showed him these faces I had drawn, independently of any desire on my own part.

As soon as Father Athanasios saw my sketches, he wanted

[1] An Orthodox prayer rope is a looped rope with knots in it, used while saying short prayers, and especially the Jesus Prayer. (Regarding the Jesus Prayer, see "The Jesus Prayer and the Hindu Mantra" on pp. 276–85 below.)

to go and pray. He arose and told me, "I'll let you be for now. We can speak again tomorrow." And then he quickly went up the stairs.

I remained alone. What had happened to me put me on edge. I felt as though someone else were using me against my will. I decided to try to free myself from this influence and control my hand. "I know what I'll do," I said to myself, "I'll draw a chapel." I tried, but it was impossible. I kept drawing those hideous faces instead. "I'll try something easier," I thought, "a dome with a cross on top." But instead of that, I started to draw the breasts of a naked woman. In exasperation, I threw the paper on the ground. What was happening to me? I felt confused and frightened. I decided to lie down, hoping that some sleep would free me from my agitated state.

The next morning, Father Athanasios came to encourage me to go and see Father Paisios. Now it seemed like a good idea, so I got directions and set out on the path.

When I arrived at the elder's cell, I pulled on the cord attached to the bell. Shortly, the elder stuck his head out the window and called out, "What do you want, my boy?" I drew near the fence and asked him, "Won't you let me in, elder?" He put the keys on a wire that ran down to where I was and told me to relock the gate when I came in. I entered the front yard, locked the gate, and started to walk up to his dwelling. When I reached the front of the cell underneath the balcony where he was standing, the elder asked me to hand him a jacket that had fallen to the ground. I picked up the jacket and stretched to hand it up to him. When the elder bent down to take it from me, our eyes met for the first time. There was something about his eyes, large and penetrating, that nearly blinded me. His sweet gaze was powerful and sacred, transcending the limits of human nature as I knew it. In a flash, I lowered my head, in awe of the spiritual radiance that was before me. I felt very small. By the time I had walked the thirty yards around the

Elder Paisios's *Panagouda* cell, a hermitage belonging to
Koutloumousiou Monastery. In the foreground is the gate.

house, I felt as though a mystery concerning the capabilities of human nature had been revealed to me.

When we met again a few seconds later, I saw a dear old monk with quite normal eyes. He now appeared to be merely an average human being, without a trace of that spiritual splendor that I had seen earlier. We sat down and began to speak. In a little while, I told him, "Elder, I don't kiss the hands of priests, because I am not a believer."[1]

"Since you're not a believer, you're doing the right thing."

We discussed various topics. He was so good and kind to me that within a few minutes our souls were quite united. On account of his virtues and discretion, I felt the immense joy of finally getting to know someone I could trust. At one point, he laughed cheerfully and asked me if he had permission to help me spiritually. "Can I take a walk around inside you?" he asked.

I trusted him so much that I said yes right away. I couldn't help smiling when he added, "My feet smell, though," since he was clearly as pure as snow with the goodness of Christ. I answered, "It doesn't bother me." Then, with great gentleness and courtesy, he stepped into my soul. I felt a luminous and healing presence being united to my soul and illumining it with a gladsome light. It was like the joy and peace of returning home after years of cruel exile. I didn't even know that in this life you could feel such a rejuvenating peace in the embrace of God. The elder shared my joy.

---

[1] At this point, the author does not realize that Father Paisios is not a priest. In the Orthodox tradition, it is customary for a priest to bless believers who approach him, and for believers to kiss the hand with which the priest has blessed them. In Greece, it is common for this process to be abbreviated and for the believer to kiss the priest's hand immediately upon approaching him, the blessing being implied. This action on the part of the believer is a sign of respect for the office of the priesthood. More profoundly, it pays honor to the fact that the hands of the priest act as the hands of Christ during the Divine Liturgy (and, indeed, in all aspects of his priestly service).

Elder Paisios at his cell.

I learned later that ancient Christians used the term "watchful intoxication" to describe the way those under the influence of the Spirit soar to great, even ecstatic, spiritual heights while nevertheless remaining calm and sober—and that is how I felt as I entered this increasingly luminous, intense state, calm and watchful all the while.

After this, I returned to the monastery a changed man, spiritually and psychologically. The monks I encountered on the way back would cheerfully ask me if I was coming from Elder Paisios. It was almost like a conspiracy. The elder's gifts could be so easily discerned on my countenance that they could all see it. And since I, a neophyte, felt as though I had been bathed in a noetic light,[1] I joyfully told these old-timers, "Yes." Indeed, I had come into contact with something extraordinary, mysterious, and divine.

But, a month later, when I returned to life in my home city, I continued to live just as I had before. Of course, I had new questions, and I bought a very fine book entitled *Staretz Silouan* that Father Athanasios had recommended,[2] but for all intents and purposes, my life hadn't changed a bit.

"You Don't Have Any Right to Interfere with My Life"

Nevertheless, after this second visit to the Holy Mountain, I felt as though an invisible, inscrutable power was influencing the course of my life. For example, I noticed that I would be

[1] The adjective *noetic* means "of or related to the mind." It is derived from the Greek word *nous* (usually translated as "mind" or "intellect"), which in Orthodox tradition has a special meaning. It does not refer to man's rational faculty, but to that faculty by which man is able to directly perceive spiritual realities.

[2] By Archimandrite Sophrony (Sakharov), available in English translation as *Saint Silouan the Athonite* (Crestwood, N.Y.: St. Vladimir's Seminary Press, 1999).

unsuccessful in my low attempts to make advances towards members of the opposite sex. When I would try to sin with a woman—to employ Christian terminology—I was confronted for the first time with unusual difficulties. This happened frequently, over an extended period of time.

Although the most reasonable explanation would have been to attribute this to Father Paisios's intervention, I felt from the bottom of my soul that the priest-monk, Father Athanasios, was responsible. So I wrote him a letter in which I told him, "I don't know what you're doing, but whatever it is, stop doing it. You don't have any right to interfere with my life."

Later, Father Athanasios explained to me what was happening: "At the time, I was a newly ordained priest and the grace of the priesthood was quite palpable. I would commemorate you at every Liturgy I celebrated. Others beg us to pray for them and to commemorate them at Liturgy," he laughed, "and you were ready to beat us up for doing the same."

The Fragrance of the Cross

One summer afternoon, a friend who had accompanied me on my first trip to the Holy Mountain visited me at my home. Although he had remained more distant from Orthodox monasticism than I, it had made a good impression on him. That afternoon he was pensive, brooding over a dilemma he had to face. As we discussed the issue, he suggested that I work with him and give him some advice. Two courses of action stood before us. We could gain a good deal of money, but would spiritually harm others and ourselves in the process, or we could lose the opportunity to make money, but we would also not cause harm to anyone. We stood at the crossroads between virtue and vice, contemplating which path we should follow.

In the midst of the discussion, I remembered Father Paisios and in my heart I called out for him to help us. I then turned to my friend and suggested that we read some prayers, and decide what to do afterwards. The astonished look on his face made clear that he was taken aback by my suggestion. I thought he was going to make fun of me, but to my surprise he instead replied, "Okay, let's read some prayers."

Monastics read a service every afternoon called Compline. I happened to have a small booklet with that service, even though I had never read through it. Since I didn't have any icons in my house, I instead hung on the wall the wooden cross that I wore around my neck, which Father Paisios had made by hand and given to me as a gift. So we started to read the service, muddling our way through it and making plenty of mistakes. Within fifteen minutes, we had finished the service, and I bowed down to venerate the cross on the wall.[1]

As I approached the cross, I found myself engulfed in an subtle and exquisite fragrance. Beside myself with joy, I called out to my friend, "Come and venerate it too!" He bent down to venerate it, and then stood back in a daze. Again he went to venerate it and inhaled deeply. He turned to me in a state of awe and said, "But it's fragrant." He picked up the cross and smelled it. Our attention was completely captivated by it. As we took turns venerating it, we noticed that this heavenly fragrance filled the room and had an unexpected effect on us. Our souls felt joyful, our minds felt light, and our entire being took part in a state of spiritual euphoria, the same "watchful intoxication" I had experienced with the elder.

---

[1] Orthodox Christians venerate icons (representations of Christ, the saints, and the angels) and crosses as an aid in prayer. In Orthodox theology, a crucial distinction is made between worship and veneration. Worship is offered to God alone, while simple veneration (honoring and reverencing) is offered to holy things such as icons and crosses, as well as to saints and angels whom God has perfected in His image. The important role that icons play in preserving traditional Biblical Christianity was the principal subject of the Seventh Ecumenical Council, a Church-wide gathering held in Nicea in A.D. 787.

There was no need for further discussion. We had made our decision. We no longer cared about the money we would lose, because we knew with certainty what was the right thing to do and we were glad that we would do it, even if we would suffer some financial losses in the process, and be unable to get the motorcycle we wanted so much. Without any delay, we arose and happily went to settle the matter in the proper way.

Looking back on this episode, I realize that what benefited us the most was not that we had been spared from getting involved in some crooked business, but that we acquired the certainty and conviction that God acts within our daily lives. We had living proof that the saints were concerned about us and had the ability to help us with our daily struggles.

From then on, I would visit the Holy Mountain frequently, at times remaining for two or three months. I enjoyed the simple and peaceful way of life, full of introspection.

First Trials in the Spiritual Life

Disturbing Sounds

I remember, when I learned that Elder Paisios had written the life of Father Arsenios of Cappadocia, how excited I was to read it, because of the great impression the elder had made on me. I shut the door to my room at the Monastery of Koutloumousiou, the closest monastery to the elder's cell, and became quite absorbed in the book, which I found truly impressive. I remember thinking, "The Hindu yogis aren't the only ones with such powers. This priest must have been a great yogi." I had already read various Hindu books on the lives of some great yogis, but this was the first time I had read about a Christian saint. With amazement, I thought, "This means that spiritually advanced people exist even in Greece and in Christianity." The more I read, the more impressed I became with Father Arsenios's holy life.

Suddenly, I began to hear noises in my room that sounded like firecrackers going off. I jumped up in surprise and looked around uneasily. Although I couldn't find any explanation, the explosive sounds continued all around me, right in front of my face in broad daylight. I didn't have a clue how to react. At last, I decided to leave and head for the elder's cell.

I was quite upset as I told the elder what had happened, but he simply laughed and said, "Don't be afraid of that imp. There's nothing to worry about. He just saw that your soul was being edified by what you were reading, and he tried to stop you. It's nothing to be afraid of." He embraced me, made the sign of the Cross over me, and sent me on my way in peace.

On the way back, I thought to myself, "You don't suppose there really is a devil, like he says?" Naturally, I didn't accept the elder's explanation. Neither my native intelligence, my upbringing, my education, my understanding of the world, nor my ideology would permit me to accept the existence of the devil. It was too farfetched. On the other hand, I couldn't just ignore my experience. At a loss for any solution, I supposed it simply required further investigation.

The Howling of Unseen Dogs

On another occasion, I was alone in my room at Koutloumousiou, reading a book on the Christian spiritual life. I suddenly felt the desire to try and pray as a Christian, in order to see how prayer differs in practice from meditation. Now, I didn't know anything about prayer or how to pray, although I knew a good deal about meditation. I decided simply to kneel and speak to Christ. After all, I was sure that Christ was a good person and that I had nothing to fear from him, whether he was a great yogi or something else.

So I arose from bed and knelt down. But, as soon as my knees touched the floor, I started to hear something howling outside. In terror, I leapt to my feet and looked out the window, but I saw nothing moving in the noonday heat. Perplexed, I decided not to proceed any further. I was afraid of getting involved with something I didn't understand.

It was as though I were wrestling blindly in the dark with an unknown entity. I had made a small step into a spiritual realm when someone slammed the door in my face, making it perfectly clear that I wasn't welcome. I no longer felt like praying after receiving this menacing threat, but I couldn't ignore that something had happened that I urgently wanted to understand.

Several days later I went back to see Elder Paisios and to tell him what had taken place. He took me by the hand and looked into my eyes with immense love. I could feel this love and his concern for my well-being, and this gave me joy. "Don't be afraid," he said. "The demons are trying to scare you away from the right path, but God won't let them hurt you. He's got them tied up, so they howl like dogs. Don't be afraid."

When I was near the elder, I felt no fear—though, in general, I wasn't really afraid anyhow, because I wasn't aware of the danger and took things so lightly. But, although I liked the elder a great deal, I couldn't simply accept what he told me. I was unreceptive, and I didn't know what to believe or how to interpret what had taken place. And, since I felt there was no solid ground under my feet, I reached no conclusion.

A Nighttime Visitor

Another time, I was staying at the beautiful little Monastery of Stavronikita, located by the sea. One afternoon, I had the opportunity to speak in private with a venerable monk in the library of the monastery's guesthouse. At one point, I told him, "Elder, I'd like you to teach me to pray." With a surprised

Stavronikita Monastery, Mount Athos.

look in his eyes, he repeated my words, "You want me to teach you to pray?"

"Yes, Elder, what should I do in order to pray? What do I have to say? How should I sit?" Being influenced by Hinduism, I imagined that there must be a special method or technique, just as there was for the meditation I practiced. He understood how little I knew, but he didn't show it. "It's really quite simple, and you must approach prayer with simplicity. Just sit calmly in some corner and speak to Christ as though He were in front of you and listening to you. And He is in front of you and listening to you. Just speak to Him as you would speak to one of your friends."

But while he was still talking, I felt as though something alien were taking hold of me and altering the state of my soul. I cut him off and told him about this change, which was preventing me from continuing and was causing me to look at him negatively. I changed my mind about wanting to learn to pray. My words startled the monk, and he looked at me anxiously. "It's all right, my child. We'll talk about this tomorrow. For now, go and take a rest." He arose from his seat and quickly left with an uneasy expression on his face. By now, night had fallen. I went to my small, solitary room, lay down, and fell asleep.

I had not been asleep for more than a couple of hours when something bearing down on my chest awoke me from sleep. I opened my eyes in fear, but I didn't see anything except the furniture in the room. Nevertheless, I felt a powerful entity putting an unbearable amount of pressure on me. I cried out in my heart, "O Christ, I can't take it anymore. Get it out of here!" Immediately, I felt the room being emptied of this heavy presence, though I could still feel it standing menacingly outside my door. I didn't dare fall asleep, and so the hours passed with me in an uneasy state of alert. Only when daylight came was I able to take a short nap.

As soon as I awoke, I went into the monastery's courtyard, where I ran into the old monk with whom I had conversed the night before. He appeared to be very tired, as though he had been awake all night. Concerned, he lovingly asked me how I was and if I was all right. I told him that I was okay now that it had left me and I thanked him—I sensed that this monk had worn himself out praying for me all night long, and that it was on account of his prayers that my evening visitor had been unable to harm me.

On the following day, I walked two and half hours in order to see Father Paisios and to tell him what had happened. Smiling, he said, "Sit down, and I'll bring you a pistol." He went into his cell and brought me a prayer rope with thirty-three knots, representing the years of Christ's earthly life, and a cross. "Guess what?" he said, laughing. "This shoots spiritual bullets. Every time you say the prayer 'Lord Jesus Christ, have mercy on me,' it's like shooting at the devil, so he won't come near you. Take it, so you'll have it to defend yourself."

I was happy to have something of his, so I took it. After talking about other subjects, I left—much better, as usual, than when I had arrived. I felt refreshed and optimistic, spiritually and even physically stronger. My problems were solved and my questions were answered. When the elder would gently tap me on the head, a habit he had with his visitors, my soul would be filled with the peace and joy of paradise, which lasted for hours. Once, I recall, it lasted for days. There was no problem, fear, or difficulty in the presence of this divine assurance, gladness, and joy.

So, I returned to the monastery of Stavronikita. One evening, the nighttime visitor returned, but this time I had Father Paisios's "pistol." Even while I was sleeping, as soon as I sensed its presence, I began shooting, "Lord Jesus Christ, have mercy on me," and it immediately withdrew from me. I continued to say the prayer and, as the visitor withdrew, I was even bold enough to attack with it. But, as I did so, I felt a blood-chilling power that made me waver. It was much stronger than I was, and pounced on me. I began to pray non-stop, "Lord Jesus Christ, have mercy on me,"[1] and it was put to flight. It was as if the words of the prayer burned it—I had no strength of my own, but the invocation of Christ's name was powerful. Then my visitor, up to that point manifest in a terrifying form, seeming as though it could squash me like a bug, suddenly changed into a fat dwarf with a cap on his head. It started joking around, gradually approaching me as though it were playing a game. I was so taken back that I almost laughed, but as soon as it came close to me I could feel in my heart its evil and threatening malice. Again I resorted to the Jesus Prayer, and again it fled from me.

[1] Information about this prayer, called the Jesus Prayer, can be found on pp. 276–85 below.

A Piece of Candy

Another time when I was at the Monastery of Stavronikita, I was reading the Gospel according to Saint Luke: *And the seventy returned again with joy, saying, Lord, even the devils are subject unto us through Thy name. And He said unto them, I beheld Satan as lightning fall from heaven. Behold, I give unto you power to tread on serpents and scorpions, and over all the power of the enemy; and nothing shall by any means hurt you. Notwithstanding, in this rejoice not, that the spirits are subject unto you; but rather rejoice, because your names are written in heaven.*[1]

I was still unsure about whether all of this was really true. Was it possible for all those great and renowned philosophers whose works I had read and admired to have been unaware of this spiritual reality? There is a reason they acquired such names for themselves—they changed the face of humanity. My thoughts turned to Marx, Mao, Johann Bachofen, Freud, Jung, Adler, Erich Fromm, Khalil Gibran, Kazantzakis, Wilhelm Reich, Nietzsche, and so many others. I recalled the thought of Buddha, the sutras of Patanjali, the teachings of Gurdjieff, the Zen philosophy of D. T. Suzuki, and the Tao of Lao Tzu. Was it possible for all these wise and learned men with such knowledge of the world and society to have made so great a mistake, and for me to have discovered a truth of which they were ignorant? I wavered in a state of uncertainty. After all, I had studied these thinkers—I enjoyed their thought and found it appealing. It seemed farfetched that someone as young in years and intellectual maturity as myself could reach the truth, succeeding where they failed.

In my uncertainty, I continued reading the Gospel, when I felt a noetic light gently and softly come over my soul. This subtle light was as pure as a diamond and entered my soul easily and peacefully. It opened my mind to depths so

[1] Luke 10:17–20.

unfathomable that they would have startled me had not this light first united itself with my soul, granting me a state of profound peace. This is when I read the next verse, *In that hour Jesus rejoiced in spirit, and said, I thank Thee, O Father, Lord of heaven and earth, that Thou hast hid these things from the wise and prudent, and hast revealed them unto babes: even so, Father; for so it seemed good in Thy sight*[1]—and then I realized that I was one of those babes.

In the twinkling of an eye, I saw how this spiritual law works throughout the world. The rich and powerful, I saw, might obtain material possessions with schemes or diplomacy. Those whose education is merely scientific, though they might gain some knowledge about the outer shell of reality, will never be able to pry open the lid of materialism and existentially enter the pure waters of true life. Others pass their days cut off from the truth about life, moving in imaginary worlds of their own creation, believing, in their pride and self-centeredness, that the creations of their minds are the highest of all goods. They worship their ideas and order their lives around them, turning their own mind into their god, and so they live within a lie, in the darkness of their hypotheses, their theories, and their ignorance. Since all these egotistically believe in themselves, they are unable to make spiritual progress. Since they consider themselves to be superior to everyone else, they can't humble themselves to receive the truth from Christ. These unfortunate souls may foolishly try to fill their emptiness with material goods, taking from those in need so that they can appear to be superior. They may try to comfort themselves through sensual pleasures.

Those who experience and live within the most profound mystery of this world are the pure and simple of heart, who resemble babes in their humility, guilelessness, and goodness.

---

[1] Luke 10:21.

They are the ones who will come into contact with true life and the fountain of life. They are like green trees bearing the fruit of life, light, and the truth—and this fruit, rather than material goods, is their wealth.

I saw then that justice is ultimately triumphant and injustice self-destructive. When the unjust cause material harm to the people they exploit, they harm themselves spiritually, much more than they have harmed the others materially. These, then, are in fact the ones who are in greater need of God's help. Divine justice filled my soul to the brim. With a profound and calm joy, I kissed the Gospel again and again. I loved everyone, and I especially rejoiced for the babes of this world.

A few days later, I went to see Father Paisios and tell him what had happened. He laughed cheerfully and said, "Christ treated you to a piece of candy from His pastry shop." Then he looked me straight in the eye and said, "There are pastries, too." I am convinced that all these spiritual gifts were given to me on account of his prayers on my behalf.

The Elder's Lesser Gifts

Those who were more advanced on the way of Christ were well aware of the elder's higher gifts and made use of them for their spiritual benefit. Most of us had difficulty grasping or indeed even recognizing these gifts because they so far exceeded our own capabilities. Nevertheless, the elder had other, "lesser" divine gifts that many of us could in fact notice.

For example, the elder knew, in a way known only to Christ, the people who came to visit him. He knew what they were thinking about, what problems they were mulling over, and the solutions to their problems. In the beginning I was impressed by this, but with the passage of time all of us near the elder observed these gifts so frequently, on a daily basis, that we came to accept them as a natural part of life. I recall once being distressed because I knew I was wearying him. He turned to me and said, "Don't be upset. The people who come here—I know their names, their jobs, their problems, what they're thinking about, and so on, but I let them talk and speak their mind so they can let off some steam." Over time, it became a habit for me not even to refer to my problem, but to listen to his response right away.

During one Lenten season, I was living by myself in a cell in the forest of Mount Athos about a two hours' walk from the elder's cell, because I wanted to learn to say the Jesus Prayer. After four weeks of prayer and fasting, I was subject to a demonic attack of an intensity that I had not encountered in my other temptations. It receded, but I was afraid of what might come next, and I wondered if the elder was aware of what was happening. Although I was sure in my heart that he knew, lingering fear and the desire to see him made me decide to go and tell him in order to be absolutely certain.

So I set out by foot on the trail to the elder's cell. Along the way, I felt the desire to eat a sweet called a *kantaïfi*.[1] I was hungry after strictly fasting for so many days. But where would I find such a sweet on the Holy Mountain? If I had been in a coenobitic monastery and if it hadn't been Lent, perhaps I could have found something, but in the midst of the forest I might as well forget it. But I couldn't get my mind off of the *kantaïfi*. I had a craving for one, and in fact I couldn't think of anything else. I tried to concentrate on the words of the prayer, "Lord Jesus Christ, have mercy on me," but within a minute or two my thoughts were again revolving around the *kantaïfi*. Although it was totally ridiculous, this struggle lasted for two more hours.

---

[1] A baked sweet with a nut filling, covered in syrup. It quickly grows stale if unrefrigerated, and it would not be eaten during a period of fasting.

When I saw the elder's cell in front of me, I became very serious and began to think about precisely what I wanted to ask him so that I wouldn't tire him out. I forgot all about the *kantaïfi* and started to look forward to our meeting. When I approached the gate to his yard and saw that there wasn't anyone else there, I felt even happier, because I would have the good fortune of having time with the elder by myself. I struck the metal bar that he used for a doorbell and waited near the fence. The elder was taking his time, but he made some noise in his cell so that I would realize he was inside. Suddenly, he opened the door, and, little by little, playfully stuck his head out. He looked at me for a moment, laughed, and shut the door.

When he finally came out, clasping something in his hands, he was serious and formal. He started to shake whatever he was holding up and down, and burst out laughing, but then he grew serious again and slowly and with great ceremony walked down to me, all the while shaking what he held in his hands to draw my attention towards it. I couldn't see what it was because he was higher than I was. When he finally reached where I was standing, he could hardly contain his laughter. He slowly lowered his hands, but, as soon as I tried to see what he was holding, he quickly lifted them above my head. This happened quite a few times: it was like a game, and we laughed like children. At last, he abruptly lowered his hands, and there, on a small saucer, I saw the rich *kantaïfi* I had desired so much. I could hardly believe it. With a laugh, he said, "Go ahead and eat it quickly before someone sees you and gets scandalized." I didn't ask him where he had gotten such an impossible thing—a baked, non-Lenten sweet in the middle of the forest, in a monastic cell with no refrigeration. I was half-afraid of receiving a supernatural explanation.

I went inside his yard. I hadn't just received the *kantaïfi*, but also a lesson: if the elder knew about my trivial desire for a sweet, how much more would he be aware of danger in my

71

spiritual struggles? I felt ashamed of my senselessness. And I had been foolish enough to think that the spiritual attack had suddenly stopped because the attackers were afraid of me. The elder was the one who put them to flight by covering me with his prayers, even when I wasn't aware of it. I thought about all these things while I ate.

The elder lovingly looked at me and gave me one of his gentle, grace-filled taps on the head. He had used his joke to give me a very serious spiritual lesson. I felt then, in the depths of my soul, that I could trust him as an unerring spiritual guide. By the grace of God, it didn't matter how far apart in space his spiritual children were from him. He was well aware of what was taking place in their souls.

Another time, when I was getting tired of struggling on the Holy Mountain, I started to think about how nice it would be to leave and return to all the material comforts of life in the world. I thought about purchasing a bicycle for riding near the shore and a small jeep for excursions in the mountains. Since I was really fixated on these and other thoughts, I made up my mind to go and see the elder. But when I went to his cell, he wasn't home, so I decided to see if he was at a neighboring cell. I found him at a distance seated on a stump, reading something to a group of monks standing around him. They were quite engrossed in what he was reading, so I stood three or four yards away so as not to disturb them. Shortly, the elder stopped reading, looked up at me, and said, "It's good to see you—how did you come over here, with a jeep or a bicycle?" The others laughed, because they thought he was joking, but I realized that he knew the thoughts that captivated me. I was ashamed for not being a little more patient in my struggles.

He then went back to what he was reading and motioned for me to come closer in order to hear him. Then, looking at me with a smile on his face, he laughed and said, "Why weren't you a little more patient? If you hadn't come so fast with that

Elder Paisios on the grounds outside his cell.

jeep and bicycle, we would have had time to finish our reading." Everyone laughed, none of them suspecting what had taken place between the elder and me.

Accounts Given by Acquaintances

One of my friends, who had known Father Paisios for many years, was in America facing some very serious problems. He wrote an urgent letter to a monk on the Holy Mountain requesting that he go and ask Father Paisios about three specific issues and then call him back on the phone. The monk got the letter and went straight to Father Paisios's cell. The elder let him in immediately and, without losing a moment, told him to start taking notes lest he forget anything. The monk didn't have a chance to say why he came or who sent him the letter, much less to refer to the questions it raised, because Father Paisios began to answer them at once.

The elder received hundreds of letters from people all over the world. Naturally, he couldn't possibly answer all of them, but, even then, he knew their contents and answered them all miraculously with his prayers. For example, I knew a girl at the university, a hippie who had nothing to do with Christ or the Church—in fact, she was an atheist. She and her family were facing such serious problems with finances and interpersonal relations that, in her hopelessness, she had made up her mind to commit suicide. Before taking that step, however, she decided to write a letter to a dear old monk she had heard about somewhere, even though she didn't know his address. She wrote on the envelope, "Father Paisios, Holy Mountain," and thought, "If it reaches him, it reaches him." Shortly thereafter, the family arguments stopped and the members of her household made peace with each other. She was taken by surprise when she realized what had happened, and this encouraged her to seek Christ. She began to live the Christian life, and, ten years later, she took the great step of becoming a nun.

The elder changed many lives. I once met a man who told me that he used to make a great deal of money showing pornographic films. He was very suspicious of Christianity, and, when he first heard about Father Paisios, he supposed that he was a charlatan and decided to go to Mount Athos with two of his friends to "expose that monk." When they arrived, the elder received them in his yard, saying, "Sit down and let me serve you something." The elder served the other two gentlemen first, and then stood in front of the first man and turned the plate upside down, letting the sweet fall in the mud. "I dropped it," he said, "but that doesn't matter. Pick it up and eat it anyway." The fellow was insulted: "How do you expect me to eat it when it's filthy?" The elder sternly replied, "And why do you give people filth to eat?" Stunned, embarrassed, and in some fear, the man got up and left, but he went back again the next day and spoke with the elder. He told me he felt then as though the ground were shifting under his feet. The conversation was brief. "What am I supposed to do?" he asked. The elder responded, "First of all, shut down your business, then come back and talk to me again." He returned to Thessaloniki, closed the business, and began to look for new work. After about a month, he again went to speak with Father Paisios, who told him to go to confession and taught him how to put his life in order spiritually. I admired the man when I heard this—at just one call to repentance he had changed his life and followed Christ, just like Matthew the tax-collector in the Gospel.[1]

There are countless other instances of people whose lives have been thus changed. Simply waiting to see the elder with the other pilgrims, I would hear about their experiences with

---

[1] See Matthew 9:9.

him, experiences that could fill another book if they were all written down.

The Elder's Teaching Method

When I first met with Father Paisios, he spoke to me very little, because my soul wasn't open to his words so that they could take root and bear fruit. Instead, he strove to create the necessary openness in my soul by praying for me. His prayer, offered from a heart of great purity, had the power to work miracles. By his prayers, I acquired knowledge and experience in the spiritual life. Whether on Mount Athos, in Thessaloniki, or wherever I might be, I could sense his prayer touching me and covering me with its ineffable sweetness and peace. I can even recall being awakened from sleep by the palpable presence of his prayers. At times, I felt his prayer approaching me softly, like a gentle, fragrant breeze. Sometimes, its presence was brief. At other times, its presence was prolonged. The variety was endless. In every case, however, it was a spiritual reality first recognized in the depths of my soul: only afterwards did my reason strive, like a good servant, to interpret and put into words the mysteries that my soul had lived.

Even now my mind has difficulty explaining how the elder taught me by his prayers. During those extraordinary moments, it was hard to determine whether his prayer consisted of his thoughts directed towards me, or whether it was his soul actually approaching and coming into contact with my own. Perhaps there was also the presence of another person or power. One would have to be as spiritually advanced as the elder in order to give a full explanation: I can only speak about my experience within the limits of my own understanding.

The elder's knowledge was knowledge from the Holy Spirit, shed abundantly in his soul. When I would sit near him, I could feel the radiance of the Spirit shining upon me and changing me. When I was far away from him, the elder's intentions would be accomplished through his prayers, which became like a channel through which God acted upon my soul, again teaching me through the Holy Spirit, the Spirit of Truth.

Of course, there are various degrees according to which people participate in the illumination that the Holy Spirit brings to the world. I had read that the vision of the Uncreated Light is considered to be the most exalted of such experiences. Once I had some questions about this and asked the elder about it. He told me, "I was praying in my cell [that is, the cell of Ypatios at Katounakia], when I saw the Uncreated Light. When the Light started to fade, I looked around me and it seemed like it was dusk. I thought, 'The sun must have set,' but when I looked up, I saw the sun in the middle of the sky. It was the middle of the day in July, but it looked like twilight to me, because my eyes were adjusted to another Light. So you can see how intense it is." To such a degree had the elder's soul transcended the experience of most others, receiving *the Spirit of Truth, Whom the world cannot receive, because it seeth Him not, neither knoweth Him.*[1]

The sins I had committed in ignorance had opened a huge chasm between God and me. The elder's prayer used God's mercy as the raw material to build a bridge across this chasm, a bridge that would allow me to receive the gift of God's love.

A Great Blessing

One afternoon, when I entered the elder's yard, I could smell a fragrance wafting through the air. I asked the elder if he was burning any incense and looked around in order to determine where the scent was coming from, but I couldn't see anything.

[1] John 14:17.

After all, we were outdoors. The elder calmly asked me if I could smell anything. And as I went to sit next to him, I simply responded that I could and that it was, in fact, very powerful. I had grown so accustomed to unusual and inexplicable phenomena taking place at the elder's cell or in his presence that I had come to just take them for granted. He once told me, "Don't give too much weight to these kinds of things or spend a lot of time investigating them, because there's always the danger that the devil's tricking you. If something is from God and you ignore it in order to be spiritually careful, God is so good that He'll find another way to speak to you that's even more obvious." In any event, I quickly forgot all about the fragrance as I got involved in an interesting conversation with the elder. When I arose to leave, I bowed to kiss his hand as is traditional, hoping that he would give me one of his spiritual taps on the head, to fill my mind and heart with joy and peace. And that is precisely what happened.

As we reached the gate I was again in a spiritual state of watchful inebriation. I suddenly wanted to take his hand and kiss it again, so I did. The elder laughed cheerfully and closed the gate behind me. Looking down the incline at me from within his yard, he started making jokes about "God's pastry shop." I felt so joyful that it was even embarrassing. I didn't want to leave his presence—where else did I have to go? He then placed his hands on my head and momentarily lifted up his eyes to heaven. I was flooded by a spiritual torrent. I felt such a fullness of life and light, of peace and joy, that it took my breath away. Words are insufficient to express what I felt: it was beyond all measurement and comparison.

I timidly lifted up my eyes to look at his joyful, yet serious face. He reached out his hand to break off a branch from a nearby bush and he gently tapped me on the head with it. Like the waters of a rushing river, waves of grace descended upon me. I was in my right mind, I was completely aware of my surroundings, yet I simultaneously felt intoxicated by the Spirit.

I do not recall leaving the elder's gate, but I do remember that I rapidly climbed the path to the Monastery of Koutloumousiou without stopping for breath. On the way, I took off my sweater, and when I entered the monastery I was wearing my t-shirt. Although the monks were quite strict when it came to the dress code, no one said anything to me. The way they looked at me showed that they were surprised but understood what had happened. Father Athanasios sighed and said, "Oh, some people wear themselves out, and others receive blessings!" I laughed at the kind way he teased me.

This intense grace remained with me for many days, and, for about a month, I was in a state of deep peace, calm, joy, and contentment. People could see a change in my face, in my movements, and in my tone of voice. After about ten days, I went to another monastery, and, the moment one of the priest-monks there saw me, he called out, "There's a very grace-filled visitor."

The Guardian Angel

> An angel, then, is a noetic essence, in perpetual motion, with free will, incorporeal.... It is not as they really are that they reveal themselves to the worthy men to whom God wishes them to appear, but in a changed form which the beholders are capable of seeing.
>
> —St. John of Damascus[1]

After much time had passed, I recalled another incident that took place that same day, which I had forgotten about

---

[1] *An Exact Exposition of the Orthodox Faith* 2.3 ("Concerning Angels"). Cf. *Nicene and Post-Nicene Fathers,* 2nd series, vol. 9 (Edinburgh: T&T Clark, 1898), p. 19.

almost as soon as it occurred. As I left the elder's gate, near where the path to his cell passes through the cypress trees, I saw a young man, about sixteen or seventeen years old, standing about a yard in front of me. He was dressed in a costly robe that resembled a deacon's vestment. He had a beauty about him that was as pure as a flower of the field, without any of the provocative or carnal features that are often found in beautiful people. I don't remember how long we spoke or what we said. I only remember that while we spoke I knew in my soul that he was an angel, my guardian angel. Afterwards, I completely forgot about this meeting.

When I did remember what happened, much later, I went to the elder and mentioned it to him. He laughed and told me, "You were a spiritual baby then, but now that you've matured a bit, God's allowed you to remember it."

The Elder's Generosity

Unfortunately I was very senseless, and I soon let these precious gifts be stolen. It was as though I had holes in my pockets. Each time I left the Holy Mountain, I was enticed into sin and wasted the precious gifts that my father had given me, becoming poorer and more wretched than I had been in the beginning.

He neither got angry with me nor gave up on me. Every time I returned in repentance, he took hold of me, lifted me up, cleaned me off, tended to my wounds, dressed me like a prince, filled my purse with gold, and sent me back again, with honors, to the world. So many times, this lamentable story repeated itself. So many times, I behaved without sense or gratitude—and yet he never lessened or limited his spiritual gifts.

Unconditional Love

*And to know the love of Christ, which surpasseth knowl-
edge.*

— Ephesians 3:19

In this world, I hadn't found any genuine love, or anyone
who really loved me for who I was. Everyone had a motive for
loving me. Girls would love men for an attractive face, a handsome body, and beautiful eyes. But if I had been in an accident
resulting in the loss of a limb or the disfigurement of my face,
no woman would have cared to stay at my side, even though I
would still have been the same person. No woman really loved
me, loved or was even interested in the deeper core of my being; rather, they were only concerned with the appearance of
my body. And the guys who were my friends loved me for my
mind, my ideas, my knowledge, and my wit; but if I hadn't
been educated, I would still have been the same person. Were I
to have suffered a wound to the head and become a little
slower on the uptake, the deeper core of my being, my soul,
would still have been the same, yet no one would have still
loved me. Even the natural love of my parents was not free
from utilitarian motives. It was colored by certain expectations
and desires for compensation in the future. They loved me because I was intelligent, because I was a good student, and because I would take care of them in their old age. No one loved
me without guile, without self-interest, or without the expecta-
tion of something in return. My real self existed beneath the
surface, apart from my being smart or stupid, handsome or
ugly, good or bad. I longed for this core of my being to be
loved without any reason or societal justification, but just because I existed.

To see how people would react, I began to cast off those

external attributes that enhanced my appearance. I began with the way I dressed, starting to wear clothes that were unattractive and in bad taste. Soon people became irritated. In fact, quite a few people became angry about this change and kept me at a distance. I was shocked to discover how false and superficial my relations with others were. Although some of my closest friends were fed up with me, I was determined to persevere until I had cast off everything false and superficial and had completely stripped and freed myself from things external. It was the only way to know who really understood me deeply—whoever would remain by my side to the end would do so exclusively for who I was.

In the end, no one remained by my side. I found the core of my being, but I was utterly forsaken and completely alone. It would have been easy to return again to the life of superficiality. After all, I had been good at acting out different roles since childhood. I could again start playing the roles of lover, friend, and son, but I didn't want to anymore. I wanted to explore and get to know my real self.

It was painful to realize, as I came to, that I had constructed a beautified, but false, idol of my self. This pain destroyed that idol. It was like a razor that cut deep, separating flesh from bone, truth from falsehood—a fire that burned the lies. I had to be like a resolved surgeon and cut out everything fake within my soul. The surgery had to take place; otherwise I would never find my way to salvation or the truth.

During this period of time, I suffered greatly in the depths of my being from a deep, bone-crushing pain. My soul was in a state of mute horror, and I felt as though my mind would be shattered into a thousand small pieces. I could barely think rationally. I was unable to sleep. I was afraid to sleep. As soon as I would start to grow drowsy, and my reason would begin to relax its control over my emotions, my soul would suddenly become like a sore oozing with a river of pain that threatened to destroy my existence. I would awaken in a state of alarm, trying to put a stop to that terrible agony. My ability to reason, that fine thread holding my mind together, was ready to snap at any moment. I was afraid I would lose my mind because of my inability to withstand the pain.

Persistently and insistently, I strove to understand this pain and to find its cause. I couldn't tell whether it was from a lack of love or an absence of truth. Perhaps it was because my life seemed purposeless. I yearned greatly for an answer and struggled to find one, but I began to wonder if the search for genuine love in this world was an impossible quest. With this in mind, I went to see Father Paisios and opened up my heart to him. I impatiently awaited his response. He became serious and said, "Man is worthy of being loved just because he's in the image of God. It doesn't matter at all if he's good or bad, moral or sinful. Man is worthy of being loved for what he is. Christ loved and sacrificed Himself for sinful, corrupt people. *I came not to call the righteous, but sinners to repentance.*[1] We should be the same way: we should love everyone without making any distinctions. Just like the sun rises on everyone, intelligent and unintelligent, good and evil, beautiful and ugly, our love should be like the love of God—love that's like the sun and shines on His whole creation without making distinctions." As Saint Paul writes in his epistle to the Romans, *The love of God is shed abroad in our hearts by the Holy Spirit Who is given unto us.*[2] At last, I felt consoled. There was someone who agreed with me and understood me, and it was Father Paisios.

Nevertheless, when I returned home, the pain remained. At times, it was more than I could bear. During the night, I would wake up weeping and unable to speak. From the utter depths of my being I would silently cry out, "My God, my God." I would strike my head against my pillow in repentance,

[1] Matthew 9:13, Mark 2:17, Luke 5:32.
[2] Romans 5:5.

thinking about how I had gone so far astray and done so much that was wrong. "My God, my God"—during those dread nights I would struggle with despair over my entire life.

Then, on one of those evenings, when I was praying alone in my apartment, I felt Him approaching me. I came to know the *perfect love* that *casteth out fear*.[1] He was so present, although He was invisible. He was so immaterial, although He was almighty. He was so unapproachable and intangible, although He was so near. He touched me, but not just on the surface. He touched the innermost depths of my being, filling me and permeating me. He united Himself with me so closely that we became as one. I was intoxicated by God, and I became like fire so that my very body burned. I wanted to be completely open towards Him, without a single corner of my soul remaining hidden, no matter how ugly or filthy it was. I wanted everything to be known to Him, so I confessed to Him and showed Him all my crooked and filthy ways, all of my vices. I longed for every corner of my soul to be visited by Him, by this vast infinite Love coming from all directions and filling all things. As Saint Symeon the New Theologian cried, "O Deifying Love that is God!"[2] This Love holds the universe together, connecting every part of it, giving it the strength to exist, and being the very cause of its continued existence.

At the same time, however, I felt so unworthy and so unfit to be with Him that I fell to the ground with my face to the floor, in order to sink into the very concrete if I could. I was so full of vice, so unworthy to exist and to be united with Him, that I wished I could stop living. I remained motionless, but this Love drew near to me, this Love that welled forth from the One Whose gaze is directed towards all things and Who pervades all things, the One Who has always existed.

[1] 1 John 4:18
[2] Hymn 5:24. Cf. St. Symeon the New Theologian, *Hymns of Divine Love* (Denville, N.J.: Dimension Books, n.d.), p. 26.

Because He loved me, He allowed me to approach Him, and He purified me and healed me, thoroughly and deeply, of all my pains and sores. He drew me gently, steadily, and safely from darkness to light, from filth to purity, from non-being into being. He granted me a more intense, true, and vital existence, not because He had need of me, but because He is Love.

I do not know how long this experience lasted. It began and ended in a single night. I do know, however, that it healed my pain, brought stability to my thoughts, put an end to my danger, and answered my questions. I learned far more than I asked. This Love granted me sure and certain knowledge: even today, I can feel its effects.

Now I know that, as human beings in synergy with God, we all have the potential to give birth in our hearts to such a love, which will ontologically transform us and deify us. Few of us give birth to this love, however, and we bear responsibility for not doing so on account of our slothfulness, fear, and involvement with trivialities. This love is the spiritual love that the Holy Spirit begets within the human soul, making human beings into *partakers of the divine nature.*[1] It is far superior to any human love—even the love of a mother is insignificant when compared to it. This all-powerful love vanquishes death, overcomes the laws of nature, and is the source of order throughout the universe, for it is the very mystery of the universe. *For God is love.*[2] Father Paisios had this kind of love for all people, for every living thing, and for all creation, and this is the reason people gathered around him. It has sustained me throughout my life, and I will turn to it for support until my very last breath.

---

[1] 2 Peter 1:4.
[2] 1 John 4:8

CHAPTER THREE

On the Brink:
Between Two Spiritual Traditions

My Meeting with Swami Yogamougananda

During this period in my life, I was open to a variety of influences. On the one hand, the prayers of the elder had a powerful effect on me, filling my disturbed soul with peace, providing it with an oasis of joy in my desert of pain, and granting me clarity and calmness in the jungle of my thoughts. Indeed, I could feel his prayers in the evening while I slept and during the day as I walked through the city. They comforted me, strengthened me, and gradually gave me the hope to pull away from a life of self-destruction. On the other hand, I didn't give up my evil habits, which over the years had become passions,[1] spreading strong roots into the depths of my soul and pulling me headfirst wherever they wished. I was trying to fill the emptiness in my life with material goods and philosophical theories, but the emptiness continued to expand, only increasing my anguish. My mind labored feverishly in order to find answers that would open a way out. I read many books and thought a great deal; I examined various philosophical systems and viewpoints. I turned to music and art, but to no avail—I found no solution, no way out.

The elder showed me much that was great and wonderful.

---

[1] Regarding the term "passions," see the note on p. 12 above.

He didn't merely say a lot of words. He granted me experiences that taught me lessons of great importance and value. When his soul touched my soul, his fervent yet sweet-tempered love moved him to grant me his own spiritual eyes so that I would be able to see, and his own heart so that I would be able to feel. In this way, the thick cloud of ignorance that encircled me began to open up, so that I could perceive the world's mysterious depth and richness. Life became meaningful without wounding me the way pleasure did. The knowledge that this other world exists was a different form of pleasure, a pleasure that never ended, but that became continuously deeper and more intense. And when this spiritual pleasure withdrew, it left joy, not suffering, in its stead.

Even now, in spite of all the changes in my life, whenever I behold the clouds, the birds, the sun, the trees, the animals, the sea, and my fellow man, I continue to feel as though I were enveloped in a mystery. And the greatest mystery, and that closest at hand, is my own self, a wondrous and unmapped world hidden within my soul. I felt that it was important to come to know this world, and I greatly desired to do so. I felt as though there were another hidden and invisible power that ruled and watched over my soul. At that time, however, I was intellectually a rebel and wanted to escape from this power.

I was exposed to other influences, quite different from the influence of the elder, on account of loose living. Also, my interest in the occult, esotericism, "white magic," yoga, Zen Buddhism, and related topics had hardly waned. I did not have a clear-cut opinion on these subjects. They seemed to be notable and encouraging possibilities that could make life easier and uncover its hidden potential.

I believed their impressive promises in spite of the elder's warnings. He told me, "Look here, my child, there are two powers in this world: God and the devil. Everything depends on who you're connected with. I'm with God. I'm with Christ. Who are they with? Satan has 'power,' too. He can work miracles of deception. He was an archangel, and he still has an archangel's power, because *the gifts ... of God are irrevocable.*"[1]

It was out of pride, the elder said, by the misuse of his God-given free will, that Lucifer became twisted and fell from heaven—and in this fall his light became darkness and he became the original inventor of evil and falsehood. The devil hates man, not only because man is called to occupy a place near the throne of God, but also because hate is the response that wells forth from his being when he looks at any creature. He wages a war to separate men from God, using every ploy, lie, delusion, guile, thought, and deed that can remove them from the light. There are people who have entered his service—some even knowingly—and through whom he works his false wonders.

I listened to all of this, but I didn't believe it. On the other hand, I couldn't quite reject it. The elder was so good and sweet that I couldn't question his character. I had seen so many miracles, so many gifts, so much knowledge, and so much holiness in him that I couldn't just disregard his views. So I remained on the fence.

Others were of the opinion that all faiths are basically the same: all religions lead to the same God, and all pathways terminate at the same place. It was only natural, of course, that each person would put effort into advertising his own "shop." The yogis said that yoga was the highest path and found fault with other paths. The Masons had something to say about everyone else, so that they ultimately came off as the best and wisest. Those involved with "white magic" claimed that their path was more suitable for the psychological makeup of

[1] Romans 11:29.

Western man, yoga being more suitable for Easterners. And so on. There was one point, however, on which they all seemed to be in agreement—that the Church was a dead, fossilized institution for the unintelligent, only to be pitied, lacking in knowledge, power, and life.

Once I went for a walk in the forest near Thessaloniki in order to assuage my pain, put my thoughts in order, and reach some conclusion about everything that was happening to me. I had been lying down for a while on the pine needles when suddenly something took hold of me so violently that I completely lost contact with my surroundings. I could neither see, nor hear, nor feel anything in the forest. I couldn't tell whether my eyes were open or shut. And then I saw an image, although I couldn't tell whether it was in front of me or simply in my mind's eye. It was of a woman with a beautiful face and long, dark hair, wearing a simple brown robe. In the place of her eyes, there were two silver fish the size of a pair of glasses. She was impressive and very attractive. She then departed from my field of vision as suddenly as she had entered it.

I sat where I was and thought about what I had just seen. It didn't upset me, because I realized it was just a message from the local ashram I would occasionally visit. A few days earlier, walking along one of the main roads of the city, I had felt as though someone were trying to entice me to visit there. I attributed my awakened desire to Swami Sivamurti, the Swamiji (which is how they referred to the highest authority at the ashram), but I didn't heed this "invitation." In fact, it irritated me, because I could tell that this desire was implanted from outside of me. This time, however, it was so intense that I decided to make a visit for curiosity's sake. I didn't mull over the subject at length—I decided I would get to the end of the matter once and for all.

A few days later, on a sunny day that dried out the grass, I

drove my car up to the suburban mansion in which the ashram
was then located. In the inner courtyard, the Swamiji was sitting with another swami, an Indian. This visitor from abroad
was a beautiful woman with a dark complexion and short hair,
a very spiritually advanced swami named Yogamougananda.
The rest of the residents of the ashram were standing at a distance, waiting for an opportunity to meet and speak with her.

I got along with people easily, and I could be very carefree
if I wanted to. I don't know what came over me, but I jokingly
called out to her, "I was searching for you in heaven, but I have
found you on earth." The Indian woman leaned over and in
English asked the Swamiji, Sivamurti, what I had said. The
Swamiji explained that when I came up to the villa I had been
looking for her.

Now, I neither liked nor disliked the Swamiji. I recall that
the first time that I laid eyes on her, after waiting in the ashram
just for this purpose, I saw through her mystique. I thought it
was ridiculous the way the crowd of young people waited so
impatiently for her to come out of her room. All of a sudden,
she majestically came forth, like a queen emerging from her
royal chambers in order to bestow gifts and favors upon her
adoring subjects. A need for people to admire her seemed to be
behind this second-rate theatrical performance, which I would
see repeated on subsequent visits. She briefly glanced at me,
but I refused to play the role of an admirer that both she and
the others expected me to. I looked at them for a moment, and
then went back to minding my own business. I was disappointed, though I knew I had no reason to assume that all
gurus shared the Swamiji's faults.

I also remember another time, when I was offered the sin-
gular honor of driving the Swamiji to the airport in my car so
that I could have "the rare opportunity to be helped by the
spiritual aura of a great yogi." I found an excuse to refuse,

because I did not want to accept the role being offered me: that of the admiring disciple who is expected to offer his services for the honor of being in the Swamiji's presence. Rather, I saw that it was part of an ugly power game she was playing in order to control those around her, and I did not wish to be responsible for participating in it. Indeed, the only reason I went to the ashram so many times was to acquire knowledge and learn about the Hindu perspective.

I sat next to them in a relaxed manner as among equals, since I was not bound by a student-teacher relationship. Strangely enough, I didn't strike up a conversation with Sivamurti, but with the Indian woman, Swami Yogamougananda. Swami Sivamurti limited herself to translating when we were having difficulty communicating in English. Swami Yogamougananda and I spoke at such length that those around us peered at us with a mixture of jealousy and curiosity. Apparently, the Indian yogi had considered my greeting to be significant. We spoke about many subjects, including the question of who I truly was: What was my nature? What were my capacities? How should I live? We spoke also about the world at large, Elder Paisios, and my vision in the forest. When I described the vision, she smiled at me meaningfully.

She told me, "The time has come for you to find your own guru. I had such questions from the age of five." "How is it possible for a child to have such questions?" I replied. "From my previous lives," she answered.

This was an impressive answer. At the same time, the Christian view espoused by the elder and the other monks flashed through my mind. They taught that there are no previous lives: at conception, a new person is created, and, after death, the body decomposes while the soul remains near God and aware of its existence, until the resurrection of the dead when all will receive back their bodies. Then, the bodies of those who are saved will be like the resurrected body of Jesus Christ: spiritual, glorious, eternal, incorrupt, and no longer subject to sickness, hunger, thirst, or the need for sleep. They will have dominion over the material world and its physical laws, as did the body of Christ after it was quickened in the Resurrection, passing through closed doors and ascending into heaven. By the power of God and through the proper use of their free will, the saved will become gods by grace.[1]

(Later, when I once asked the elder about the transmigration of souls, he told me, "Look here—this is one of the devil's biggest traps. Someone who believes in it says, 'Oh well, it doesn't matter if I don't pull it off in this life: I'll succeed in the next one.' So he gets lax spiritually. But the devil knows that there won't be a next time. That schemer thinks, 'Sit still and let me get my hands on you just once, and we'll see what happens afterwards.'" The elder then looked at me and said, "Now, write that down. Yes, write it down!")

I then asked the Swami, "Why do the monks say that you are on the devil's side?"

"They are ignorant, because they are at a lower level."

"No," I responded, "that's not true! They are not at a lower level. They know many things."

I had the elder in mind. I recalled the many miracles he had worked, such as the time he had taken by the hand a man paralyzed from birth and enabled him to walk around the room. The elder had told me many details of my own life that even I had forgotten. He would feed wild bears by hand, for nature was obedient to him. He saw and conversed with saints, angels, and the Virgin Mary. He could be in a distant location without having traveled.

[1] In Orthodox theology, this process is referred to as "deification" (in Greek, *theosis*). See pp. 262–63 below.

Nevertheless, miracles were not the reason that I cried out with a resounding "No." My objection was based on something deeper and more hidden. The elder was a God-bearer. He had God in his heart and in his soul. Each of us could feel the grace of God in the elder's presence. Christ's words were incarnate in the elder's life: *If a man love Me, he will keep My words: and My Father will love him, and We will come unto him, and make Our abode with him.*[1] God had made the elder's heart His home. The thousands of people who visited him would relate their experiences of him with gratitude. Their testimonies were the elder's fruit. Truly, *he that abideth in Me, and I in him, the same bringeth forth much fruit.*[2]

Of course, at the time I would hardly have been able to express this deep sense with the clarity I have just now. Nevertheless, this knowledge was a part of me, and it made me object to what she said.

She continued, "Neither God nor the devil exists. We are already further advanced, beyond good and evil. After all, what is evil? What is sin?"

I answered, "When you harm, hurt, upset, or kill someone, or even your own self, you are committing a sin."

Our conversation ended with this disagreement. We arose and went our separate ways. I stayed around the ashram for a little, though, because I had found some acquaintances there. At one point when I was alone, Yogamougananda approached me and asked me directly, "And whose side are you on?" I playfully answered, "I am beyond good and evil." But she became serious, stared at me with an intense look, and continued, "If only God and the devil existed, who would you side with?" I replied, "The monks say that you are with the devil." "So what?" she said.

Did she mean, "So what if the monks say that?" or "So what

[1] John 14:23.
[2] John 15:5.

if we're with the devil?" The way that she put it made it more than a question: it was an invitation. And, though her words were few and ambiguous, her posture, her countenance, and the tone of her voice were eloquent and clear as a bell. By non-verbal means, I felt her saying, "We're with the devil and we're having a great time. Come along for the ride—what are you afraid of?"

I felt physically attracted to her, or perhaps I was just affected by a *Tantra*-related phenomenon of some kind.[1] In any event, it seemed that—by some means unbeknownst to me—she had managed to inflame my soul, so that I suddenly felt a rush of desire pushing me to answer, "I am with the devil." I was jolted by this unexpected attack. I struggled to use my reason to regain my balance after this overwhelming wave of desire, so powerful that it nearly washed me away. I tried to understand this extremely strange experience—such a manifestation of power surprised me. "Since she has this kind of power," I thought, "I should have been careful around her." So many things were happening to me at once. She stood in front of me and continued to gaze at me intensely, her countenance dominating her appearance.

I managed to gain control over the irrational impulse of my soul, and did not yield to say what was so strongly fixed in my mind. And so I answered, "I am with God." I wanted to continue, but her face immediately grew dark. I didn't have time to discern whether she was angry, threatening, or full of hatred, because she made an about-face and left without saying another word. If she hadn't left so abruptly, I would have told her, "But I like rebels, and I've been a rebel all my life." Afterwards, I never saw her again.

Later, I learned other facts about this swami. From a young age, she had been a disciple of a guru and later became one of

---

[1] The *Tantras* are Hindu or Buddhist scriptures that discuss a variety of esoteric topics, including meditative and sexual practices.

the closest disciples of Satyananda.[1] She gave lectures and lessons in Greece. Many considered her to be quite advanced and at a high spiritual level, a reputation she even had at the central ashram of the movement in Mungir, India, as I was able to confirm when I went there a few months later.

Silva Mind Control

Some time before I got to know the elder, I had come into contact with Silva Mind Control, now known as the Silva Method, through a book of the same title that my cousin gave me. In this book, José Silva, a once-poor man from Mexico, claims that he has discovered a method by which one can make use of the mind's hidden potential. Putting this method into practice for himself, he became the wealthy founder and leader of a worldwide organization whose goal is to spread this method throughout the world. Today, this organization has offices even in Greece. Its members pay for participating in seminars that are held from time to time, form groups, and try to attract younger people to the seminars.

The method is based on the scientific observation that the brain generates different kinds of electromagnetic waves when one is awake, when one is in a deep sleep, and when one is between sleep and wakefulness, or in a light sleep. The waves that correspond to the state between sleep and wakefulness, generated when the brain is at the alpha level, are called alpha waves. Now, the members of the Silva Method movement claim that the brain can perform other functions, or can make better use of its potential, when it is at the alpha level. They teach a method by which a person can consciously "descend to the alpha level" at will and without falling asleep, by counting

[1] Swami Satyananda Saraswati (born 1923), regarded as a yoga master and guru both in his native India and in the West. See chapter 4 below.

backwards. Supposedly, when someone is at this level, he can make use of the hidden potential of his mind.

All of their views are packaged in scientific terminology. At no point does one hear about yoga or Eastern religions. On the contrary, Western views on science and psychology are presented, thus attracting individuals who place great trust in scientific knowledge. One would have to enter into the organization in order to begin to suspect its difficult-to-discern connections with Eastern mysticism. Only when one has become more involved with them do they begin to speak about how one can also use, for example, yoga and occult techniques in order to further one's potential.

Of course, I did not realize all of this then. So when I learned that an introductory lecture on José Silva's method was being organized at the Center for Macedonian Studies, I was very interested in attending. I went and heard the entire presentation. It vaguely reminded me of yoga, with which I was already familiar, though someone who had never been involved with yoga would never have suspected such a relationship.

At the end of the lecture, I asked the speaker a question that had been on my mind. "The human mind naturally functions in such a manner that it is found at the alpha level for only a limited period of time every twenty-four hours. You are suggesting that we interfere with this spontaneous natural process, attempting to alter it or replace it with another way of functioning, trying to remain at the alpha level as long as we can. But how do we know that this isn't dangerous? How can we be sure that this defiance of nature will not produce some sort of imbalance or psychosomatic injury? For example, how do we know that this will not have an adverse affect on our nervous system, even if the injury does not manifest itself at once? The brain's endurance may have certain limits. What will happen if we systematically and chronically violate its normal processes? How do we know that it will withstand such stress?"

The teacher simply answered, "Don't be afraid: we know what we're doing." In other words, I was simply supposed to believe them and believe in their wisdom. A doctor or other scientist, I thought to myself, would have brought forward experimental proof—measurable results. He would have explained, for instance, how a certain drug or a certain procedure was tested on a group for a certain length of time, how the members of the group were examined, and what were the findings in terms of positive results and negative side effects. But these people did not merely lack scientific evidence based on experimentation—they were not even prepared for a scientific discussion, but were merely trying to pacify me with assurances. How much, I asked myself, can someone trust a person he doesn't know? Can he trust him with his motorcycle, his car, his home, or his bank account? Would it make sense to give him free reign over his mind, mental processes, and psychological balance? I was amazed by how many people did trust them.

That year, I didn't go back to their seminars, but two years later, several months after my meeting with Swami Yogamougananda, I did return. One day, I was sitting at the Majestic, a shoreline café popular with students. There, I met an acquaintance of mine, who told me that he was going to take part in the first lesson at a seminar for Silva Mind Control, and I decided to accept his invitation to accompany him. The seminar was held in a conference room in the Electra Palace Hotel on Aristotle Square, one of the finest hotels in Thessaloniki. It would last for four to five days, and the fee was about half of a student's monthly wages. I met the teacher and told him that I didn't have enough money, so he allowed me to attend free of charge.

Why did I make a snap decision to go back, after having so decisively rejected the movement before? In part, surely, just in order to have something to do, but I believe I had other motives, unknown to me at the time. For one thing, I had a desire to excel and to stand out from the crowd. Mind Control promised to help me to make use of my hidden potential and to utilize my entire mind, in contrast to the rest of the mass of humanity. I could help others—which really meant, be superior to them. In this way, then, the passions of my soul were masked by the beautiful ideas of making spiritual progress, searching for the truth, helping humanity, and so forth. (Of course, these were goals to which I was genuinely attracted, but on their own they couldn't really account for my sudden change of mind.) Many of us, perhaps, were also moved in some degree to participate by boredom and inner emptiness; by loneliness and a desire for belonging; and by the simple, basic wish for companionship, especially with the opposite sex.

The first day of the seminar went smoothly and everyone was quite pleased. At the end, I tried to meet with the teacher in private. He was a well-dressed man with a muscular physique, around fifty years old. His name was Paul, and he was second-generation Greek-American of Cypriot origin who lived in New York. He spoke Greek well, and we took a liking to each other. Since I was reading the works of Mihail Ivanov, a practitioner of white magic, I asked him, "Do you belong to the Universal White Brotherhood?"[1] He answered that he should think so. As our conversation proceeded, he could see that I had read a great deal about yoga, so he told me that he was a yogi. That surprised me a bit, because I had never

[1] Ivanov (1900–1986), known to his followers as Omraam Mikhaël Aïvanhov, was a disciple of Peter Deunov, also called Master Beinsa Douno (1864–1944). Deunov was the founder of the Universal White Brotherhood, an esoteric organization based in Bulgaria, and Ivanov was the founder of one of its largest international centers, in Fréjus, France. Ivanov's works include discussions of magic. He began to be called "Omraam" after a 1958 trip to India, during which, he related, the name had been bestowed upon him by a guru.

imagined seeing a yogi in a suit. He told me that he practiced *kriya* yoga[1] and had had Paramahansa Yogananda as a guru. At present, he was working in Greece to make some money. I knew of his teacher from one of his books, which I had read when I was a university freshman, and I would have liked to have met him.

We continued our conversation, and I could see that Paul was an advanced yogi. I told him how I felt as though whatever I did changed me and affected me deeply. "My actions, my words, and my thoughts alter my soul. I don't know how I should live, and I don't know where I should go. It's as though I'm sculpting myself daily, but without a design, without a model, and totally at random. I shouldn't continue living my life in this way, but I don't know how to live." He replied, "The next time that I come to Greece, in the spring, six months from now, we will spend a day together, but now I don't have enough time." "In the spring," I retorted, "I will be in India." I was surprised by my own answer—I had wanted to go to India, but had not seriously thought about when. I was also surprised by how quickly Paul and I had become so close. I felt that Paul had influenced me in some unknown way—today, I believe he had put me under a light hypnosis.

On the second day of the seminar, I was waiting in the lounge of the hotel for the beginning of the real instruction or initiation. Now, by this time I had come to know Father Paisios. So, by experience, I had some feel as to whether something sounded Christian or not. As I sat there, I was wondering

[1] *Kriya yoga* was popularized by Paramahansa Yogananda (1893–1952), founder of the Self-Realization Fellowship in the United States, who claimed it was an ancient form of yoga, a method for radically accelerating one's "evolution." In it, the practioner mentally directs his "life energy" to revolve around "spinal centers ... which correspond to the twelve astral signs of the zodiac" (*Autobiography of a Yogi* [Los Angeles: Self-Realization Fellowship, 1998], p. 210).

if I was doing the right thing. I thought about what Father Paisios had told me, and in my mind I begged him, "Elder, if this is evil, prevent it from taking place. Don't let it happen." Shortly thereafter, with the arrival of some girls and other participants, I completely forgot about my inner reservations.

We began the seminar by loudly intoning the word *Om,* which Hindu teaching considers sacred, in order to purify the atmosphere from spiritual interference. The seminar proceeded, but the students who were repeating the course began to get frustrated. During the breaks, they began to voice their gripes and complaints. I couldn't figure out what was going on. I really liked Paul and didn't enjoy listening to him being criticized.

As it turned out, Paul was beginning to suspect that I was the source of the difficulties. After the break, he began the next session with some jokes in order to break the tension. While he was telling the jokes and walking around the room, he tested me to see how I would respond to his actions. For example, he would suddenly give me his open hand to see my reaction. I responded spontaneously and positively, grabbing his hand firmly without even thinking about it. He did three or four tests of this sort, finishing with one that I had read about in a psychology book. It was then I realized that he had doubts about me and was testing my feelings about him and the seminar. It seemed strange, because I only had good feelings in that regard. In any event, I responded quite positively to all the tests.

He decided to go ahead with the initiation, but within half an hour of exercises, the returning students were again frustrated and grumbling. It didn't take long for their dissatisfaction to come to the surface. Two or three of them began to get fed up and complain openly. They defiantly asked, "Is there a spiritual shield over this seminar or isn't there?" For the new students, the question was hardly comprehensible. What was a "spiritual shield"? What were we being shielded from? Was there some danger? Who was threatening us, and who was shielding us?

The returning students minced their words in answering these questions. Nevertheless, they did stress that there was an interference making our initiation very difficult on a spiritual level: on other occasions, it had proceeded much more smoothly.

In the end, the sessions were broken off for a day. Paul announced that Maria, a former student of his, would continue the instruction, since he was not able to do so personally. That's when the thought flashed through my mind: What had I asked Father Paisios to do? Didn't I pray that he would prevent the initiation from taking place if it were something bad? Maybe the elder's hand had been in the unsuccessful outcome of the last meeting. I still wasn't sure, because there could have been a thousand other explanations. I decided to continue to go to the meetings, but I simultaneously prayed to Christ, and also asked the elder, to make it even more obvious in my eyes if there was something evil about the seminar.

After a space of one day, Maria came up from Athens to lead the meetings in Paul's place. She was a pleasant woman around thirty years old with light-brown hair. The initiation continued without any obstacles for everyone else, but I kept on encountering unexpected phenomena. For example, during a certain exercise we all had our eyes closed and had supposedly descended deep into the alpha level. We were supposed to picture in our minds images that Maria would name. Maria had selected these images in advance, and was directing us from one to the next without any pause, so that they resembled a movie playing in our minds.

Suddenly, while I was smoothly performing this exercise, it was as though an interruption jammed the film. Instead of seeing what Maria was describing, I saw a demon with an ugly, cunning face, complete with tail and horns. He didn't appear to be threatening or hostile. On the contrary, he was joking around and seemed to be well disposed towards me. This apparition took me by surprise. I wondered what this creature was and what he wanted from me. The interruption lasted only a few seconds, and afterwards the exercise proceeded normally. No one else was aware of what happened to me. During the rest of the exercises, I saw the demon many times in various ways.

Finally, I decided to ask Maria about it. When the instruction for the day was over, we went and sat in a corner of the lounge, where I described to her what had happened and asked for her opinion. She carefully listened to what I had to say, without being surprised or making objections. She accepted what had happened and told me that such phenomena occur in the spiritual realm.

She told me that, though she practiced yoga from time to time, she found certain errors in it and considered it to be an inferior path to the one she followed. The Mind Control seminar, she told me, was for beginners: if someone wanted to advance, he would have to find a personal teacher. She then began to speak to me about her own teacher, who lived in France. I gathered that he was a follower of Gurdjieff. She said that he helped her a great deal, although she had to pay him a considerable sum. She worked at least twelve hours a day apart from the seminar and would meet her teacher four or five times a year and give him nearly all of her money. She considered her connection with him to be worth such a price. Now, I could see that Maria was a bright young woman. She had a law degree and had traveled to many places, and I couldn't understand why she would give her teacher all of her annual earnings. I also wondered what kind of spiritual teacher would drive such a hard bargain. I thought of Christ, Whom I also considered to have been a spiritual teacher, telling the first disciples, *Freely ye have received, freely give,*[1] and I thought of Elder Paisios, who followed this teaching to the letter.

In any event, having heard her views and suggestions, I

[1] Matthew 10:8.

again posed the question: "Why did the demon appear in my mind?" She smiled kindly and said, "Apparently, the polarity of your cells attracts him." In other words, she maintained that I was somehow organically related to the devil at a cellular level. I found such an explanation astonishing. "So why did the demons appear to Christ?" I asked her. She started to squirm and said, "You ask difficult questions." And with that, she left. I surmised from her comments that she had two aims: to bring me into contact with her teacher, and to convince me that I had a connection with the demon I had seen, and a connection I should look at in a positive light.

The seminar was nearly over and had raised a number of questions. I wondered whether Maria's exposition to me of her views and the manifestation of the demon were not, in fact, the answer to my prayerful request to Father Paisios to make it more obvious in my eyes if there was something evil about the seminar. Indeed, a short time afterwards I asked the elder if he had heard my prayer and extended to me a helping hand. He smiled, and lovingly said, "Would I leave someone like you without any help?"

We had supposedly gained certain abilities from these meetings, such as the ability to diagnose someone's illness at a distance. We had, they told us, gained the capability of healing the sick. We had supposedly learned to foretell the future using a crystal ball—yes, a crystal ball, like the one used by a cartoon witch, was part of the bill of goods they were selling us. We supposedly had the ability to create our own future, by influencing events to our advantage such that we might, for example, find a good job or become rich, as did José Silva. We also, supposedly, had the ability to avert undesirable events such as car accidents.

When we were practicing with our teachers, the method seemed to work, but it's hard always to establish claims like this with certainty—after all, anyone can provide his own rationale for what takes place around him. So I decided to test the method on my own: I would use it to make an improbable situation arise. There was a girl whom I had split up with about a year before, who disliked me so much that she painstakingly avoided coming into contact with me. I had tried in vain to meet her on many occasions, but in that whole year I hadn't been able to see her at all. She was absolutely inflexible. So I decided to use the method for about a week in order to make her try to find me, without my even lifting my little finger.

After ten days, this girl, who previously had not even wanted to lay eyes on me, was looking for excuses and opportunities through various acquaintances to approach me. I didn't make the slightest advance—on the contrary, I made myself more distant. Finally, an invitation to visit her at her home arrived by means of a common acquaintance. I didn't respond. In a short while, the invitation was made again. Again, I didn't respond. Finally, she herself called me on the phone, asking me to meet her, purportedly because she had something to give me.

What had taken place was astounding. I couldn't help but wonder whether this method was in fact akin to witchcraft. In the back of my mind, I asked myself if demons were, in fact, the entities arranging these situations on my behalf—maybe the monks were actually right when they said that people in such organizations work with the devil. I couldn't believe that I had been given such power because these entities loved me, and I didn't know what I would have to pay in exchange. Who was really serving whom?

At a healing meeting that I arranged I also discovered an illness that my father had. When I went and asked him about it he confirmed everything I had predicted. There were many other such incidents, too many to recount. I found these powers to be quite scary, and in the end I would completely refrain from using the method.

A Visit to the Holy Mountain by the Scruff of My Neck

In spite of all my experiences on the Holy Mountain, in spite of my relationship with Father Paisios, when I was back in the world, I quickly returned to my old ways. Also, yoga and Silva Mind Control techniques remained a part of my life. At some point, I had a feeling that I wasn't in good shape. In fact, I was in a state of turmoil. So, I decided to return to the Holy Mountain in order to see the elder. But I encountered unexpected obstacles. The first time I tried to go, although I set my alarm to wake up in time to catch the bus, I overslept anyway, because the clock broke during the night. Then I decided to go on the following Tuesday, but, on Monday night, a friend came to visit from Athens. I told myself that I would go on Thursday, but then, on Wednesday night, I ended up sleeping at someone else's home. Growing annoyed with these failures, I decided that I would not let anything prevent me from going to Athos on Sunday morning. On Saturday evening, I didn't go out, so that I wouldn't get mixed up with anything that would prevent my departure. And then a friend came to my house and wanted me go out with her, because she felt bad and wanted someone to keep her company and console her. What could I do?

One afternoon, I was at the home of a friend who had also begun to visit the Holy Mountain. I told him about the perplexing difficulties I was having in making a visit, concluding that if the elder didn't give me a helping hand, my trip to Mount Athos looked most unlikely. Immediately, I felt a refreshing peace as I heard my friend tell me to sleep at his house that night. I told him that I didn't have money or clothes with me, but he told me he would give me money, clothing, and his backpack as well. So, I slept at his house, and the next day I took the bus for the Holy Mountain.

From the time my friend made his invitation until the time the bus departed, even in my sleep, I felt as though I were surrounded by that refreshing peace. It was as though someone were keeping me company in my very soul. I knew that again the elder had extended his helping hand and grabbed me by the scruff of my neck, disentangling me from the world.

When I arrived, I immediately went to see him. He tenderly took me in his arms, seeing that I was at the brink of a breakdown, and suggested that I go stay as a guest with Father Christos, an ascetic friend of his, until I calmed down a bit. He told me to come and see him whenever I wanted to and that I could learn iconography while I was there. I agreed and went to stay with the ascetic.

The Theotokos Who Keeps the Gate: Portaitissa

This period was my first attempt to live like a Christian. Father Christos lived alone in a tiny house in the midst of the forest. Every afternoon, the two of us would tend to our small garden. To buy anything, one had to walk about an hour by foot along a path that was often overgrown with brambles. It was so quiet that we almost never saw another living soul. Once a week, a neighboring monk would come over for Divine Liturgy. Sometimes, Father Christos served Liturgy with only me present, so that a fortnight would pass before we would see anyone else. Moreover, he and I didn't spend much time together: I would read a patristic text out loud for an hour in the morning while he would paint icons, and in the afternoon we would work together for about two hours in the garden. After the main meal, it was time for Compline.

I spent my time reading about the Orthodox Christian Faith. I read ancient texts written by ascetics and spiritual men ages back, one thousand to seventeen hundred years ago. I also read more recent books, three hundred to four hundred years old, by other men who greatly struggled and labored in the spiritual life. I also read the works of holy men who had died only of late. It was the spiritual experiences of these writers that provided them with their knowledge. They wrote about the mystery of man—his greatness and his fall—and about what is hidden in the human soul and mind. They wrote about God, because they knew Him so intimately that they could feel Him and see Him. They wrote about how they lived with God, how and why one loses intimacy with Him, and how one can find it once more, in a fuller, purer, and more blessed way. I was astonished by the fact that their views and experiences were the same, though they were separated by as much as fifteen hundred years, and I asked Father Christos about this. He told me that this is what is meant by "Orthodox tradition." As I would come to discover, this ascetic and hesychast[1] was a living link in that living tradition. I would realize that he had been able to clarify the issues that these texts raised because he lived as their authors did and had the same experiences of *Jesus Christ, the same yesterday, and today, and forever.*[2]

And so I tried to live a life of prayer, the study of patristic texts, and spiritual struggle, but my spiritual path was still an uncertain one. From time to time, I would practice different yoga exercises, meditations, and the like. Also, my soul was still strongly attracted by witchcraft, and that attraction manifested itself in this setting. Although our outward life was peaceful and routine, our inner spiritual life was quite intense. On the one hand, there were clashes, battles, struggles, fears, disturbances, and uprisings. On the other, there were divine gifts, experiences of divine grace, the tangible sense of God's presence,

---

[1] A hesychast (from the Greek word *hesychia*, meaning *stillness*) is one who practices inner stillness and concentration in the context of pure noetic prayer.
[2] Hebrews 13:8.

the opening of the mind to a more profound understanding of the Scriptures, a thirst and hunger for the divine, a physical and spiritual sweetness, desire for and ease in saying the Jesus Prayer, knowledge of self given from on high, sweet tears, and the contrition of repentance. I wrote poems in praise and love of God, and also for Father Paisios, by whose prayers I felt that God was granting me all these blessings.

Sometimes, we experienced in a mystical way the presence of the saints, especially on their feast days and during vigils. These experiences calmed me, giving me joy, support, strength, courage, and the will to continue this fertile, if arduous, life. My soul came to know a reality beyond the five senses, being deepened as it descended into hell, soaring as it nearly touched heaven, and coming into contact with a world that the soul alone can know. I remember writing to a friend of mine that I had never lived a life that was so rich and so full of meaning.

Among my many experiences at that time, I remember one significant experience that stands out from the others. The fifteenth of August, the feast of the Dormition of the Theotokos, was approaching, during which time the entire Holy Mountain would celebrate from one end to the other. All the monasteries in the garden of the Most Pure Virgin would hold vigils in her honor, glorifying and rejoicing in the protectress of the Holy Mountain.[1] We also prepared to go to the monastery to which our cell was attached in order to participate in the vigil.[2]

On that day I had a fierce battle, given my spiritual

[1] Traditionally, the Virgin Mary is considered to be the special patron of the Holy Mountain. In Orthodox tradition, the Virgin is known as the Theotokos (lit. *Birthgiver of God*) or the Mother of God, titles that emphasize the literal reality of God's having become a human being, *made of a woman* (Galatians 4:4), in the Incarnation.
[2] Typically, individual monastic cells or small communities are "attached to," or organizationally a part of, a larger monastery.

immaturity. For some of the advanced fathers, such a battle might have been humorous, but for me it was all I could handle. Suddenly, my mind was filled with thoughts. If on a regular day, there would be, for example, two or three thoughts in my mind per minute, suddenly there were hundreds of thoughts passing through my mind every minute, at such a speed that they created an unbearable pressure, a pressure that was only exacerbated by the confusion it caused. Even more troubling and unnerving was the fact that all the thoughts were negative, evil, and ugly, and they were all urging me not to go to the vigil. It was as though a talkative person, full of guile and evil, were continuously whispering in my ear, making malevolent comments about people and their lives. I would try to repel them and put everything in a reasonable order, but, under such a continual bombardment, I couldn't get a word in edgewise.

Soon, my head was aching and I fell into despondency. Had it been just another human being bothering me, I could have distanced myself from him and calmed down, but what was I to do, afflicted by so many evil, hideous words, when they would follow me even to my bed? What would I do if this continued for three or four days? This was the first time I faced such a noetic battle, or warfare with thoughts, which are referred to by the Orthodox with the Greek word *logismoi.*[1]

I knew that I wasn't myself, and I tried to react by repelling the passionate thoughts, but to no avail. In fact, the onslaught only intensified: it was as though I had simply stirred the thoughts up. I tried to say the Jesus Prayer, but the resistance was so great that I quickly weakened, yielded, and stopped

---

[1] Resistance to negative thoughts in general, particularly judgmental or cynical thoughts, is an important aspect of traditional Christian life. Such thoughts may arise from demonic influence or simply from fallen human nature. In addition, occasional periods of intense struggle with demonically generated evil thoughts may form part of a Christian's spiritual struggle, particularly that of a monastic, dedicated entirely to prayer.

trying. I was simply too weak to go on, unbelievable as it may seem. Father Christos took one look at me and understood thoroughly. "The bees are swarming," he said with a smile. "Let's see if you will be patient." Indeed, my thoughts were like swarming bees, and their stings were painful. I was unable to sleep that night, because my plight continued. I prayed mechanically, but my heart was unable to participate.

By the morning, sleeplessness had left me weakened and with a throbbing headache. I thought my mind would become unglued from the pressure of this rapid flow of capricious thoughts. In the afternoon, we went down to the monastery, where they gave us a room to rest in for a few hours before the vigil. I lay down, but my mind found no rest. When I entered the church at the beginning of the vigil, I was dead tired, still suffering from my condition, which exhaustion had only aggravated. I wearily settled into one of the choir stalls near the chanter's stand.

A sweet monk named Father Savas, who was from a neighboring cell, approached the stall where I had collapsed. He would sometimes come to Father Christos's cell for Liturgy, and the elder had told me that he had been a monk for many years and was both experienced and advanced spiritually. He smiled at me. I felt better just looking at him and sensing the love between us. "What's going on?" he asked. "How is your struggle going?" "It's difficult, elder," I answered. As I lowered my head to kiss his hand, he pulled it away and gave me a gentle tap on the head. Suddenly, the storm subsided, the clouds parted, and, to my relief and joy, a sense of calm descended that swallowed up all of my assaulting thoughts. What divine power was hidden in that wrinkled old hand! Overjoyed, I lifted up my head to look him in the face. "Come on," he said, "let's go chant a bit." And so I cheerfully followed him to the chanter's stand. We sat next to each other and chanted to our Most Pure Virgin. I felt so much at ease seated next to him, and I enjoyed the

Elder Savas, who lived alone in the Kapsala area of Mount Athos,
in a cell attached to Pantocrator Monastery.

beauty of being sheltered, if for but a moment, under his spiritual wings. In between chanting, he told me, "Don't be afraid of
the demon that's bothering you, because he's powerless. Just
imagine what he did to me this morning while I was praying
with my prayer rope. He made me drowsy, and, when I nodded
off, I saw him making fun of me. I pounced on him to drive him
away. He fled, and as he was fleeing I asked him where he was
from. He shouted back, 'From Iconium, I come from Iconium!'
and then he disappeared. He was from Asia Minor, where there
were once many temples where idols were worshipped. After
waking up, I could still hear him shouting from the ravine like a
swine or some strange wild beast. He does all of this in order to
frighten us so that we'll stop praying, but he's powerless and all
he can do is make empty threats from a distance. God has him
bound and doesn't let him go free, otherwise he'd already have
killed us all and torn us apart. Don't be afraid: the Most Pure
Virgin protects us, and so do the saints."

Iviron Monastery, Mount Athos.

What did I have to fear? I was sailing in an ocean of joy now that this elder had revealed to me his spiritual strength, rescued me from the stranglehold of thoughts, and driven away the demon that was bothering me. I rejoiced in the fact that God had revealed to me another genuine monk. As the vigil progressed, other people came between us and I was separated from the elder. After that, everything continued as normal.

We rested after the vigil, and, by the time I woke up, Elder Savas had already left the monastery for his little hesychast cell. We would stay for the meal in the refectory, and then, at my request, we would go to the Monastery of Iviron for Vespers in order to venerate the icon of the Most Holy Virgin *Portaitissa*.[1] Upon waking from sleep, I found myself again in the same plight, with my adversary now more savage, more aggressive,

---

[1] This icon of the Most Holy Virgin *Portaitissa* ("the Keeper of the Gate") is also commonly known as "the Iviron Icon." Through it God has worked countless miracles throughout the centuries.

The chapel in Iviron Monastery that houses the *Portaitissa* Icon.

Icon of the Most Holy Virgin *Portaitissa,*
Iviron Monastery, Mount Athos.

and more determined than ever—but, now that I knew what was going on, I tried simply to scorn the one who had been so humiliated by Elder Savas.

As we approached Iviron, a gust of wrath was unleashed and the battle became even fiercer, with vicious and wicked thoughts of blasphemy assaulting me. My mind could hardly restrain the multitude of evil thoughts rushing in one after the other, making demands and giving orders. "Run away!" "Leave now!" "Don't go to the *Portaitissa!*" "Run for it!" I couldn't keep the thoughts out—resistance had proven futile. I just longed for a break in this violent torrent and a lessening in the vehemence and number of thoughts so that my mind wouldn't be pushed to the breaking point. This crowd of thoughts in my mind suffocated even my simplest thoughts such as "Where did I put my flashlight?" or "I'll take my sweater with me." There was simply no room whatsoever. In my suffering, I became downcast. If I hadn't had that experience with Elder Savas, I would have yielded to the thoughts and fled far from the Holy Virgin *Portaitissa*, far from Father Christos, and far from the Holy Mountain. But, remembering the ascetic's words, I tried to be patient and staggered in the shadows.

When we reached the monastery, most people had already left. The few visitors present were already with the monks in church for Vespers. I felt dizzy, confused, and in pain, but I made my way into the church and soon found myself with a few other people in front of the icon of the Most Pure Virgin *Portaitissa*. It is a large icon about five feet tall, veiled in part by a golden covering. The Virgin's crown is inlayed with precious stones. It is the most famous icon on the Holy Mountain and also the most miraculous.

I was so faint that I didn't hear the chanters or even notice who was standing next to me. My mind was so captivated that I was incapable of thinking properly, but I was able to lift up my eyes to the icon and beg weakly in my mind, "My Most Pure

Lady, help me." And then I beheld, hovering over our heads, a luminous cloud as bright as white lightning and as translucent as clear water. My inner condition changed as with the flip of a switch. My mind was utterly cleansed. Not only did the bad thoughts vanish, but even my ordinary thoughts disappeared. The thought process in my mind was brought to a standstill, and another process or kind of perception was set in motion, reflecting another way of existence and another way of knowing, in the deep tranquility and calm quiet of a serene mind.

The cloud's light was pure, sacred, exceptionally precious, and filled with a kindness and a power that was diametrically opposed to my own spiritual state. I felt myself to be covered in filth, reeking with a moral stench. It was beyond my understanding how that cloud could condescend so much as to deign to approach us, to display such love and tenderness to us. In my ecstatic state, I nearly had the desire to beg it to depart from me—I felt painfully unworthy to be in its presence. Nevertheless, it continued to pour out gifts of inestimable spiritual value. It was like the most fragrant spiritual myrrh flowing into the reeking mire of my soul, which was seething with evil. I was a breath away from spiritual death, and the Most Holy Virgin granted me life. This wonderful vision naturally induced my soul to beget knowledge, understanding, healing, strength, repentance, gratitude, sensitivity, love, reverence, joy, sorrow for my sins, and the hope of life eternal. But my efforts to sketch even a pale reflection of this inexpressible treasure of life seem so futile that I will break off my description here.

I am not sure how long this transformation lasted, in which my soul was suddenly translated into the realm of eternity, while in my body I remained quite under the influence of time and space. I do recall, however, that when I came out of church after the conclusion of the service I still could feel its effects. I met Father Christos and we began to walk up to his cell. In the meantime, my former ordeal again began to plague

ON THE BRINK: BETWEEN TWO SPIRITUAL TRADITIONS

me, so that I was again unable to think and lost any appetite for conversation. I even forgot what had taken place in the church—I could only remember that something important had happened. I told him, "Something happened in the church, elder, but I don't remember what it was to tell you about it." He looked surprised, but attributed my strange explanation to my present struggle with the "bees" that were again swarming around me, so he made no further comment.

Gradually, daily life returned and I reverted to that state we call normal. Although I had completely forgotten about the incident at that point, it began to come to mind as the months passed, becoming increasingly clear. When a year had rolled by, I could clearly recall everything. Apparently, God had His own reasons for bringing on my forgetfulness and for later allowing me to remember the incident. Years later, I spoke with a certain hermit about it when I visited his cell. After he had carefully listened to what I had to say, I asked him, "Elder, what was that cloud?" And his answer was, "It was the grace of the Most Holy Virgin."

A Spiritual Helmet

I often experienced spiritual warfare involving combat with passionate thoughts, although not as intensely as at the time just related. The second time I had such a relentless fight was when I was trying to grasp the difference between Orthodox Christianity and Eastern religions. I had decided to make a systematic effort to examine representative documents describing the views of Orthodox Christianity and yoga and other Eastern belief systems. I found books and journals from both sides, bought a thick notebook, and began to systematically document and compare the two perspectives, including my personal experiences in both camps.

Through this effort, I hoped to find answers to my

questions about the existence of God, who the true God is, and which is the true religion. Perhaps all religions are but different pathways leading to the same true God. Or is there only one religion or path that leads to the truth and to God?

I hadn't made much progress in this endeavor when I was again subjected to a spiritual attack by thousands of savage thoughts, each making its own demands and giving its own orders. Recalling my similar experience earlier, I decided to struggle with the thoughts and overcome them on my own, but I was very soon reminded of my spiritual weakness. With my mind whirling about, I was unable to put up any resistance and finally gave up trying. I tried to take courage by remembering the counsels of Father Savas and Father Paisios, and the spiritual gift I had received while standing before the icon of the Most Pure Virgin *Portaitissa*.

After putting up with these thoughts for three days, I traveled to Elder Paisios's cell. I was so weary, so physically and spiritually exhausted that I could hardly walk straight. The sun had gone down and darkness had nearly set in. Now that everyone had left, the elder was by himself in his yard, getting ready for his nighttime vigil. He smiled as soon as he saw me, and asked, "How are your spirits holding up?" It was a joy and a source of encouragement just to see him. Although I felt faint, I found the strength to smile back and say, "Oh, Elder, I can't continue anymore. I can't take it any longer."

He laughed as he approached me, saying, "Have a seat, so we can put things in order." He then gave me a tap on the head—and, immediately, the flood of evil thoughts was brought to a halt. But this didn't just bring an end to my suffering. My mind didn't simply return to a normal state, such as it is in as I write these words. No, it entered a deeper, more distant realm, of quiet tranquility, great joy, and profound peace. Another Spirit had been united to my mind and, out of kindness, had freely imparted to me that which was His by nature. I am afraid and ashamed to say it, but perhaps it really was that Person that Christ called the Comforter, for He truly comforted me.[1] It made my trial seem trivial, and I would gladly have suffered another such trial, if it would have meant receiving such consolation. I was too abashed to speak about it, so I only asked, "Elder, what was happening to me earlier?" "Well," he replied, "that imp"—that's what the elder called a demon—"was bothering you. Don't be afraid. It was just a battle. When you're having a hard time, come over here so I can fire off a bullet to help you. Say the Jesus Prayer. Wait a minute and I'll bring you a spiritual helmet." With a cheerful laugh, he went into his cell and came out with a brown monastic cap. "Someone forgot it here, and now he's left the Holy Mountain." He took the cap, made the sign of the Cross over it three times, and put it on my head. He then smiled and said, "Let me take a look at you. You've become a fine soldier. Now those impassioned thoughts won't come near you. They'll hit the helmet and bounce right off it. That's why the officers in the army would yell at us about wearing our helmets on the battlefield. Just be careful not to lose it."

He then gave me a fatherly kiss on the forehead. He loved me so much. And for my part, I felt great joy at having a spiritual father whose spiritual strength and wealth were such that the enemy was a nonentity before him. How effortlessly he had made the enemy take flight! What now did I have to fear? If I found the struggle tough going, I would just come to the elder and the battle would be over immediately. My soul was filled with a deep and fearless trust. It was already nightfall when I left, having taken my fill of the elder's paternal love. At the back door, the elder was smiling and called out, "I'll be on the lookout. When they give you a hard time, I'll fire a bullet or two." Actually, he lifted the entire burden of my spiritual

---

[1] That is, the Holy Spirit: *And I will pray the Father, and He shall give you another Comforter, that He may abide with you forever* (John 14:16).

warfare, because I was a coward and lazy (as indeed I still am). As long as I wore the "spiritual helmet" that the elder gave me, I had spiritual peace instead of impassioned thoughts. I was able to rest up fully.

Nevertheless, in spite of his forewarning, I lost the cap. He didn't give me another one in spite of my requests, though he helped me in other ways. Many times I would go to see him, and he would give me a gentle tap on the head, imparting the grace of Christ. How I yearned for and looked forward to these blessings of his, outwardly so innocuous! Once I came to understand who the elder was, I didn't dare ask for such gifts of grace, as I had when I was still naïve about the spiritual life—instead I received them timidly, with awe and joy. It was his way of sharing spiritual blessings, and so pedestrian did it seem that he could use it for this purpose even publicly, when his yard was crowded with pilgrims. (Of course, I was far from the only one who understood what this casual gesture concealed, for by it many others would also receive grace according to their needs.)

A Decision

I could see that it was no easy task to acquire the truth. I faced my own temptations and the opposition of evil powers. On my own, I wasn't able to find an answer to my questions about God, the world, and man. Later, the elder would tell me that, if God does not help man spiritually, it is impossible for man to approach the truth, and that this is why Christ came into this world. But I was unable to call myself a Christian. Although I had seen so many wonders in the presence of Father Paisios, I still disagreed with him and had misgivings about his explanations. I didn't want to be deceived yet again in this life. "He may well look at the world like that," I thought, "but reality is far greater than his perspective on it.

He may well have part of the truth, but other ways of thinking and other religions may have other parts of the truth." Perhaps I was simply under the sway of his strong personality and the atmosphere of the Holy Mountain. If I would distance myself from him, I thought, perhaps I would see things differently.

So I decided to give the Hindu yogis the same opportunity I had given the Orthodox monks. Although I had been acquainted with yogis before becoming acquainted with Father Paisios, I had never gone to India, their heartland and center. I decided to open up my soul to them just like I had opened up to the elder. I decided to live with them and let myself be shaped by them, just like I had lived with and let myself be shaped by Orthodox monks. As a symbolic gesture, I took off the little cross that the elder had made me with his own hands, in order to go to India utterly unbiased, open, and well-intentioned, for I believed that yoga was also a path towards God, and a path that was more suitable for me.

This is how I ended up in India in various ashrams with swamis and gurus, trying to gain experiences in their world as well. For the next months, the two worlds of Orthodox Christianity and Indian Hinduism would wrestle with each other in my soul.[1]

Was this tactic of mine without its dangers? No—in retrospect, I see that I was in great danger, and I could never have ridden out the storm relying on my own abilities. Rather, I was helped, or, to be more precise, saved through God's intervention, which aided me not only in my spiritual problems, but also in many everyday, worldly difficulties. Had God not helped me in this way, I would have been utterly destroyed.

---

[1] The author's trip to India took place from November 1982 to March 1983. He was twenty-five years old at the time.

CHAPTER FOUR

Inside the Ashrams of India

Some Introductory Remarks about India

India is a vast country about half the size of Europe, with a landscape that includes arid deserts and tropical forests, spacious plains and majestic mountains, the most stunning of which are the Himalayas—the world's highest mountain range, which covers India's entire northern region. This immense land has many climates, with temperatures that range from the burning heat of the south to the bitter cold of the north. The southern, tropical zone is known for its monsoon rains, dense vegetation, and oppressive heat, while the northern, inland zone is distinguished by its glaciers and isolated regions completely cut off from the rest of India by snowfall. Naturally, there are plenty of local variations in climate as well. India's population is composed of numerous races, from the dark-skinned peoples of the south, to those with fairer complexions and Indo-European features in the central regions, to those resembling the Asiatic peoples in the north. In India one finds a mixture of every ethnic group.

All the major religions are represented in India and each has at least a million followers. Although most people are under the impression that all Indians are Hindus, this is far from the truth. In addition to the Hindus, the Muslim population is quite large, and there are also Christians, Buddhists, and Sikhs.

Religious competition is quite intense and results in bloody clashes that have left thousands of victims. The clashes between Muslims and Hindus at the time of Gandhi and the clashes between Sikhs and Hindus today are among the most striking examples. In fact, the number of casualties is so high that it is perhaps more accurate to speak about a long-standing war than about occasional skirmishes.

Surprisingly enough, English is the common language in India among both tourists and Indians. There are so many local dialects, and the differences between dialects are so great, that Indians from different regions are frequently unable to understand one another.

It is worthy of admiration that such an immense and populous land was able to unite and form a country. Of course, the government has had problems from its very inception, with the secession and partitioning of the two sizeable regions of Bangladesh and Pakistan. Conflicts between these nations continue to break out from time to time.

Although I have no desire to praise British colonial rule, which was dictatorial and exploitative, it did leave certain legacies that were significant in the attempt to forge a unified Indian nation. The British were responsible for providing an impressive first-rate railway system that linked India's vast distances. They also left behind a fine postal service that continues to serve the nation. And, finally, the British are the source of the language that continues to be used throughout India.

All of this, combined with the racist attitudes of the colonizers, helped instill among the region's inhabitants an awful feeling of inferiority vis-à-vis white people. This, I found, had persisted. Even though the colonial period had outwardly ended, the souls of the people were marked by the legacy of their subjugation, which was frequently found expressed on their faces and manifested in their gestures. The appalling economic disparity between India and Western Europe, a Western film industry that portrayed white men as Superman and James Bond, and alarming overpopulation that could cause the individual to feel crushed or lost, all contributed to this phenomenon.

For this reason, I discovered, many Indians attached a strange sense of importance to conversing with white people or to having a relationship with them. I met many educated Indians who within half an hour of contact asked me to give them a note, a letter, or anything else that would prove that they had some connection with a white person from the West, so as to increase their standing in their community. For example, I once visited the clinic of an upper-class Indian doctor in his sixties. He was so pleased with my presence that he extended the visit with polite conversation about subjects of common interest, and, in order to convince me that he had connections with other white people, he pulled out a letter from a student in Europe sent over two years ago, which he had carefully stored away.

White people always stood out in India when I was there, except at the marketplace in New Delhi and the airport at Mumbai (Bombay). Anywhere else, I would become an object of attention. Once I was traveling for several days with an Englishman and, while visiting a city, we stopped to pass some time looking at a beautiful house. We were immediately surrounded by about thirty to forty Indians, standing at a distance of about six to ten feet and staring at us with admiration. My companion was amused and to my shock began calling them—and this is no exaggeration—as though they were a pack of animals, like a shepherd would call his sheep, and they submitted to his mockery and abuse. I was irritated both by the Englishman's sense of superiority and by the Indians' passivity.

Along with this sense of inferiority, however, there also exists an underlying strain of belligerence and jealousy. Even older yogis who are educated and advanced are prone to such psychological conflicts. But this usually only comes to the surface in larger or smaller crowds. I remember once, when I was in Benares,[1] my companions and I had an argument with a rickshaw owner. Although we paid him a decent amount of money for our ride, he wanted more. After all, we were white tourists, so surely we had enough money to be able to pay ten times the normal rate. Of course, we understood that we would pay more than his local passengers, but he wanted even more than this usual fee, upon which we had agreed. We had been in such situations before and, since we no longer had any interest in such incessant arguments, we firmly and calmly held our ground. After the rickshaw owner had complained and cursed us, he left, muttering what seemed to be threats in his own language. When I ran into him again on another road a few hours later, he started to pick a fight with me and called for help. At this point I saw three or four middle-aged men running towards me from the back of an alley, making threatening gestures and clenching their teeth. They were followed by a group of busybodies ready to stir up a fight just for the fun of it—it didn't require much thought to guess whose side they would be on. I was so taken aback by this turn of events that I just stood there awkwardly. But, to my even greater surprise, when this hostile mob was within six or seven feet from where I was standing, their intimidating threats vanished away. Instead of taking revenge or venting their hatred, they simply stood there looking rather helpless and even ashamed. This transformation was so comical that I almost started to laugh. We looked at each other for a while and then I continued on my way while someone muttered something under his breath. Even today I ask myself if what happened reflected an Indian complex vis-à-vis the whites, some fear in connection with their former oppressors, or if maybe someone's prayers protected me.

[1] It is also called Varanasi or Banaras. Located in the state of Uttar Pradesh in northern India, on the left bank of the Ganges River, it is one of the seven sacred cities of the Hindus.

A Meeting at Benares

Our travels in India began with a reservation in a second-class sleeping car of the train from New Delhi to Varanasi, or, as Westerners call it, Benares. The passenger car was so jam-packed that it was difficult to breathe: here as elsewhere in India, people were in such droves that they were literally falling all over each other. I had to use my boots as a pillow for fear that they would be stolen—after all, a nice pair of boots like that could be very tempting to thieves. We still hadn't gotten used to the lack of sanitation, which was so dreadful that in the beginning the only foods that didn't make us squeamish were fruits with skins, such as bananas, avocados, and papayas, and some bread that we bought at a luxury store in New Delhi. (Since the bread had come wrapped in a paper bag, we could at least pretend that it would be protected from the swarms of flies.)

At night, once the peddlers selling peanuts, tea, and various snacks had finally stopped their interminable rounds and the conductors had checked our tickets and locked our train car, we opened up our beds. Now that only those with beds remained in the car, we could relax a little bit.

In the bed across from me was a girl from the West. I couldn't tell whether she was a European or an American. It didn't matter, though, because all Westerners there felt like compatriots. In Europe, the differences between a Greek and a German or between an American and a Frenchman might seem striking and significant, but in India all these differences simply disappeared in the face of the enormous political, economic, and religious differences between India and the West. In India, we were all simply Westerners—which usually meant rich, educated, well-fed, and well-traveled, our circumstances being in sharp contrast with those of the vast majority of the Indian

INSIDE THE ASHRAMS OF INDIA

people, whose utter destitution we could all feel. We were able to understand each other, because we had so much in common. We listened to the same songs and liked the same writers. As young people of the West, we were all a part of the same international rock culture, subscribing to the same ideologies and resembling each other a great deal regardless of whether we were hippies or members of some other movement.

Now, since the girl in the bed across from me was traveling alone, we thought she would feel a bit safer in our company. My friend Noni, who had been at the university with me and was now an architect, tried to approach her. The girl's name was Kikis and, though she was initially wary about contact with strangers, a journey lasting three days and two nights was enough time for her to get to know us better.

There was a continuous problem with the water—there was never any guarantee that it was drinkable. This is why so many people were suffering from various illnesses, ranging from diarrhea to hepatitis. The scores of vaccinations that we received in Greece hardly protected us. Apart from the issue of whether or not the water was potable, it tasted and smelled bad. Kikis had a canteen, which turned out to be the solution to the horrible taste and smell. After we squeezed lemons into the canteen, the water tasted a bit better, and we humored ourselves with the thought that it somehow made the water more sanitary. We shared the canteen until we reached Benares.

When the conversations had died down one night in the train, I tried to put my thoughts in order and interpret what had happened to me, in order to find some answers to the questions that had brought me to India.

My thoughts naturally turned to the elder, whose prayers wouldn't let me forget him. I would recall the elder frequently in India, but this wasn't just a memory of a loved one like my recollections of my parents or my girlfriend. It was something more significant and deeper than that, a powerful experience of the present, not the past. Suddenly, as I sat there, I felt a great love flood my heart and engulf my entire being, embracing me with tenderness and sustaining me with peace. In a way known only to God and the elder, our souls came into contact at the level of our very beings. Although we were separated by vast distances, our souls were joined by an infinite love, and I mysteriously felt the simple truth of his nearness and his loving desire to protect and fight beside me.

I often wept when I felt this love. It made my heart grow soft with gratitude and with love for him in return, although I realize that my love was just a dim reflection of his own, which blazed like the sun. Indeed, he loved me greatly, incomparably more than anyone else. Even my mother's love, in comparison, was as no more than the flickering flame of a candle in the presence of a fiery star. This love graciously surpassed all things, transcending the spiritual law, covering my deficiencies, and paying in my stead, like a loving father, the penalties that I owed. The elder would only limit this fervent and impetuous love when doing so would result in my benefit, edification, and progress. When I would act wrongly, I would become ashamed, because I realized that it was my sin that kept my mystical contact with the elder from lasting longer than it did, or even being continuous.

Without exaggeration, I can say that I felt his love every day I was in India. Of course, I had felt it in Greece also from time to time, but in India it was a part of my everyday life. But, in spite of that love, my never-ending questions didn't leave me. That the elder loved me, I had no doubt—but what about the truth? What was the truth? Yoga remained very appealing to me. I found Hindu philosophy and practices to be fascinating. This was an exotic universe of mysterious, supernatural phenomena, which attracted me with the allure of the unknown,

Ganges River, Benares (Varanasi), India.
Photograph by Jon Rawlinson, October 2006.

the taste of adventure, and promises of overwhelming magnitude.

During my first afternoon in Benares, I took a walk by myself along the shoreline of the Ganges River. There was a variegated crowd of people swarming in such suffocating numbers over the shores of the Ganges that it reminded me of an anthill—it was difficult to distinguish a single individual. Nevertheless, among them I noticed a handsome young man in his early twenties, sitting calm and detached in the lotus position, a yoga position in which one's legs are crossed in a difficult manner. His silence in the talkative tumult, his motionlessness in a sea of unruly movement, and his indifference to the everyday preoccupations that concerned most people made him stand out. At first, I passed by him with indifference, thinking of him as just another show-off. Couldn't he find someplace better to meditate in, like some quiet corner?

I continued to walk for many hours alongside the colossal buildings and past the steps of the temples leading down to the shores of the Ganges. I was entranced by the sight of the *sadhus*[1] in their nakedness, the beggars with their cups, the families of pilgrims taking their sacred baths in the Ganges, the peddlers crying out to advertise their wares, and the drug-using Western hippies diving into the Ganges and smoking *chillums*[2] with their Indian friends. The incredible colors of the Ganges as the sun set were enchanting.

I recall sitting at a makeshift café, consisting of a straw canopy hung over four pieces of wood quickly set up on the stone steps of a temple to idols. It was right on the road. Most of the patrons were Indians, although there were also two or three hippies from the West. While I was drinking my tea with milk, the man sitting next to me offered me a chillum. It was an Indian social custom simply to light up the chillum and pass it along to the person sitting next to you, the way I might have offered someone a cigarette in Greece.

After a return walk lasting several hours, I reached the spot where I had first seen the young man. To my surprise, he was still in the lotus position. I found this quite remarkable and impressive, because I knew what it meant for someone to sit in the lotus position for hours. I had also done exercises to acquire flexibility. But, although my body was fit and flexible, and although I had a belt in Kung Fu, I wasn't able to sit for more than fifteen minutes in that position. I stood nearby for a while in order to observe him.

---

[1] A *sadhu* is a Hindu renunciant and practitioner of yoga, considered a holy person by the Hindus.

[2] A *chillum* is an Indian pipe, traditionally made of clay, in the form of a small, narrow funnel the size of a cigar. It is normally filled with a mixture of tobacco and charas, which is a powerful type of cannibis used traditionally in India, especially by devotees of *Shiva*. Charas was legal in India until 1985, and even today its use continues to be widespread.

Bathers in the Ganges River, Benares.
Photograph by Dan Kamminga, August 2006.

Sadhus in India, November 2007.

After two or three minutes, he stopped meditating and came towards the place where I was sitting, where he had left his belongings. He had a calm face, and three horizontal parallel yellow lines painted across his forehead, which, as he later told me, symbolized the god *Vishnu;* a red dot also painted there symbolized the third eye. There was something peculiar about him. Even by Indian standards, his dress was so poor that I was surprised to discover that he was a Westerner when he approached me. There was, however, something about him that bothered me. I didn't believe deep down that he was really the person he was trying to pass himself off as. It seemed to me that he was, rather, merely playing the part of an illumined yogi, deceiving others, but first of all deceiving himself.

He told me that his name was Pavis and that he used to live in Germany with his German father and Iranian mother. After living in India for a year, he ran out of money and lost his passport. Although there was nothing worse that could happen to a Westerner, he was calm and collected about the situation, saying that he left it all in the hands of God and his *karma.* That is what he said, but not what he believed, because he knew that he could count on his parents. As he told me, "If I write them and ask them for money, they'll send it to me within a week." At present, however, he preferred to play the role of a yogi or an anchorite. Although he didn't ask me directly for money, I could see he was hoping for some, so I gave him five rupees anyway.[1] He later also hit up my female friends, who gave him some money because they felt sorry for him.

In any event, we struck up a conversation that quickly turned to the familiar topic of the quest for existential fulfillment in Hinduism and yoga. I told him about some of my experiences with hypnotism, Silva Mind Control, and the elder. I also mentioned some of my questions that I couldn't seem to

[1] At that time, one dollar was worth ten to twelve rupees.

answer. He then began to tell me various stories about his guru, or teacher: "My guru says this; my guru does that." His guru had an ashram up in the Himalayas, which Pavis visited for a week, seeing, as he told me, many exciting things, which still left him amazed, astonished, and spellbound. He said that his guru's name was Babaji.

Now, in India, the word "Babaji" has two meanings. In day-to-day speech it is used as a respectful term of address for an elder person. In the sacred texts, however, it means "most high," "venerable," and "divine," and it is the name used for a yogi-god who descends to earth in order to teach very advanced disciples, who will then become gurus themselves. I recalled when I was nineteen years old, reading a book entitled *Autobiography of a Yogi* by Paramahansa Yogananda. Among the many teachings expounded in this book was a reference to this Babaji—who supposedly was such an advanced yogi that he became an immortal god who taught yoga to human beings and was the guru of the gurus. He would take the form of a young man, appearing over the centuries to a few exceptional students. He was said to fly in the air, pass through walls, become invisible in the midst of large crowds, heal the sick, and raise the dead. In a word, he was one of the deities of the Hindu pantheon.[1] I reread this book shortly before departing for India and gave it to a

[1] *Author's note:* The biography of the Eldress Gavrilia, *The Ascetic of Love* (Helen Anthony, trans., 2nd ed. [Athens: Series Talanto, 2000]), discusses how she met the great guru of that time, Sai Baba, who maintained that he was the highest god, superior to all known gods. He performed various impressive magic feats with the help of evil spirits. "Madeleine Bachon, an old French friend, recalls: 'I remember [Eldress Gavrilia] telling me that when she was in India, working in a hospital, Sai Baba who was then rising in fame happened to pass by there. He had in his company some Americans who marveled at his magical 'tricks' such as the 'transpositions' and 'materializations' of various gold and silver jewels. When he saw her, he gave her only a few pebbles from the river. It seemed he recognized her spirituality and was unable to do anything'" (pp. 51–52).

friend to read as well, and the week before our departure we had been joking that we were going to meet him.

So when Pavis called his guru "Babaji," at first I thought he was using the everyday meaning of the term. As he continued to relate different stories about him, however, I began to realize that he was talking about the great Babaji.

"Wait a minute," I said. "Are you talking about *the* Babaji?"

"Yes," he answered.

Surprised, I asked again, "You mean the great Babaji?"

"Yes," he replied emphatically.

"You mean the one who is mentioned in the sacred writings?" I asked once more, just in case I had misunderstood him.

"Yes," he answered, even more firmly.

This left me awestruck. Pavis then began to explain how Babaji was on earth in our days and began to tell me about the book *Autobiography of a Yogi*. I cut him off, however, and told him that I had already learned about Babaji from that book, just like everyone else who knew about him in the West.

Pavis's stories were amazing, but his contention that Babaji was now on earth was even more amazing. I immediately decided to go and see this Babaji with my own eyes and draw my own conclusions. After all, that was why I had come to India. I asked how I could find him, and Pavis gave me the necessary information about roads, buses, and the village closest to Babaji's ashram, called Haidakhan, which was located high in the Himalayas, far from any other inhabited place.[1] His final instructions were, "Follow the river and you should reach his ashram within four miles. Be aware, however, that many start out for his ashram but get lost and never reach it, even if they know the road."

[1] Because his ashram was located in Haidakhan, this alleged incarnation or manifestation of Babaji came to be known as "Haidakhan Babaji." He began his public teaching in 1970 and died in February 1984, less than two years after the author's encounters with him.

"Is it really that difficult?"

"No, but the guru doesn't want them to come. Even when they take local guides, they still get mixed up, because they aren't qualified to reach the ashram. He drives some away as soon as they arrive; he allows others to stay for a day, a week, a month, or longer, depending on each person's worthiness. In order to go there, you have to be pure and have good *karma*."

While we were talking, it had already grown quite dark. I saw my friends taking a walk nearby, and I called them over so that they could meet Pavis. After making plans to meet Pavis again on the following day, my friends and I got up and went to the filthy hovel we called our hotel. Along the way, I related what he had told me. My female friends quickly became interested, with the exception of Chryssa. Chryssa, whom I had met at the university, where she was studying French Literature, was hesitant, and she became a bit frightened when I told her that I was planning to go and see Babaji.

On the following day, Noni came into my room quite excited, because she had found in our hotel someone who had gone to Babaji's ashram. This man had a photograph of Babaji, which was apparently enough to convince Noni that she also wanted to meet him, and to inspire her to tell me about what an amazing person he must be. When I met the man whom she had run into, he took me to his room, where a vigil light was burning in front of a photograph of Babaji, whom he worshipped as a living god. I found it mystifying how this drug-using hippie and rebel from the West who was raised in a supposedly Christian society had become a religious Hindu. I wondered what happened to him and what he—and others like him—saw in this man. Pavis wanted to return to Germany and start a monastery in honor of Babaji, and here this man worshipped him as a god.

He showed me an old photograph of Babaji, taken years ago when he was a frail boy between eighteen and twenty years old. The person in the photograph had an incredibly flexible body and was sitting in the lotus position. There was, however, something peculiar, even supernatural—or perhaps just unnatural—about one of his eyes, which was disproportionately large. His gaze was vehement and the expression on his face was terrifyingly odd. Everything about him gave me the impression that he was a personality worth exploring.

The girls met with Pavis, who gave them the relevant information about the trip. Noni would come with me, and Chryssa would follow along because she didn't want to be left alone. We were all eager and curious.

We remained in Benares for about a week. I would regularly see the hippies gathering on the terrace of the hotel and getting high. I also noticed families of Indians on the neighboring terrace making handicrafts for ten cents a day. We visited Buddha's tomb, and bought various inexpensive things in the city. Kikis took us to the finest hotel in the city, which also had a rather clean restaurant where we decided to eat a meal. We had gone hungry so long that we were thrilled with the food and gradually began eating in almost any available restaurant and shopping for sweets at the various stores. We bought some Indian clothing and took off our Western clothes. This change in our garb and appearance helped us to blend in better, and, in a short while, we learned how to move about in India with ease.

Kikis's line of business was exporting small merchandise. She would shop for items such as beads and fabrics and sell them in France, making enough money to cover the cost of the airline ticket and the other expenses for her next trip. While she was in India, her boyfriend was in Africa plying the same trade. They intended to purchase some property in Brazil, where living was less expensive. They were drug users on a daily basis, using hashish and other more serious drugs, such as opium, cocaine, LSD, and mushrooms. We spent our time with Kikis every day, except for two days during which she was shut up in her room after taking opium and would come out only to use the bathroom to vomit.

When we told Kikis that we intended to return to New Delhi, she said she would join us. We were delighted to have her come back with us, because she was a useful guide and pleasant to be with. When we told her that we were going to find Babaji, she tried to warn us that various gurus take advantage of young people in their searches for meaning in life.

In general, she had reservations about the gurus, and was even negative towards them. Her position was not based on philosophical differences or ideological clashes, but on her experiences and the experiences of some of her close friends, about whom she told us some stories in an attempt to help us. One of her girlfriends had a guru in South India who accepted disciples from Europe. He was not a great guru, like Rajneesh[1] or Maharishi,[2] with their thousands of followers, but he had disciples. They would write him letters and seek his advice on important matters and decisions in their lives. He would answer them and meditate for them. His disciples were duty-bound to send him money every so often, which enabled him to avoid working and to live quite comfortably. Now this girl had become his disciple—and, after a short while, his mistress. Over the next several months, however, she came to her senses and saw how exploitative a situation she was in. Naturally, she left him, and when she would encounter young people from the West who were sincerely searching, she would try

---

[1] Bhagwan Shree Rajneesh (1931–1990) was an Indian guru who propagated a controversial teaching according to which higher consciousness could be attained through unrestrained sexual activity. The wealth and gifts showered on him by his many, largely Western, devotees caused additional controversy. Towards the end of his life he took the name Osho, under which his followers disseminate his teachings today.

[2] Maharishi Mahesh Yogi (1911–2008) was a Hindu religious figure who founded the Transcendental Meditation movement.

to prevent them from falling into such traps by relating her own experience.

I imagine that this young lady often heard the answer that we gave Kikis: "Yes, of course there are charlatans, but *our* guru isn't one of them." In fact, in our pride we secretly thought that we were too smart to be deceived. We would easily be able to recognize a phony guru. Why couldn't the others recognize that someone was simply faking it? Perhaps they weren't as sharp as we were.

Our Trip to Babaji, "God in the Flesh"

It's not easy to travel in India. In general, travel in a foreign land is difficult because of unknown tongues, misunderstandings, and misinformation. In India, matters are even more challenging. People are so crammed into the buses that there are some who travel on the roof of the bus, eating, smoking, and sleeping there. Despite the many adverse conditions we encountered along the five-hundred-mile trip to meet Babaji up in the Himalayas, our trip proceeded in an unexpectedly smooth manner. In fact, we always found someone who helped make our life easier, and that person was usually a follower of Babaji.

For example, at the beginning, the girls tried to get tickets for our train two times, but without success. In the past, we never had such difficulties with the trains. On the third try, we all went together. I don't recall precisely what the problem was, but I do remember waiting at the counter in front of an employee who had no desire to help us and with a line of people impatiently pushing us from behind. Finally, since we simply couldn't get a ticket, we got out of line in a state of frustration and disappointment. Then, an Indian, who spoke English rather well, approached us and told us just what we needed to do, and, within fifteen minutes, we had our tickets in hand.

When we went back to thank him for helping us, we discovered that he was a follower of Babaji. He then gave us additional instructions regarding the bus we needed to take from New Delhi.

So, we headed straight for New Delhi. In the evening, I could hear in my sleep the tea-peddlers loudly calling out at every station, "Tea, Tea, Tea!" I felt keyed up and excited. I wondered if this person really was *the* Babaji. I believed it was possible. After all, I had seen so many miracles on Mount Athos with the elder and had been exposed to a variety of extraordinary phenomena through hypnotism, yoga seminars, and Silva Mind Control. All these experiences had made me certain, without a shadow of a doubt, about the existence of the spiritual world. Of course, if Babaji were god in the flesh, as his followers claimed, that would be a spiritual wonder beyond all the rest.

Hinduism teaches that all faiths are essentially the same and come from the same source. Only the forms differ. Naturally, Hinduism, and especially yoga, is the best and most perfect form. The swamis[1] told me that Jesus Christ was a great guru, whose final ashram and chosen resting place, "New Jerusalem," was in the Himalayas, to which Christ traveled after preaching in Palestine. Other yogis put Christ at a higher level, as one of the nine incarnations of God, like *Krishna* and Babaji. Though I wasn't wholly convinced, it seemed to me that this understanding could indeed be the truth.

The elder, on the other hand, used to say, "There are two powers in the world: God and the devil. Everything depends on who you're working for." Several months before my departure for India, an abbot on the Holy Mountain spoke to me. He came to a table where I was eating by myself and exchanged

[1] The title "swami," meaning "owner of oneself," is given to Hindu religious teachers to honor their mastery of yoga and devotion to the gods.

some small talk with me. Then, out of the blue, he said, "Look here, we say that we are with Christ and want you to be united with Him, but who are the others with, and with whom do they want you to be united?" I wondered at the time why he said that to me, since we weren't even talking about the subject—I wondered if his words were inspired by God.

Now, on the train for New Delhi, those words rang in my ears. Just what, I asked myself, is this Babaji? Is he a sorcerer, yogi, god, or *avatar?*[1] What does it mean to be a sorcerer and how does a sorcerer differ from a saint? They both work miracles, but who is telling the truth? Who is right? The purpose of my trip to India was to answer these questions by examining matters firsthand. My intention remained fixed. I had gone to the Holy Mountain, now it was India's turn: I wanted to speak with her holy men face-to-face and be shaped by them, giving them the same opportunity I had given the monks on Athos.

In New Delhi, we stayed in a bungalow with a fairly good-looking exterior, located near the central bus station. It was expensive, costing fifteen rupees[2] a night in contrast to five to six rupees a night charged at a hotel. Nevertheless, we decided to settle in there for the night, and to go to Haldwani, a town at the foothills of the Himalayas, in the morning. When we asked them for some blankets to cover the filthy mattresses, they told us it would cost five extra rupees. It seemed like extortion, but we gave them the money anyway and took the blankets, which were so grimy and unbearably soiled that it was nauseating just to touch them—at least we could take comfort in the fact that we decided to place them over our sleeping bags. As in the desert, it was hot during the day and cold at night.

[1] That is, a deity manifested on earth in bodily form.
[2] Approximately one dollar and fifty cents.

A short while after turning off the lights in order to go to sleep, I heard Chryssa screaming and felt a cat walking over my legs. Someone quickly flipped on the lights, revealing five or six huge rats crawling on our beds. They weren't the least bit startled that we had discovered them. In fact, when we threw our shoes at them, they just looked at us with indifference. That night, we slept as best we could, with one eye open and praying that God would protect us from being bitten.

The next day, we went to the central bus station, which was inundated with a thick and lively crowd. There were scores of ticket counters, numerous platforms, and all the signs were in Hindi, written in a Devanagari script used also for Sanskrit that was as foreign to us as Chinese. Finally, after a good deal of searching, we found the right platform, but now we had to figure out how to recognize our bus. Buses would pass by from time to time—some were early, others were late, and none of them had any signs. As if that weren't enough, as soon as a bus pulled up to the platform—and, in fact, while it was still in motion—a mob of Indians would start running beside it, tossing packages through the windows and doors and climbing up its sides. By the time the bus came to a halt, it would already be filled up inside and covered on the roof with people. Meanwhile, I would stand there with my backpack, wondering if this was the bus we had to take, while my friends would ask those standing nearby. Under such conditions, we felt we were at an impasse. It seemed impossible to get on the bus (and the tickets were sold on the bus, so only those who managed to board could get them).

While I was pondering how to get around this situation, an Indian man approached me and offered us the perfect solution. He said we could take a taxi to a certain intervening bus station where we would be able to get on the bus, since a number of passengers would have gotten off en route. I called my friends over and the six of us got in a taxi and we were off. On the way, we learned that this man had also seen Babaji and was one of his followers.

Just as the man had said, we were able to find seats on the last bus of the day for Haldwani. It was still early in the afternoon, so we could enjoy the Indian scenery. I struck up a conversation with a sincere and educated Indian man about my age who was sitting next to me. He was a Sikh from the upper class. I learned a great deal from him about life in Indian society.

The trip lasted many hours, during which he smoked his chillum two or three times. As it grew later, I asked him when he thought we would arrive at our destination. To my dismay, he said "Around three o'clock in the morning." Once again, the information we had received had turned out to be wrong. What were we supposed to do at three o'clock in the morning in a strange city? With everything closed and no police present, we were bound to be targets for the packs of hoodlums roaming the streets. Somehow, we had to get off the bus without being observed or noticed—such thugs usually lurked around the bus stations, lying in ambush. I had taken some walks at night in New Delhi, so I already had a taste of the nightlife in India. And this time, I had to worry about two girls at my side.

Fortunately, the station was not crowded when we arrived and no one harmed us. We only knew the name of one hotel, but when we mentioned that name to the rickshaw drivers, they looked at us with a blank stare. Finally, I said the name "Babaji" to one driver, who seemed to understand. He loaded up our belongings and took us through some dark back streets, stopping in front of a certain house, where he said, "Babaji." A sleepy but polite young man came out and asked for a high price, which we agreed to pay just so that we could get some sleep.

The next morning, we had an opportunity to speak with the young man and for my irate friends to complain about the exorbitant fee. He also happened to be a follower of the guru.

In fact, the guru had put him in charge of serving the visitors who were coming to see him. "Many times," he told me, "I can feel the presence of the guru, who mystically visits us, leaving behind a distinctive odor." I learned from him that the guru appeared in the region out of nowhere, as a young man around twenty years of age. No one knew where he came from or had seen him before when he was discovered by some shepherds. He meditated for forty days and forty nights. When he opened his eyes, a multitude had already gathered around him. They asked him, "Who are you?" And he answered, "The Babaji." At first, they laughed and didn't believe him. He withdrew to an ancient temple in the mountains. In a short while, respected yogis from diverse parts started coming to see him. They recognized him as an incarnation of Babaji by means of certain marks he had on his feet, and they worshipped him. Afterwards, he gathered his first disciples and made his presence felt throughout the entire region. Foreigners from all parts of the world began to come to see him.

Later, I had a conversation with this young man's father, who maintained his Hindu principles adamantly, with a fanatic's passion. I was struck by the fact that they had, in a prominent place, a painting of the Annunciation of the Virgin Mary. It was a work in Renaissance style, portraying an angel offering a lily to the Most Pure Virgin. I found this quite bizarre and wondered whether it was there to make Western visitors feel at home, or if perhaps the intended message was that, just as Christ was an incarnation of the Deity, so was Babaji. I later verified that the painting was supposed to convey the view that all faiths are one and the same, regardless of whether the god being worshipped is Babaji or Christ.

The town had a large population, although by the standards of overpopulated India it was considered to be merely a village high up in the Himalayas. It was also where the public transportation system ended. We had to find some means to go about six miles further up the mountain road, then take a footpath leading to an ancient temple, and finally walk another four miles in a certain riverbed. We tried to find a taxi, but all the fares were exorbitant. Then, a very kindly Indian gentleman of about fifty years old approached me and asked if I was going to see Babaji. When I responded affirmatively, he offered to go with us, since he was one of the guru's followers. I was delighted to find this unexpected help.

He explained that taxis could not cover the difficult terrain, and that a larger vehicle would be required. So we began to look for a truck or some other more rugged means of transportation. Seeing that I was a Westerner, the drivers insisted on high prices. I told the Indian gentleman that my friends and I were willing to pay extra, but he insisted on bargaining with the drivers until he got us a fair rate. Finally, we piled into the back of a truck with about six others and began our ascent on the narrow road up the mountain. In this way, we overcame our final obstacle. Whenever we had encountered some insurmountable hurdle along our journey, a hurdle that would have brought our trip to a screeching halt, a follower of the guru had always turned up to help us find a way around it. This made an impression on all of us and predisposed us to look favorably on the guru and even perhaps to believe in and admire his unusual capabilities.

In the Himalayas at the Ashram of the Teacher of Teachers

The terrain of the Himalayas along our ascent was peculiar, its numerous small jagged peaks comprising a larger mountain formation. It was as though someone had used hundreds of hills to fashion one large mountain. In between these hills, which were covered sparsely by tall trees, there was a valley formed by the erosion of a side river with a wide riverbed. This exquisitely beautiful valley was wrapped in luxuriant green, adorned with lovely flowers, and embellished with the icy, crystal waters of a flowing stream.

There were about ten of us walking through this valley, including some Indian strangers who had joined us. The beautiful landscape made an impression on us, but there was something that moved us in a strange way. The air seemed electric, so that the entire area was quivering. It was as though the countryside could hardly withstand such power and energy, so that the very mountains trembled in order to keep from breaking into pieces; and I felt as though I were in the midst of a continuous earth tremor. Although one of our party normally loved to look at scenery, this time she wasn't interested in the beautiful landscape and didn't rave about it as usual. I soon realized that she was frightened, if not scared to death.

I was cautious and speculated about what was taking place. Another friend kept looking around and shaking her head in bewilderment, saying, "Oh my goodness, what's going on here?" She was also amazed, not by the beauty, but by the abnormal feeling caused by the power we could sense in the air. We were all stunned and curious. The Indians, however, didn't show any sign of having the same reaction we did.

After about three miles, we made a turn and saw the Haidakhan ashram in the distance. It was situated on the top of a hill, where an ancient Hindu temple stood together with some old buildings and other, more recent ones. It was reached by climbing some two hundred steps up its steep slope. At the base of the hill, there was a flowing river next to which some Westerners were working, gathering round stones from the stream bed in order to build dry stone walls. Strangely enough, there seemed to be no reason for them to be building the walls: to me, the task appeared meaningless.

Near the river basin, there was a pyramid about sixteen feet tall with a fire burning continuously in front of it, as well as other symbols made of stone. Everything I had read about in various occult books or books about white magic—everything I knew about these subjects—came to life in this place. I felt odd looking at this assortment of symbols and other objects whose uses in witchcraft I had read and heard about since childhood.

I was subconsciously drawn towards living alone and apart from the world, and I thought that I wanted to become a yogi. I recall when I was talking with my friends in junior high, I would tell them that all I wanted was a room in the woods, a plate of food, and free time to develop my inner life. And now, I had all of these things at my disposal.

That tantalizing world which I had spent so many hours exploring in a piecemeal and limited way, and which seemed to be the only thing of real importance in this life, was now within my reach in all its entirety and richness. I had reached the source and center where what my books had described theoretically became living and practical experience. This was the source of Carl Jung's psychoanalytic theory of the unconscious and Hermann Hesse's ideas for his novels. This was the foundation of the books of various yogis such as Vivekananda as well as the various books on the supernatural by Lyall Watson. This was the wellspring of Fritjof Capra's book *The Tao of Physics* and Aldous Huxley's *The Doors of Perception*, which had so influenced the hippie movement. This had inspired Ivanov's books on white magic, Gurdjieff's strange teachings, Helena Blavatsky's Theosophical Society, and Alice Bailey's writings on witchcraft. All these people had been influenced by ideas and views emanating from India, and ultimately from the spiritual center of India, the ashram.

I had seen and heard about various ashrams, but there was something special about this place. It was as though everything were condensed and complete. After all, Babaji was the guru of the gurus and the teacher of the teachers. This is what they said, and I verified it by questioning other yogis, many of whom desired to be accepted one day into his ashram.

I am utterly convinced that if I hadn't gone to the Holy Mountain and had the experiences I did with Elder Paisios, I would have remained in that ashram and become a disciple of Babaji. But having heard another perspective from a man with undoubted spiritual power, I was somewhat skeptical. Moreover, the numerous miracles I had witnessed and spiritual experiences I had had by the elder's prayers were qualitatively different from anything I had experienced through yoga and related practices up to that time. They were deeper and purer than what I had experienced with various gurus, and I had known quite a few of them. I couldn't consider the elder to be a member of an inferior faith, as all the groups influenced by Eastern religions portrayed Christianity to be, because I had never encountered anyone of his caliber with whom to make a comparison. At the same time, I couldn't ignore those in Eastern religions, towards which I was already favorably predisposed on account of my earlier experiences. I was there, after all, in order to be open to the voices of mother India—that is why I had taken off my cross and made the journey that I had.

We approached the foot of the hill where the ashram was located and stood before the river, which separated us from the stairs leading to the top. Suddenly, the crowd that was carrying the stones became agitated. Everyone turned towards the top of the hill and began loudly shouting, "Bhole Baba Ki Jai!" which I later learned was a cry of glorification and honor, meaning "Victorious Holy Father." That is when I saw Babaji for the first time. He stood for a moment at the top of the hill. He was about thirty years old with jet-black hair down to his shoulders. He looked like he was about five foot seven inches tall and had a large belly—he was nothing like that frail boy in that old photograph of him. He was clad in expensive fabrics

The Haidakhan ashram.

and wore soft fur boots from the West. He quickly came down the stairs, leaping spryly from one step to the next, and seeming quite pleased with the crowd's cheers, which he accepted as completely natural. His whole demeanor seemed to say, "Yes, I am who you proclaim me to be: a victor and a saint." It was impossible to miss the fact that he was the absolute master in the ashram—one who was not only obeyed but also worshipped.

At that point, something strange happened to me, which reminded me of my experiences under hypnosis. Suddenly, while I was watching him come down the stairs, I lost consciousness for an indeterminate period of time. I was standing there, but my mind and self-consciousness had been seized and taken somewhere else. I was not aware of my body or my thoughts: for a moment, it was as though I no longer existed. Even now, there remains a startling empty space in my memory about what happened to me during those few seconds—or were they minutes?—during which my very existence seemed to have dissolved away. When I regained consciousness, I became aware of a broad smile pasted across my face. My first thought was, "Why are you standing there smiling like an idiot?" I felt violated—it was as though someone had forced me to smile when I didn't feel like smiling. I found this very unsettling, but it also piqued my curiosity.

In the meantime, Babaji had come down the hill, giving orders to some and blessings to others. Soon, he approached the visitors. The others had already bowed down before him and received permission to stay in the ashram. The only ones left who hadn't made the slightest motion were my friends and I. We were too rattled to speak and felt very ill at ease. I really didn't know what to do. When he came within about fifteen feet of where I was standing, I shuddered with apprehension and broke out into a cold sweat. I was taken aback by his features, which were somehow not quite human. Of course, this being in front of me had a human body and form, but there was nothing else human about him: it was clear that his soul was hardly human at all. I would have found it more credible and less shocking for someone to claim that he were a figment of my imagination or some extraterrestrial being. Everything about him was strangely alien, and his eyes were charged with a terrifying intensity and power.

Although I was terror-struck and confused, I remained aware of my surroundings. Babaji was accompanied by four or five yogis with black fabric draped around their bodies and holding in their hands spears with tridents at the top symbolizing the god *Shiva*. One of them drew near me, looked me straight in the eye, and with a stern and imposing voice ordered, "Take off your shoes and worship him!" As he said that, his pupil became so unnaturally large that it eclipsed his iris, which now seemed to be entirely black. From my knowledge of witchcraft I immediately recognized this as a ploy for

Babaji ("Haidakhan Babaji").

achieving domination. "So, they resort to magic tricks like that," I thought, and in spite of my fear I completely ignored the yogi. I slowly approached Babaji, but I didn't dare get nearer than ten feet—it was as though there were some sort of sinister field surrounding him. I stammered, but managed to say to him, "*Namasté,*" the polite, everyday greeting used by Indians. He pointed towards the road for the ashram. He had accepted us: we were allowed to stay.

As I walked away from him, the tension I had felt when near him began to diminish, and I began to reflect on just what this astounding individual could be. Surely, no human being could have such gargantuan power. I felt a dire need to uncover the identity of this enigma, whatever he was—god or devil, sorcerer or saint, man or something else entirely.

It was already late afternoon when we began to climb the steep stairs leading to the mountaintop where the ashram was located. A stark naked man, a Westerner in his thirties, ran past me shivering from the cold because he had just come out of the river's freezing waters. I had read about yogis taking extended baths in cold waters in connection with certain *asanas,* or yoga positions, with the aim of altering the biochemistry of the body.

Indeed, everywhere I looked, I was reminded of what I had learned from books about the life of yoga and the life of witchcraft, teachings I had desired to put into practice for many years. I looked at witchcraft as something quite positive. Nevertheless, at the same time I could hear the voices of the elder, the Holy Mountain, and my Christian experiences clamoring to dissuade me, warning me about the devil transforming himself into an angel of light in order to deceive.[1] Still, I didn't really believe those voices, continuing to waver between the two outlooks.

As I continued to climb the stairs, afraid, astonished, and very curious, I suddenly felt someone invisibly approach me, granting me comfort, calmness, and strength. At the same time, I clearly heard a voice in my mind—which, in retrospect, I believe to have been that of my guardian angel—saying, *I am the Lord thy God.... Thou shalt have no other gods before Me.... Thou shalt not bow down thyself to them, nor serve them.*[2] I felt at peace as I began to fathom the profundity of meaning contained in those words, which I found far more remarkable than the unusual way in which I had been reminded of them.

With that voice still resounding in my being, the steps came to an end, and I found myself face-to-face with a small open-air Hindu temple, complete with statues of various deities from the Hindu pantheon which were worshipped by the residents. One had to pass through this temple in order to

[1] Cf. 2 Corinthians 11:14.
[2] Exodus 20:2, 3, 5.

enter the ashram; and, to walk through it, visitors were required to take off their shoes, because it was considered to be holy ground. The statues were draped with flowers and other offerings, apparently tokens of idol worship that had taken place. One god had the body of a human and the head of an elephant; another god was a monkey with humanoid features; yet another had six arms and four legs. I thought to myself, "If these aren't idols, what are?" For me, it was a revelation that these Hindus really were idolaters just like the Greeks and the other ancient peoples before the coming of Christ.

At that point, I considered how frank the Orthodox Faith is, clearly and categorically stating its separation from and opposition to Hinduism. The Hindus, on the other hand, presented matters in such a way as to suggest that every faith was nearly the same and that only narrow-minded fanatics refused to recognize this. Now, however, I became convinced that this approach was deceptive, because it was not, after all, a secondary figure—a narrow-minded priest or monk, for example—who the Christian Faith recorded as saying, "Thou shalt have no other gods before Me," but the God of the Bible Himself. Indeed, this crystal-clear injunction against polytheism and idolatry was the very first of the Ten Commandments, so revered by Christians. But the Hindus ignored this, suggesting that the Christian Faith was compatible with and even similar to Hinduism. But as I stood there in the midst of the idols, considering how great the differences were between the faiths, it was hard to conceive of what they could mean. The yogis at the ashram in Thessaloniki never talked about the Hindu gods, but now here they were before me. What did the one and unique God presented in the Old and New Testaments have to do with the god *Shiva; Ganesha,* the god with the elephant head; or *Hanuman,* the monkey god? But, though this all became clear to me at the time, it would not remain securely or clearly fixed in my consciousness.

A festival in honor of the elephant-headed god *Ganesha* in Mumbai, India, 2006. At bottom left is a figure of the god *Hanuman*.

As I made my way through the temple carrying my shoes, I noted a shiny jet-black statue of a fat young man in the lotus position, the only touch of white on it being the whites of his eyes. I later learned that this well-polished porcelain statue, black as a moonless night, portrayed Babaji and was created by his disciples from Italy. It was also in the temple and worshipped together with the other statues. The people in the ashram really believed that Babaji was a god, a god incarnate. And so the residents worshipped him every morning and every evening, passing in front of him one by one while he sat comfortably on a dais. They would usually fall prostrate to the ground in front of him and give him gifts. He in turn would take their gifts and give back part of them as his blessing. The whole process lasted at least two hours, if not longer.

In various prominent places throughout the ashram, there were hanging on the walls photographs of his feet, which supposedly had markings that enabled the other yogis to recognize

153

him as the teacher of teachers, an *avatar,* or incarnation of Babaji. All I could see was a naked pair of chubby feet. I really wondered how many people knew the telltale markings, or if such markings even existed. Perhaps the whole tale was just sensationalism. I was more impressed by a painting of flames forming a heart of garish red and orange colors. I encountered that painting frequently in the various buildings in the ashram and eventually learned that it was the guru's emblem.

Although I had been separated by now from my friends, who would be staying in another part of the ashram, I was still with people with whom I had a lot in common, since at least half of the residents of the ashram were Europeans and Americans. When the food was distributed, we ate in scattered groups. We then began to gather in an old building which had a roof supported by large pillars, but which did not have walls, being open on three sides. I was among the first to enter, attracted by the beat of the small drums and the singing of Hindu religious hymns called *kirtana.* Soon, everyone else gathered and the pavilion was packed. Then Babaji made his entrance with his entourage, the five or six yogis who made up the tight circle of his closest disciples. Interestingly enough, they were all Westerners.

At this point, Babaji reclined on his dais, and the others began to pass in front him to worship him and offer him gifts. There was something so uncanny about him that I couldn't take my eyes off him. I had the same reaction to him that I had when I first met him, the only difference being that I was now about fifteen yards away, and I tried to come to some conclusion about this baffling creature. I was engrossed in his every movement and expression, hoping to find some clue to his identity. I could see him incessantly practicing much of what I had read about in books about witchcraft. On the wall behind him hung a large embroidered tapestry portraying three mountain peaks and a peculiar depiction of the sun. I had seen this symbol before in a book on witchcraft I had read in Greece, which presented it as the secret symbol for high magic, and I recognized it at once.

Although there were variations in how intently and whole-heartedly each person worshipped Babaji, everyone was certainly focused on him. Three times I was approached and urged to worship him, but I didn't budge. I simply tried to look at him straight in the eyes. Babaji's eyes roved around the room and at a certain point our eyes did in fact meet, although he wasn't looking at me purposely. As soon as this happened, I lost all contact with my surroundings and fell into an ecstasy. It was as though I were looking into my chest, and in that inner darkness I saw my own heart in the most lurid colors and engulfed in flames. The very next moment I regained consciousness and realized what had taken place. I was quite impressed and continued to watch him carefully.

Again, someone approached me and told me to go before him, but I didn't reply. "And what am I supposed to do?" I asked myself. "I guess what everyone else is doing: worship him!" But I refused to go, because I couldn't figure out just what Babaji was, and the idea that I was required to worship him without knowing why was frightening. It was obvious that he had power—great power—but I would not bow down to him only for that. I wanted to know: Was he humble, did he speak the truth, did he love?

Suddenly, Babaji became tense, straightened himself up, and sat in the lotus position. His acute concentration and vigilance were obvious. His eyes became as dark as coal and as piercing as lightning. A man was in front of him worshipping him unreservedly with a deep devotion that could be seen in his whole demeanor, and especially in the recurring prostrations that he made without any scruple whatsoever. He had also offered Babaji many precious gifts. Babaji fixed his powerful eyes firmly on the man, who suddenly folded his hands together in front of his chest, as though giving a traditional Indian greeting, and moved his legs together. Although the man's body became as rigid as a stone column, he began to tremble where he stood and to leap up and down in a most unnatural manner, as though he had springs attached to his heels. He began uttering the most deafening groans and moans, like a wounded cow or an enraged bull. Babaji kept the man in this state for about a minute. He then let him go for a moment, but, before the man could come to, he seized him even more vehemently, so that the man began to vibrate like a jackhammer and wail at the top of his lungs. We were all flabbergasted by the shocking spectacle taking place before us. Babaji then released the man, relaxed a bit, and laid back to watch the rest of the people pass in front of him.

A woman standing next to Babaji spoke to the crowd, informing us that the guru had just granted the man illumination. I found this explanation to be rather problematic since, according to the Hindu worldview, in order for someone to reach illumination, or *samadhi*, he must struggle many times and live many lives as a yogi. If Babaji was able to grant this man illumination in a few minutes, he had greatly abbreviated a process of spiritual development that usually requires many cycles of reincarnation. Anyone who had embraced the Hindu worldview and accepted what the woman claimed could only conclude that what Babaji did proved he was a god.

Even a Christian, I knew, would consider the guru to be supernatural—but by virtue of his being demon-possessed. That is to say, a Christian would have said that the spiritual power he displayed was in fact the power of the evil spirits that he permitted to dwell within his soul. Everyone who worshipped Babaji, therefore, would come under a demonic influence to a greater or lesser extent. That is, the man we had just seen, by worshipping Babaji, would be in fact, like the rest, worshipping the demons dwelling within Babaji, and in this way giving these demons the power to enter into him. We would have witnessed, not the acquisition of enlightenment, but the process by which the demons seized possession of his soul.

I stood there wondering which of these two utterly divergent perspectives was, in fact, correct. I needed to find a criterion by which to determine what this teacher of teachers really was: if I could only find the proper set of scales, I would weigh him in the balance in order to discern whether he was a sorcerer or a saint. I somehow had to find a gauge that would indicate if he was a god or a devil.

In a short while, Babaji stood up and headed off with his disciples. He passed by me without my realizing it even though I was trying to get a closer look at him. I was only able to see his back: he somehow managed to restrain my mind so that I couldn't look at him when he walked past me. I decided to take a walk on the grounds of the ashram and ran into my friend Noni, who was very distressed and disturbed. She told me that our friend Chryssa was bedridden and losing a great deal of blood on account of her menstrual cycle—that the amount of blood loss was abnormally high. Chryssa was so frightened that she was unable to get out of bed. Noni then made some unseemly comments about the fact that all the women in the ashram slept under Babaji's apartment. We spoke a bit longer, and then went our separate ways.

Babaji stayed in an apartment that had a special entrance and was cut off from the other buildings. The multicolored, shiny tiles covering the apartment's outside walls were no doubt intended to be decorative, though I found them rather tacky. When I approached the entrance, a European man standing there stopped me and told me that I wasn't permitted to enter for various reasons. The man was a bit embarrassed and depressed, because they had made him take up a ridiculous pose as the guard of the entrance to Babaji's chambers. He was wearing a silly little hat as a helmet and held a reed in one hand as a weapon and a mat in his other hand as a shield. He felt out of sorts and wanted to justify himself. I felt sorry for him, so I sat down and let him tell me his story. Although he had known the guru for a number of years, he had come here this time particularly because he wanted to get a promotion in his company and decided to beg Babaji to use his powers to help him. "Of course," he told me, "I could have simply written a letter, but I preferred to come in person." I was astonished that he would agree to be made such a laughingstock just for a promotion. The skeptic in me wondered if they were making a fool of him on purpose—if this were just a way of imposing authority over him in order to train him to be absolutely obedient.

In the evening, I slept in a large room with ten others who were all about my age. We not only had similar knapsacks and sleeping bags, we also shared the same mind-set and way of life. One of these young people told me that he made a living teaching people in America how to breathe. "Imagine," I thought to myself, "teaching yoga breathing exercises qualifies as an occupation. Soon, they'll be teaching us how to walk."

The next morning, I awoke at dawn and climbed up the hill outside of the ashram in order to practice my morning meditation as did the rest of the residents. On my way back, I met Noni, who told me that we were late and that it was imperative for us to attend the morning ritual in front of the guru, which was to take place in the courtyard in front of Babaji's apartment. When we arrived, they rebuked us for our intolerable tardiness, a sign of disrespect for the guru. We pushed our way into the crowded courtyard and I sat down in the back in order to watch the captivating ritual. Unwittingly, I offended the others by doing this. Someone came over and sharply reprimanded me for daring to sit in a sacred place, since there was a temple there with photographs and drawings of the gods, animals with human features and humans with animal features.

The ritual was basically the same as that of the day before. Babaji, that strangely aberrant creature, was again the central attraction. On the one hand, it was terrifying to look upon him, but, on the other hand, he was just a young man who happened to be overweight. I watched him, struggling to find some sign that would uncover his identity.

In the middle of the line, there was a couple from Australia with a four-year-old boy. Suddenly, Babaji asked them to bring the child to him, and one of the yogis in his entourage went and took the child from his mother. The child was peaceful as the yogi held him in his arms, but as soon as he came close to Babaji, he began screaming and bawling with the most heart-wrenching cries. He even hurt himself while desperately struggling to get away from the guru. The parents just stood there, making no objection at all. Babaji then took the child in his arms and put his thumb in the boy's mouth and his index finger in between the boy's eyebrows. Abruptly, the child fell into a deep sleep, or perhaps he was simply hypnotized. In any event, Babaji kept the child in that state for the entire duration of the ritual.

I believed then and still do that small children have better instincts than adults, because they're so innocent. Their intuition springs from the fact that they use their heart to directly experience the world, without the mind interfering and confusing the heart with various speculations that may have no basis in reality. The child's negative response and fear made an impression on me, especially when I recalled how the children mentioned in the Gospel embraced Christ with trust and joy.

Again, they approached us and urged us to go and worship Babaji, but neither Noni nor I moved an inch. Our friend was still bedridden and losing blood, which the yogis referred to as a purification and a blessing from the guru. After everyone, except us, had passed in front of him, we dispersed. In a short while, our hosts told us to leave the ashram, because they were not pleased with our behavior. What had we done wrong? We hadn't worshipped Babaji. Why, I would wonder later, had the others worshipped him—the ones who, like me, had never met Babaji before? Was it the wonders he had performed, the confident authority of his disciples, or even some fear of them? Perhaps it was a combination of the three; in any event, it seemed that the life of the ashram functioned as a sort of psychological program directed towards encouraging this worship.

My friend was relieved and cheerfully started to gather her belongings, but I felt torn. How could I leave without coming to a definite conclusion? I was not about to leave India with empty hands and my objective unachieved. I decided to request to see the guru. They went to ask the proper party and shortly thereafter led me to Babaji.

As I entered his courtyard, I made the sign of the Cross and asked God to help me. As I drew nearer to Babaji, I felt as though he were influencing my mind, causing it to no longer function properly. When I was within about six feet of him, I looked around for a place to sit, because I thought we would have a conversation. Babaji gave me a dirty look, as though he both feared and loathed me. He had been sitting comfortably, but now he shrunk back in his seat, turning away from me in disgust. He loudly shrieked, "Get out!" I was flabbergasted by this response and looked at him in disbelief. He shrieked even more loudly, "Get out!" I said, "Only one question." "No questions here," he bellowed, "Get out!" I made an about-face and left in a daze. I was astonished—what was I to make of his behavior?

I ran into one of my friends, who happened to be coming out of the gate to his courtyard. "We're definitely leaving," she said. "Are you coming along?" I decided to join them on the journey back on the assumption that I could always return later. As we walked away from the ashram, one of my friends turned to me and said, "What was wrong with that fellow who ordered us to bow down and worship him? There's a certain sweetness about our religion, but he was downright savage." I could not believe what she was saying. Both my friends were hostile towards Christianity and favorably inclined to yoga and witchcraft.

During our return trip to New Delhi, we met a Brahman who was a disciple of the guru and a Dutch lady who had also spent years in India as his disciple. The Brahman told us that his wife was insane, but that he considered that insanity to be sacred. In the course of our conversation, he made no attempts to hide his racist disdain for Indians of lower castes. This bothered me so much that when he offered to let us stay at his home in the foothills of the Himalayas, I refused, to the Dutch lady's great surprise. She helped us return to the capital city of New Delhi, where we decided to stay in the ashram of Sri Aurobindo.

At the Ashram of Sri Aurobindo in New Delhi

Located in the suburbs of India's capital, this ashram was left for years without a guru after the death of the founder, Sri Aurobindo, who was widely regarded as a saint in India.[1] His disciples now ran the ashram and continued to follow his path. The ashram ran a private elementary school, junior high school, and high school attended by the children of rich Indians, which provided it with a good income by Indian

[1] Sri Aurobindo (1872–1950) was an Indian guru educated in the West, who, after an initial period as an Indian nationalist leader, developed a philosophy of cosmic salvation through spiritual evolution. He wrote extensively; and, after his 1910 relocation to the French colony of Puducherry in southeast India, a community formed around him which in time would be formally organized as his ashram. He retired into seclusion in 1926.

standards. They also rented rooms to tourists like myself, at about the same rates as those of a good hotel. I was to stay in an isolated room as I requested, so as to have ample opportunity to reflect on the events of the past few days and to come to some kind of conclusion about them. The ashram had a laid-back and calm ambiance, quite unlike the spiritual intensity of Babaji's ashram in the Himalayas.

The residents of this ashram were wary of Babaji and seemed to have a negative opinion of him. When I spoke with them about him, they asked, "How can he claim that he is god?" They instead followed the esoteric path of Sri Aurobindo, whom, as his title suggests, they considered a saint.[1] I found corroboration of this conclusion about their devotion in an outdoor memorial in the courtyard of the ashram, where I would frequently see Indian and Western patrons of the ashram come and worship a stone in the shape of an egg, containing ashes from Aurobindo's funeral pyre.

In the ashram, I met a retired Indian doctor and homeopath who offered his medical assistance to the poor free of charge. He was a good man, a conscientious Hindu, and a practitioner of yoga. He spoke very highly of the Guru Satyananda, whom he had known before he and his ashrams had become famous. Interestingly, he expressed his admiration for Alexander the Great, in whom he had become interested owing to Alexander's conquest of parts of the Indian subcontinent. He even told me that there were Indians who believed themselves to be the descendants of Alexander's soldiers.

I also encountered many people from the West living in the ashram, such as a childless couple in their forties from Holland, who had decided to remain in India, join the ashram, and teach at the school. They were quite happy to learn that I had studied physics and could work as a teacher. They gave me

---

[1] *Sri* in Sanskrit literally means "beauty" or "majesty." It is a conventional title of respect used with regard to Indian holy men or saints.

a tour of the school building and hinted that, if I were interested, I could find work there.

I had many conversations with the teacher from Holland about topics relating to the spiritual life. At one point, he told me that what I was saying was "just Christian nonsense." Now I found this to be an astonishing statement from someone who had never investigated Christianity beyond the confines of his former Protestant surroundings, where what passed for Christian faith was a watered-down mixture of moralism and humanism. Understandably, we had trouble communicating with each other. My statements were based on experiencing the Holy Spirit and the grace of Christ, while his position was based on the experience of a rationalistic Protestant Christianity, a Christianity cut off, tragically, from the ancient Church of Christ, and deprived of its wisdom and mysteries.

Of course this man had changed his religion and become a Hindu, because he yearned for something more than barren moralism. He tried to convince me that Hinduism was true, but I contended that the existence of so many gods was hardly plausible. Instead of answering me, he changed the subject and began to tell me about the mysticism and magic in Sufi orders. (Indeed, I doubted that he could answer me, and I suspected that he, too, had difficulty accepting Hindu polytheism—thus accounting for his interest in Sufism, a monotheistic tradition.) He said that he knew a remarkable woman, a teacher of Sufism with extraordinary capabilities. He offered to introduce me to her, but Islam did not interest me.

After spending a few days as carefree tourists in the capital of India, my friends and I decided to go our separate ways. They wanted to go to Nepal for a vacation and not get mixed up anymore with gurus, ashrams, and the like. Their experience with Babaji had turned out to be too much for them—they simply wanted to enjoy some rest and relaxation.

So we parted, agreeing to contact each other in New Delhi before we were to return to Greece.

I decided to visit the mother ashram of Guru Satyananda's movement. I already knew about this movement from its office in Greece. I hoped to meet Satyananda himself, so that, by direct contact with him, I would be able to compare him with Father Paisios and come to some conclusion about Hinduism and Orthodoxy. After all, both men were living expressions of their respective spiritual traditions.

At the Ashram of Guru Satyananda in Munger

After a long train ride in the direction of Calcutta, I found myself on my own in the small Indian town of Munger,[1] built on the edge of the Ganges. At this point, the gray waters of the muddy Ganges ooze along a wide riverbed flanked by sandy shores. To me, the unclean water was so filthy that it was too disgusting to look at, but, to the Indians, the water of the sacred river was fit for bathing, for drinking, and for taking home as a blessing.

I was famished when I got off the train. A short distance beyond the train station, I spied what looked like a restaurant—a small straw canopy over two tables with some large, black kettles on a wooden bench. Despite the dirty water used for the cooking and the swarm of flies, I headed straight there. Most Westerners wouldn't have had the stomach to eat in such a place—as I didn't during my first ten days in India—but now I was used to it. Hunger and exhaustion had overcome all my qualms. I ordered three dishes and some yogurt, which I actually enjoyed. It made me wonder if we Europeans are too fussy about cleanliness.

After this satisfying meal, I found a taxi to take me to the

---

[1] Often spelled "Monghyr," its name during British colonial rule.

INSIDE THE ASHRAMS OF INDIA

ashram, because I didn't know the way. We shortly pulled up in front of a tall closed iron gate, behind which stood a middle-aged woman wearing the orange robe of a yogi. I told her that I wished to see the guru. With a stern expression on her face, she responded, "Wait here." She sent a young child to ask a question of someone, while I waited outside the gate. It was clear that she wasn't taking a liking to me. In the meantime, I began to take in the surroundings. The ashram was located on a hill with a number of buildings around the top and a tall apartment building under construction at the center of the hilltop itself. The complex was surrounded by walls a bit higher than the average person and was roomy inside, with trees, gardens, courtyards, and work sites.

In a short while, the child returned and said something in Hindi to the woman. They then opened the outer iron gate and let me in the ashram. We started climbing the peak, and then stopped and waited in silence for about fifteen minutes until a Western swami about thirty years of age came down to meet me.

We went into a room, and an interrogation of sorts began, in which the swami tried to learn everything he could about me. "Who are you? Where are you from? Whom did you know in Greece? Do you have any illnesses? Do you take any medication? Do you use drugs? Do you smoke marijuana?" Although his job was unpleasant, I found him a likable man who seemed to take to me as well. I told him, "I would like to see the Guru Satyananda." "He's not here," he responded, "He's in Australia." I made no attempts to hide my disappointment at hearing this unexpected news after traveling so far. My reaction made such a good impression on him that, as I could see, his estimation of me increased such that I would be allowed stay in the ashram if I wanted to.

Ultimately I decided to stay, so he gave me the rules of the ashram to read and told me that I must observe them.

Residents were required to hand over all of their cash, their passport, and their tickets. Smoking charas, drinking alcohol, and making trouble were strictly forbidden. Residents were also expected to pay one hundred dollars a day. I almost gasped when I read that they wanted so much. I could survive in India for a month and half on a hundred dollars, and I had only brought two hundred and fifty dollars with me from Greece. I told him that I didn't have that much money, so he said he would take me to the president of the ashram to determine whether I would be accepted or not. I hoped this would be their final assessment of me.

We walked down a long hallway and entered a room with three robed swamis inside—a middle-aged man, a man in his thirties, and a young man around twenty years old. To my great surprise, the young man, named Niranjan, turned out to be the president. The others looked to him for instruction, listened to his words with respect, and agreed fully with whatever he said. He was very thin, just skin and bones, with a shaved head, large eyes, protruding jaw, and an unattractive but kind face. He spoke with a calm and pleasant voice.

While he was speaking to the others, outwardly paying no attention to me, I felt a presence invisibly approach me and realized that he was going to engage in something like I had experienced when I was involved with Silva Mind Control. I didn't have anything to hide, so I sat quietly and calmly, not resisting his searching. The very air in the room had changed. It was as though some kind of disembodied psychic energy emanating from the young man was trying to probe my mind. This search, however, just skimmed the surface of my mind without penetrating more deeply into my soul. He was no doubt looking for some sort of sign to help him make his decision.

Although this searching was more powerful than what I had encountered in Silva Mind Control, it was still but child's play next to Elder Paisios, when he had "walked inside me" with help of the Spirit and descended into the very depths of my soul. Nevertheless, I was impressed by Niranjan's demonstration of capabilities not found in the average person. What struck me in particular about him was that he seemed to be able to do this mental searching effortlessly and inconspicuously, while speaking with others. When the others left, he immediately turned to me and told me that I was accepted. I would pay something, but only five rupees a day,[1] not the one hundred dollars that was normally required. (A few days later, I asked a construction worker about the fee, and he told me that he received a four-rupee wage per day. So, for India, I still paid well and certainly covered my expenses at the ashram.)

After the usual formalities, I decided to ask Niranjan precisely what he had been doing to me. He was apologetic and said, "I am sorry, but as the president of the ashram I need to know what kind of people we are allowing in here." I said, "It doesn't matter," but I didn't like the idea of someone searching me in this way, without my knowledge and permission. The elder had always asked for my consent. Nevertheless, I couldn't hold back my curiosity, so I asked him what he saw. He responded that he saw good things, but didn't enlarge on it. He then called for someone to show me where I was to stay.

My room on the ground floor had a toilet and a sink where I could take a sponge bath. My bed consisted of a grimy mattress on top of some boards, surrounded by a mosquito net. Even though I had grown used to filth during my time in India, I found this mattress so disgusting that I removed it and put my sleeping bag directly on the boards.

At sunrise, we would have a breakfast consisting of a large cup of tea and some tiny doughnuts. We then went to a large hall before starting our workday and for about half an hour

---

[1] Approximately fifty cents a day.

chanted some selections from the *Bhagavad Gita*, one of Hinduism's sacred books. At noon, we lined up in front of a large pot with plates in our hands in order to receive our rations, which we ate with whomever we liked. Afterwards, we disbanded into smaller groups to learn yoga techniques or participate in other activities. I usually attended the *nintra* yoga session.[1] Afterwards, there was more work to be done until sunset, when everyone, men, women, and children, would gather together in a large hall for *satsang*[2] or for *kirtana*.

Later, I learned that the Sanskrit verses they chanted then were devotional texts for the worship of the guru and the various gods from the Hindu pantheon, such as *Krishna, Shiva, Parvati,*[3] and *Vishnu*. I was not a polytheist myself, and, having been introduced to yoga as a non-religious practice, I thought of such worship as the keeping of certain traditional customs. Despite all I had seen, I couldn't bring myself to admit the possibility that these people were polytheists like the ancient Greeks.

One evening when there was a full moon, they prepared an altar by digging a pit, decorating it beautifully, and lighting a fire. They then began a ritual dance around the fire, chanting, and at regular intervals casting in by the handful a blend of wood splinters, rice, and flowers. When I saw one of my friends joining in, I did as well, regarding the ritual as a very picturesque scene. As soon as it was over, I asked a German swami named Prakash what we had been doing. The forty-five-year-old woman told me that it was a sacrifice to a

---

[1] *Author's note:* As I was told, *nintra* is a form of yoga created by Guru Satyananda.

[2] The term *satsang* as used here refers to a meeting between a guru and his disciples and guests, in which questions on spiritual subjects can be posed.

[3] *Parvati* is the wife of the god *Shiva* and, according to some Hindu communities, the benevolent aspect of the goddess *Shakti*. She has two children: the elephant-headed *Ganesha* and the six-headed *Skanda*.

certain god, whose name I no longer recall, so that the god would help us and wipe out our sins. She told me that she had often seen the people of Munger gather on the shores of the Ganges in order to observe this tradition. She also said that, in accordance with Hindu tradition, such rites are to take place during a full moon, so that the people can confess their sins to the moon and thereby undergo what they call a "purification." I felt ill at ease with the idea of confessing my sins to the moon, and I was astonished by the fact that she believed in it.

Some of the People in the Ashram

Niranjan, the President of the Ashram

On my second or third day in the ashram, I ran into Niranjan in the hallway. He was friendly and quite willing to give me his time. Our ensuing conversation quickly reached the crux of the matter, when I asked him for his opinion about Christians and Orthodox monks. He answered that they were also on a spiritual path, but at a low level of spirituality. All of my past experiences came to the surface of my mind, and spontaneously I replied, "But I can't accept that. It's not true." I tried to explain my position to him, but it visibly disturbed him, and shortly thereafter we went our separate ways.

I instinctively compared the elder with the Indian yogi whom I had met in Thessaloniki, who was presented as being advanced and at a high spiritual level. She seemed small and inconsequential in every way next to the elder: in terms of spiritual power, in terms of miraculous gifts, in terms of knowledge, and above all in terms of all-powerful love. Every yogi that I had known during my life was a spiritual nonentity in comparison with Elder Paisios.

Niranjan was perhaps displeased with my refusal to accept his view because the yogis taught that, when someone who is inwardly detached tells the truth, his words will be accepted by another person. Although I had heard about this and read about it in books, in the ashram it was considered to be an absolute spiritual law. Since my soul did not accept his words, he may have seen the encounter as an indication of some inward attachment on his part, and hence a weakness or defect in his perfection, in spite of the fact that he was himself supposedly a great yogi, the successor to the guru, and a guru in his own right, with his own disciples. In any event, Niranjan never again had an extended conversation with me.

An Educated German Lady Named Prakash
    I don't know the Christian name of this lovely and distinguished lady known to us as Prakash. She took me under her wing and had frequent conversations with me. She was the wealthy, educated wife of a powerful and influential man in Germany, where they had lived a worldly life seasoned with social gatherings and vacations abroad. She related to me how she had felt that her former way of life was terribly empty, revolving around senseless trivialities such as what clothing to wear or how expensive a certain fabric was. In order to make her life more full in some way, she opened a health food store. It kept her busy for a few years, but it didn't relieve her inner emptiness, which was only compounded by the fact that she couldn't relate to her husband. She asked him, "What do you want out of life?" He answered, "I want success, and to become as hard as stone, so that I am insensitive to everything."
    In her emptiness, she began a patient search for some goal in life, a deeper meaning to existence, and a new way of being. After she had become acquainted with yoga and met the guru, she abandoned everything, shaved her head, put on an orange

robe, became his follower, and began to practice yoga. She told me that her children came to see her one or two times a year and begged her to return to them, to take off her clerical robes and act once again as a mother. She, on the other hand, took great pride in standing above cultural differences and assigned family roles, which she found to be amusing. At the same time, I sensed in her soul a hidden, painful conflict occasioned by this new life.

She believed that her husband would be reincarnated in the next life as a rock, because that was his desire. More strikingly, she believed that his attitude towards life was predetermined by his *karma*. I was surprised that, in spite of all her education, she would not consider her husband's behavior in the light of psychology, but had turned to an unverifiable, deterministic metaphysical interpretation. Perhaps the former was too painful for her and promised too much labor. In other words, if she had accepted a psychological explanation for her husband's perverse emotional condition, she would have had to face her responsibility as his spouse to help him change it (the same responsibility, of course, that he had towards her). But instead, she had separated herself from, and even abandoned, her family, including her children, and told herself that matters could not be otherwise. It seemed to me then, as it does now, that a metaphysical point of view that so utterly relieves a person of responsibility may, to begin with, be easy and painless—but that the consequences of a mistake in this area can be enormous and can even destroy lives.

This intelligent and kindhearted woman was fond of me and interested in seeing me become a swami. She frequently encouraged me to remain in the ashram and tried to dispel my worries about my parents. If I hadn't encountered Orthodoxy and gotten a sense of its depth, I would hardly have differed from this woman, who could find no nourishment in the dry barrenness of the German Protestant milieu, in which authentic Christian life was virtually dead. I could understand her dissatisfaction with the materialistic way of life in the West, which was essentially atheistic.

Shivaraja

On my second or third day, the yogis told me that there was another Greek man present at the ashram, who could help me adjust to its closed society. Naturally, I was interested in meeting him, but when we became acquainted I learned that the man, whom they called Shivaraja, was in fact an English-man about thirty-five years of age, who had merely spent five years illegally in Greece, teaching English.

Shivaraja was a married man and a college graduate, who used to have a good job in electronics. However, he was ex-tremely interested in spiritual phenomena, and, after some bi-zarre spiritual experiences, he abandoned his family and homeland and came to Greece where he became acquainted with Satyananda's ashram. Although he never joined the Greek branch of the ashram, he did become involved with it and practiced yoga techniques. One day, the director of the ashram told him that they were planning a trip to India and wanted to know if he was interested in participating. He told her how much money he had and that he didn't know if it was suffi-cient. In a few days, he was told that it was enough, so he gave her his money and shortly set out with the rest of the group for India. He stayed in Munger with everyone else in the group, but when the day for the return trip arrived, the director told him that he would not be returning to Greece, because his money didn't cover the cost of a return ticket. He was thus compelled to remain in India.

When I met Shivaraja, a year had already gone by since he had been left behind. He felt horrible about his situation—as though they had deceived him and made him a prisoner. He cursed the Greek director and said that she was a very evil woman. He had never lived outside of the ashram, and he was under the impression that the chances of survival in India were much bleaker than they really were, as I knew full well from my month-long wanderings there. Those in the ashram cultivated such fears. Once, when I requested permission to make a visit to a neighboring city, they told me that it was too dangerous on account of the high crime rate in that region. Ultimately, however, they gave me permission, and I took Shivaraja with me to the Ganges, where he took a bath in spite of his quite apparent revulsion for its muddy gray waters. (He had endless rationalizations for why he did it, with which he was probably trying to convince himself rather than me.)

He was frightened and didn't dare move from the ashram or oppose its wishes. He told me that he intended to write some friends to send him money for a return ticket, but he didn't want them to send the money to the ashram because he was afraid they wouldn't give it to him. I remember asking him, "Why don't you go tell Niranjan, the president of the ashram, about your situation and ask him to loan you the sum with the promise that you'll send him back the money as soon as you reach Europe, or give it to their ashram there?" "No," he replied, "not that." He wouldn't hear of such a solution, because he obviously didn't trust anyone.

Since Shivaraja didn't trust the members of the ashram with financial matters, I couldn't understand how he could trust them with his body, practicing various techniques that, as they themselves affirmed, brought about physical changes. For who really knew what these changes were, or whether or not they were harmful? I was further mystified by the fact that he would entrust them with his mind and his soul by submitting to their spiritual direction, since it was certainly plausible that, just as they had misled him with the ticket, so they were now misleading him, guiding him through mental gymnastics that could lead him to a worse state.

When we were alone, I shared my thoughts with him, because I found his attitude to be not only irrational and inconsistent, but also insincere. Because he had had a bad experience in dealing with them, he had become cunning in order to protect himself: in the hope of deceiving them, he always seemed to be happy, good-natured, and obedient, although he found the life of the ashram to be boring, and the food even more so. I remember him going on about "rice, rice, and nothing but rice." He said, "Here they tell us how we have to eat fruit, but cram rice down our throats." He also reminisced about Greek cuisine, which he liked very much. I felt genuinely sorry for him, but I didn't have the money to help him.

Benoît, the French Aspirant of *Samadhi*

Benoît was a sarcastic twenty-five-year-old Frenchman, in good shape, who had worked as a fireman and had practiced *kriya* yoga to the point of becoming quite adept. He wasn't especially bright, but he was by no means stupid. Benoît wasn't a follower of Satyananda, but a visitor to the ashram who paid dearly for his stay, and for a period of time we shared the same room.

One day, I caught some Indian yogis reading someone's palm and foretelling his future just the way I had seen Gypsies do in Greece. Apparently, palm-reading has its roots in India. I asked them to read my palm as well, and they responded that it would cost ten rupees.[1] Now, according to the *Yoga Sutras* of Patanjali, which is one of the most important works in Hinduism, yoga is a path to the ultimate spiritual good, while *siddhis*—supernatural abilities like flight, changing form, and knowing the future—have to do with the world of the senses.

[1] Approximately one dollar.

Siddhis are held to be a natural consequence of a yogi's spiritual development, but focusing on them or using them for gain is despised for being at a low level and as unworthy of those with spiritual potential (who ought to be pursuing *samadhi,* or enlightenment).[1] Notwithstanding, lowly palm-reading was not beneath these Indian yogis when they could make a profit from it. In any event, I paid them the fee and they told me, among other things, that I would meet a guru who would love me very much. When I told Benoît that, he told me that, when they read his own palm, they told him that he would reach *samadhi* within two years. Of course this made him very happy, even ecstatic. "Now," he told me, "I will have to work very hard in order to achieve it."

I found it farfetched that those peculiar bodily exercises could be sufficient to achieve *samadhi.* I had always thought that an individual's moral choices played a decisive role. I couldn't conceive of someone reaching *samadhi* if he, for example, murdered, was full of craftiness, or deceived others and took advantage of them, just because he flawlessly performed certain exercises and rites—as though man were but a machine whose conscience was irrelevant. When I questioned Benoît about this, he replied, "Why yes, it will take place automatically, just by putting these exercises into practice." I could hardly swallow such an answer, which I found rather simplistic and irrational for someone who was only two or three years from *samadhi,* but Niranjan later affirmed that this position was the general view of the yogis.

Benoît told me about a French karate master and sorcerer with many amazing abilities, whom he paid a good deal of money to be his teacher. This man had been the one who

[1] In Hinduism, *samadhi* is the final goal of the practice of yoga. A person who has reached *samadhi* is said to have attained complete self-collectedness and to have become identified with the object of his meditation.

advised him to come to India. Once, he told me, when two thugs in the French subway attacked his teacher with knives in order to steal his wallet, the sorcerer disposed of them with a few well-placed kicks, without even putting down his briefcase. This teacher was an admirer of Pythagoras and promoted his tradition, and Benoît sincerely believed him, considering himself to be a devotee of Pythagoras as well.

I couldn't help being skeptical about the high spiritual level of a teacher who would resort to violence in order to protect his wallet. In fact, I found such an idea downright amusing when I recalled a similar incident involving Elder Paisios. There was a young man who had grown up around a Buddhist monastery and spent a lot of time around the elder. Even though the elder was kindly trying to help him, the young man decided that he wanted to test the elder's strength, and he grabbed Father Paisios from behind and tried to crush his frail body with his muscular arms. Irreverently, he said, "Hey, let's see if Saint Arsenios can help you now!"

As the elder told me later, "As soon as I heard him say that, I felt as though he had uttered blasphemy. I moved my hand slightly, like this, and immediately saw him cast six feet away and slammed against the wall. He afterwards came over and made a prostration, and I told him to ask forgiveness of the saint." From this example, I concluded that God protects spiritual people in a spiritual way, and not with their own use of the martial arts, which (apart from being potentially injurious) hardly reflect the character that befits a saint.

Luke, the Would-Be Yoga Instructor

Luke was also a Frenchman, around twenty-five years old and a disciple of Satyananda, who had come to the ashram in order to become a yoga teacher. I held him in high regard on account of his genial character, and for years afterwards we would correspond from time to time. He was a humble and kindly soul who didn't try to pass himself off as someone important and learned. I remember him for his goodness and compassion, and for the time he gave me a wool hat when I was cold after shaving my head. I never saw him being jealous or crafty, and he never made fun of others or insulted them.

He was a quiet and peaceful man, an introvert who didn't say much about himself and didn't make acquaintances quickly. Nevertheless, after a while I did get to know him, and I learned that before he came to India he used to live with his parents in a village in southern France. Luke hadn't gone to college and had trouble finding employment. Nevertheless, although he had financial difficulties, he paid the ashram the normal fee out of his savings. He yearned to be freed from the strictures of a limited budget and believed that he could gain that freedom by means of yoga. In fact, he was obsessed with the idea of riches through yoga, which someone had planted in his head. It seemed that this promise had drawn him into yoga in the first place. He used to tell me, "When I make some money, I'll come and visit you in Greece." He really believed that he would become wealthy through yoga. Ten years later, he was in the same straits, a poor man still living in the ashram and still writing me that when he made some money he "would come to Greece." His address never changed, nor did his hopes for wealth diminish in spite of all those years slipping away without any result.

Kabirina, a Yogi's Heartthrob

In the ashram, there was a large building that served as a printing house devoted exclusively to printing Guru Satyananda's books. It was run by an advanced Indian swami around thirty years old, whose *siddhis* were beginning to stir. The other inhabitants of the ashram were truly in awe of this swami, whom they said had "awakened the serpent of *kundalini.*"[1] The printing house where he worked was full of *mandalas,*[2] signs with strange clusters of geometric patterns painted on them in vibrant colors that supposedly conveyed certain messages to the subconscious, as Jung postulated in his theory of archetypes and the collective unconscious. These striking *mandalas* had been drawn by an American swami living in the ashram, under the direction of an Indian swami who had seen them in his dreams.

I worked in this printing house for several days, folding pages that were to be bound as a book. Once, while I was working, I suddenly felt an irresistible desire to draw, which I automatically obeyed by sketching some strange but impressive geometrical patterns. This drawing didn't require any special effort on my part or even the use of my imagination—it was as though I were mechanically obeying a suggestion arising from or implanted in my soul. When the person working with me insisted that I show them to the Indian swami in charge, I let him take a look at them. He encouraged me in a friendly manner, saying, "Seven leaves. Seven is a very spiritual number." For quite a few days I continued to be in this strange state, enjoying drawing the patterns on paper or on the ground, and showing them to the swami. Several times I

---

[1] *Kundalini* is a cosmic energy spoken of as a coiled serpent because it is said to reside at the base of the spine. To "wake" it is to cause it to rise, through energy centers, up the spine to the head, an attainment that is considered to be highly profitable for the aspirant. *Kundalini* yoga is a type of yoga that has this as its particular goal.

[2] A *mandala* is a concentric, often circular, geometric design. The *mandala,* and the patterns of particular *mandalas,* are significant in different ways in different Hindu traditions. However, speaking generally, it is taught that a *mandala* acts as a focus point for divine beings or cosmic powers, and meditating on it can bring one closer to enlightenment. *Mandalas* are also used in ritual and serve a particularly important role in Tantric initiation rites.

even formed such patterns using mounds of earth. I had had precisely the same feeling when I first met Niranjan, the president of the ashram, in his office.

While I was working in the printing house, I laid eyes for the first time on an Indian woman named Kabirina, a swami who was slightly younger than I was. We needed to talk about some issue concerning our work. As we looked into each other's eyes, we unexpectedly began to smile, excited at our pleasure in getting to know each other. There was something erotic about the sudden thrill we felt, standing there in the middle of the printing shop with everyone else seated on the floor around us. We felt so gay and happy that we almost started laughing. We made the moment last as long as we could, then we went back to our respective tasks.

Over the next few days, the swami in charge of the printing house started acting hostile towards me. Once, when we were carrying some boxes with papers, he sharply rebuked me for being careless. I tried to make light of his remark, so that we could just forget about it—I considered his comments to be unfair and, after all, didn't really consider him to be my boss. But he looked at me with a threatening glance and spoke to me even more harshly, giving the impression that he was able to hurt me if he wanted to. I was about to reply to him when the American swami who was carrying boxes with me turned towards me with an alarmed look on her face and whispered, "Shhh!" Her fear startled me so much that I immediately obeyed her. The girl and I had become friends, so I accepted her advice when she suggested that I go and work elsewhere. When I later asked her why she had been so scared, she said that I was in great danger, because he was a very powerful yogi.

I was much more careful for the next few days, and I came

to the conclusion that this powerful yogi was jealous because he wanted to have some sort of romantic relationship with Kabirina, or perhaps because he already had a relationship with her. Of course, there was not supposed to be any sexual activity in the ashram, and for this reason the men and women lived separately, in different buildings, but what went on in secret was another matter. One day, I didn't go to work as I should have, but instead rested in my room, and I heard two women swamis outside laughing and talking quietly. One of them mentioned that a certain male swami tried to convince her to have sexual relations with him, but, because she didn't care for him, she shunned him.

I mentioned this to Tony, a British yoga teacher with whom I spent a good deal of time, and he didn't dismiss the possibility of something of that sort taking place. In fact, as I was scandalized to learn, he was interested in finding a way to take part in such activities. He laughed and told me that he strove to get his fill of sexual experiences so that the desire would go away. Although the yogis publicly regarded this path—of having a lot of sexual relations in order to make oneself bored with them—as inferior, Tony more or less supported the idea, and followed it in his life. This was diametrically opposed to what I had read about in the yogis' books. But then, Tony was a yoga teacher whereas I was a mere student. He had known yogis up close for years, while I had only known them from a distance, for a short while.

Years later, as I was preparing to write this book, I read one of the guru's newer books, which completely settled this issue in my mind. The guru publicly admitted that there is "a path on the left" whereby one can reach a state of "ultimate awareness" by means of an ecstatic experience in an orgy, but he also noted that the yogis don't broadcast the existence of this path. They keep it hidden, he wrote, because people must be mature in order to accept it.[1] Apparently, the time was then ripe for them to speak openly about what was kept secret only a few years back. It made me wonder what other secrets were being hidden from us until we had matured.

Tony, the English Yoga Teacher

Tony was an intelligent and physically fit Englishman of medium stature. He was the son of a minister in the Anglican Church and had studied mathematics at a university in England. At some point, he had become involved in yoga, *kriya* yoga to be precise, and had abandoned his home to become a follower of Guru Satyananda. It was from him that I learned about the *Tantras* and the Hindu idea of the "spiritual" use of sex. At first, he eked out a living by working as a yoga teacher in seminars for beginners. Afterwards, he decided to travel around the world and then spend the rest of his life in one of the guru's ashrams.

One day, when we were having a conversation about the *Bhagavad Gita*, he asked, "Did you know that Christ was an eminent yogi?" I responded, "So Christ was a yogi and *Shiva* is God?" He didn't answer. He had a preference for *Shiva*—the god of destruction according to Hinduism, an image of whom

---

[1] *Author's note:* It is worth investigating where this "path on the left" ultimately leads the practitioner of yoga who follows the *Tantras* to their logical conclusion. It is not unreasonable to suspect that they lead to the very orgiastic rites in honor of the idols that characterized the religions of the ancient world, such as the cults of Aphrodite, the ancient Greek goddess of sexual love and beauty, or Astarte, the ancient Middle Eastern goddess of sexual love and war. The international press has reported that Bhagwan Shree Rajneesh, who had such a large following in the West, would dope his followers with drugs such as hashish, LSD, and cocaine and initiate dances that he would direct into sexual orgies in order for his followers to experience freedom. During these events he would have any woman or boy he desired for himself. I personally know individuals who were his followers, who have privately confirmed those reports.

hung in his room—over the God of the distorted Anglican Christianity he had rejected. He used to smoke charas and had taken LSD several times, and he confessed to me that he secretly continued to smoke in the ashram, especially before the *santsang*, so that he would have more vibrant experiences. Indeed, I once caught him red-handed getting high with two other members of the ashram. He admired Niranjan, but he put down the Indians who weren't swamis, and still had all the airs of the ruling class of the British Empire. He gave me the *Bhagavad Gita* and some of the guru's books in English, and we traveled together for a few days.

My Second Encounter with Babaji, at Allahabad

All the yogis in Satyananda's ashram were impressed by the fact that I had met Babaji and visited his ashram in the Himalayas. They would come and ask me various questions, inquiring for example into the ashram's precise location (a difficult question to answer). It was quite apparent that they wanted to meet this living legend, and that their estimation of me had increased because I had. Even Niranjan, the president of the ashram, admired him and was curious. Babaji, he told me, "is at the highest level," expressing what seemed to be a universal opinion in the ashram.

Now, I knew that the next month Babaji would be coming for a few days to Allahabad, one of the many sacred cities of the Indians in the Ganges basin. When I asked permission to go and see him, they were amazed that I intended to go to that particular city on those particular days. They considered me to be lucky, because the religious feast that would be occurring in that city takes place only once every twelve years. Moreover, important yogis and impressive gurus from all over India would be gathered there for three days to worship the Hindu pantheon, and I would have the great honor and blessing to be present with them and to be helped by the energy and atmosphere that they would generate. Niranjan considered the fact that an un-initiated foreigner knew the place and day of this event to be an encouraging omen, so he gave me permission to travel. (That is to say, he gave me back my passport and money, which, when I first arrived, the ashram had required me to surrender.)

So I boarded a train, and after a long journey I arrived at the classical Indian city of Allahabad, with its multi-story wooden houses, patched together with mud, and an occasional more modern structure held together by cement. It was like a village, laced with small narrow roads, but of enormous di-mensions, shrouded in darkness and overflowing with filth. Standing at the edge of this chaotic city, I realized that there were no large thoroughfares I could use to keep my bearings in its labyrinth, and no maps to chart my way. Merely entering would surely entail getting lost.

I went straight to the hotel next to the station and booked a single room in order to rest, and I decided to look for Babaji on the following day. Although the probability of my finding him was very low, I believed that he would arrange everything as he had before. After my afternoon meal, throwing caution to the wind, I decided to explore the city. It grew dark as I wan-dered through the pedestrian-filled streets. From time to time, I would enter a back alley, where I would listen to the din of life in overpopulated and poverty-stricken India. Considering the amount of human and animal waste and dirty water in the streets, I don't believe the city had a modern sewage system. I was wearing a pair of boots, which made it a bit less repugnant to walk through the city; the Indians, however, walked bare-foot. Although electric streetlights were rare, there were fires lit here and there where the Indians would warm themselves and gather for conversations that would last for hours. Many didn't have anywhere else to go, so they would also sleep there, next to the sidewalk.

This night, however, was different than normal: There were also present yogis who had chosen various places to loiter. One yogi might settle for a small opening between the buildings, while another might camp out in a yard or in some park. Still another might take up his lodgings under a tree. People would gather around them, sitting down and taking off their shoes in order to spend the night chanting the entire *Bhagavad Gita*. Some yogis would play small instruments to accompany the singing. The most pious sat near the yogis; the others would stand at a distance for a while and then leave. I walked around taking it all in.

Eventually, I attached myself to an ever-increasing group surrounding a thin guru, who was dressed in an orange robe and seated in the lotus position, with a book open in front of him. His hair and beard were snow white, and his face was calm and beautiful. He sang with a melodic voice, while with his right hand he played a small instrument with a tiny keyboard. He was a model yogi, just the way I imagined a yogi should be, and I suppose it was for this reason that I was attracted to him and decided to observe him.

Suddenly, I became aware that I was jerking my head back and forth, as though I were trying to rid myself of something that had sat on top of it. I rubbed my eyes vigorously in order to awake from this condition. In the meantime, the crowd became alarmed and recoiled from me in fear, and many even fled the group. I felt sure it was the work of the yogi. Nevertheless, when I came to, I looked at him indifferently and thought, "You huckster, you're nothing to write home about." To me, he seemed to be showing off. I blamed him, but I wasn't angry with him: I had lost all interest in him and his powers. Shortly thereafter, I returned to my hotel and went to sleep.

When I later reflected on what had taken place, I realized that I couldn't tell when I had lost control over my senses. I didn't know when this state had begun, how long it lasted, or what I did while I was in it. I only remembered trying to get out of it. In retrospect, I saw that the hypnotic trance might have ended immediately after it began: perhaps the yogi had attempted to control me through hypnotism, but failed. Or, on the other hand, it might have gone on for an indeterminable period of time, and only at the end, when he released me, had I begun to awaken and react. In any event, the crux of the matter is that he secretly and suddenly encroached on my person without my consent, showing no respect for me—in fact, using me.

It's worth noting how the people recoiled in fear. Experience obviously warned them that something evil and fearful was taking place. If they had experienced positive results from such phenomena, they wouldn't have fled—on the contrary, they would have happily drawn near. But I suppose that I had become used to such things, even if I didn't know the mechanism by which they took place; and, instead of being afraid, I simply brushed him aside.

Nevertheless, I was curious. Although I hadn't been able to see, hear, or touch anything, I had felt something encircling my head, touching it, and letting go. At the time, I couldn't discern whether it was an energy or a spirit. But it felt like a vexing and undesirable little cloud lingering and bringing with it a hostile, foul, and utterly repulsive evil presence. Later, I would come to believe that the yogi with a beautiful face had sent an evil spirit in my direction.

The next day, I arose early in order to find the "guru of gurus." I had an address on a piece of paper, but in the chaos that surrounded me it was meaningless. Even for an Indian in my position the problem would have been insurmountable. Nevertheless, I remained calm, because I believed that the one who had guided me to that peak in the Himalayas would somehow intervene and draw me again to himself. Eventually, I asked someone, who examined the address and told me that I had to go to the other side of the tracks, since beneath the address were printed the words "Civil Lines."

When I reached the station and crossed the train tracks, I realized just what it meant to live in the "Civil Lines" neighborhood.[1] I was now in another world, with large parks, expansive boulevards, and wide avenues lined with aristocratic European-style homes surrounded by large yards and gardens. Everything was impeccably clean, so unlike the city I had entered the night before. There were so few people out that the roads were nearly empty, except for a few cars, which seemed minute against the backdrop of the vast thoroughfares.

Apparently, the railway line, which could be crossed only at a few elevated bridges, also served as a barrier that divided the Indian city from the area where the English colonizers had built their homes and parks. The economic inequality between these two worlds was enormous. Hunger, wretched conditions, and the struggle for survival marked life on one side of the tracks, while extravagance and luxury were the traits of life on the other side. Of course, the English colonial masters, the aristocracy of an earlier age, no longer lived in these homes. The new Indian aristocracy had taken their place.

For those caught in the trap of wretchedness and poverty there was no way out. This also included some of the Western Europeans and Americans who had come under the influence of various writers who cultivated the myth of India. Such Westerners were usually involved with drugs or became drug users in India and, as soon as their money ran out, they would

---

[1] Older cities in India are frequently abutted by areas with the name "Civil Lines." These spacious neighborhoods were built by the colonizers to house the ranks of the British civil service. (The term "lines," in this sense, originally had the military meaning of rows of temporary shelters in an encampment. The attractive housing in the "Civil Lines" areas, of course, hardly resembled a military camp. They were, however, deliberately and regularly laid out, in contrast to the slowly evolved Indian cities.)

sell their passport in order to buy more narcotics. Their embassies would help them in the beginning, but then, when they would use that help to acquire more drugs, they would be driven away. And so, these abject youth would sleep on the pavement in a dark despair that nearly drove them mad. The smooth-talkers who deceived them with pleasant-sounding lies, enticing myths, and empty promises surely share the blame for their predicament. Hermann Hesse, for example, surely bears some responsibility for the droves of young people that he goaded to India with his books.

If someone were to have stolen my wallet, which contained my money, passport, and return ticket, I would automatically have found myself in such tragic straits. And such a scenario was not implausible. My wallet contained the equivalent of two years' pay for a working Indian—surely, there were those who would risk committing a crime in order to lay their hands on it. Of course, that was a frightening scenario that I tried to avoid dwelling on.

In any event, I found myself strolling through civilized Allahabad, observing its residents and catching a glimpse of their little palaces, including the home of former Prime Minister Indira Gandhi. Along the way, I asked about the address, but no one had ever heard of it. I sat on a bench, made an oath that I would give ten rupees in almsgiving to a poor Indian, and asked Babaji to help me. At that point, a young man around twenty years of age passed by me riding his bicycle. I made a motion for him to stop in order to show him the address and, like other Indians I had met, he appeared to be flattered to speak with a Westerner. He told me that he knew the owner of the house, a very wealthy book distributor and publisher with business connections abroad. The residence was about two miles away and he offered to take me there on his bicycle. So I took him up on his offer, and in a short while we were in front of a mansion with a fairly large number of people milling about outside and, from the sound of it, an even larger crowd within. My companion was hesitant about entering the inner courtyard, presumably because he was of a lower caste than the house's owner, who was a Brahman, but I was in a hurry and rushed in.

The courtyard enclosed a formal garden complete with a sizeable lawn, statues, and a fountain. It was a lovely day: the sun was shining and there wasn't a cloud in the sky. The disciples of Babaji's inner circle, all Westerners in their thirties, were sitting on the grass by themselves—they were his permanent entourage, and no one dared draw near them. I recognized the yogi we had irritated at the Haidakhan ashram, when we didn't obey his order to take off our shoes and worship Babaji.

Nevertheless, I walked towards them and sat next to them on the grass. I struck up a conversation with one of the more familiar and likable members of the group, a fellow who was always stark naked wherever he went and carried around a yellow fabric to spread out on the ground whenever he wanted to lie down. He told me his story. He was a Dutchman from Amsterdam who didn't at all care for life in Europe. So, in his twenties, he decided to go and live in the tropical islands of Fiji. On his way to Fiji, he passed through India, where he met Babaji at the Haidakhan ashram. Until that point, he had had no connection with yoga or religion. When he found himself face-to-face with Babaji, he told me, Babaji made him feel tiny, as though he were merely two inches tall, and Babaji a colossal mountain. Babaji told him in a commanding voice, "You will start a business." "I will start a business?" he answered, his voice betraying shock and fear. "Yes," Babaji responded, "you will. Now go." Leaving the ashram, the Dutchman made his first business agreement. Within three years, this insignificant, impoverished, drug-using hippie became an international businessman who used a jet for his continual business trips, making about a million dollars a year in profits. "Of course," he continued, "I did all these things through Babaji's power. Later, Babaji told me to stay with him, and so I abandoned everything and began to practice yoga."

At this point, I directed the conversation to my own concerns and told him, "I don't like to work."

"Then don't work," he responded. "What do you want, a quiet life?"

"No, I want to learn what's going on in this world. It's all an incomprehensible mystery to me. I don't understand anything."

"I've been with him three years, and I still don't understand anything," he replied.

"I don't know who I am or where I'm going. I don't know what I should do in this world. I don't know what the significance is of events or of my own actions. Do you do things you don't want to do?"

"No, I'm free and do whatever I want."

At this point, the others called for him, and he got up to leave. I asked where he was going, and he told me that he was going to have a smoke. I asked him if I could come along too, and he invited me. While they were preparing the chillum, I told them, "I get frightened when I'm in front of Babaji." "Don't be afraid," one of them answered. Another man smiled and said, "Don't be afraid to be afraid." He then lit the chillum and inhaled deeply, for an amazing length of time. I don't know what his lung capacity was, but when he let out his breath the entire room filled with smoke. The others followed suit, with the same results. When my turn came, I tried to make a dignified attempt, sucking in as much as I could, but I was rather pathetic in comparison. In spite of that, it made me so dizzy that I felt as though I were about to faint. The following times, I only pretended to participate: the blend was just too strong for me. I felt unsteady as I went out into the mansion's inner courtyard.

About three hundred people, attending various events, were present, including two or three *sadhus,* or Indian ascetic hermits. There was a goodly number of Europeans as well, including a blond girl in traditional Indian dress that I had met in New Delhi. The poor girl thought she was Babaji's wife and tried to behave accordingly. No one made fun of her, but they also weren't paying any attention to her. I felt sorry for her because she seemed so ridiculous. It seemed to me as though she had gone off the deep end. During all these years in India, she only rarely got to play the role that was the heart of her fantasy world. In reality, she was just another ornament in Babaji's court. Was there no one who tried to bring her to her senses and open her eyes? Indeed, from what I learned from a friend of hers in New Delhi, the guru only encouraged her behavior. Perhaps he had had relations with her and thus led her to believe that she was his wife. All the Indians seemed to look towards the fair-headed race that was once their country's master with awe, jealousy, and hatred. Perhaps Babaji was not an exception. I remember similar stories told by other girls who had been abused by gurus.

Those with whom I had smoked had taken up their places behind Babaji as though they were his bodyguards, and everyone else started to file past him in order to worship him and kiss his feet. His disposition would change with each person. Sometimes, he would be harsh. Sometimes, he would be kindly. Sometimes he would joke with the person. The fellow who originally gave me the address wouldn't leave me alone, insisting that I also go in front of Babaji. I was afraid, and wanted to put it off. At the same time, I felt bad about putting him in a difficult situation, so I went forward. The moment I stood in front of Babaji he grew fierce, and I was literally paralyzed by fear. With my mind, I barely managed to whisper, "Help!" and immediately he softened and asked me, "Who brought you here?"

"You did," I answered, ignoring all of those who were but instruments of his will.

"Where have you come from?"

"Munger."

He motioned for me to move along, and I gladly distanced myself from the strain and fear of being in his presence. I tried to determine what I found so terrifying, asking myself why I felt such anxiety and fear. Was it the strange look in his eyes or his great power? Father Paisios also had great power and his eyes at times had an otherworldliness about them—but I was never frightened around him; on the contrary, I felt quite safe.

It was now time for the meal, so we sat down on the ground in rows and each received a large leaf, about a foot long, that held potatoes, greens, and some spicy boiled rice. The man who had given me the address kindly sat next to me and told me that he had opened up a small business, which made him wealthy by Indian standards and offered prospects of even greater wealth, as he was still in the beginning stages. The guru, it seemed, distributed wealth to at least some of his followers, such as this man and the eminent book publisher who had opened up his home to us. This publisher and his family had vacated their rooms for the guru and his disciples. The expenses for such hospitality must have been enormous, since all the guests stayed in his mansion for about four or five days until Babaji went elsewhere. Everyone present had to be fed and given a place to sleep. The family's behavior in general made it clear that they recognized that their wealth came from the guru. As one of his disciples put it, "Naturally, everything they've built is through his power." Now, it was the guru's turn to receive some benefit from the transaction.

The Worship of Idols

After everyone had finished the meal, the sacrifice began. In the courtyard was a permanent altar where they lit the fires for sacrifices. They brought pans piled high with some sort of mixture that included plenty of ghee.[1] Babaji offered the sacrifice with the help of his closest disciples, while the master of the house stood nearby. Babaji was chanting various hymns to the gods, and every so often he would take a large spoonful of ghee and throw it on the fire, filling the air with the smell of burning butter. Everyone followed the two-hour ritual with piety, though the master of the house had a strange look on his face, as though he were trying to preserve his wounded pride. After the sacrifice was complete, the Dutch yogi took ashes from the blackened spoon that they had used in the ritual and placed a dot between the eyebrows of the believers. I was so impressed by the rite that I went forward for him to put a dot on my forehead as well. It never occurred to me to ask to *whom* the sacrifice had been offered. Once again, the influence of Christianity made it difficult for me to come to terms with the fact of real polytheism and idol worship. And having smoked the charas hadn't helped, either.

Afterwards, I could see the guru moving about the crowd with ease, but no one approached him or crossed his path. I lost track of him when he went towards the western side of the buildings. In the meantime, the people were forming a line. I thought they would pass in front of him as on previous occasions and, since I was ready to leave the mansion, I got in line as well. I didn't intend to worship him like they urged me to, but simply to greet him, a polite gesture in response to his hospitality.

It was a long line and I couldn't see what was happening at the front. As I drew closer, to my surprise I saw Babaji emerging from behind some trees. Before I could ask myself whom it was the crowd was actually greeting, I found myself in a temple with about twenty two-foot-tall statues, guarded by stern Brahmans keeping an eye on those in line. Babaji climbed up a

---

[1] Ghee is clarified butter, traditional in India, and is made from the milk of cows or buffalos.

tree to watch us. Three people in front of me worshipped the idols, left money, and went their way. At this point, I was ashamed to get out of the line and insult them. There was no way to leave discreetly, so I went forward and worshipped the idols, although inwardly I prayed to Christ.

Thus did I transgress the commandment I had heard so clearly when I ascended the steps of Babaji's ashram: *I am the Lord thy God.... Thou shalt have no other gods before Me.... Thou shalt not bow down thyself to them, nor serve them.*[1] Without realizing it, I had spent the entire day participating in the Hindu worship of idols, by following a ritual sacrifice made as an offering to them.

Unfortunately, at the time, I didn't think about the Christian martyrs who lost their possessions, their loved ones, and their very lives in the midst of terrible tortures by idolaters, in order to avoid casting a mere handful of incense into a fire in honor of their idols. If I had thought about this at the time, if I hadn't been under the influence of the charas I'd smoked, if I hadn't allowed myself to be swayed by my warm feelings for the Dutch former hippie, if I hadn't let the demands of etiquette trick me into getting into the line—perhaps I would not have ended up doing what I never intended to do.

Demon Possession

Afterwards, when the guru had retired and the crowd began to break up into smaller groups, I decided it was time to leave. So I found the Dutch yogi, who was sitting on the lawn, and went over to tell him goodbye. I sat next to him on the grass, we chatted a bit, and finally I told him, "I'll see you again," and gave him a friendly slap on the thigh. With that touch, I felt something come out of his body and enter my own—it was as though a powerful force had engulfed me. He looked at me in

[1] Exodus 20:2, 3, 5.

astonishment and, without saying a word, quickly rose and rushed away. I was taken aback by both what I felt and by the naked yogi's reaction, but I couldn't understand what had happened to me or with what I had come into contact.

I got up and set out for the hotel by foot. It was a long walk lasting many hours: I started out around four o'clock in the afternoon and arrived at midnight. It was also a strange walk: I felt so energetic and powerful that I wasn't afraid of anyone or anything. As I walked, I felt consumed by an arrogant pride, by the feeling that I had everyone in my clutches and could utterly defeat them. I was superior—an indisputable ruler. The sensation of freedom that arose from this feeling of fearlessness and power was intoxicating. I thought to myself, "I have never walked so freely on the earth in my entire life."

Such thoughts were soon manifest in action. It had grown dark as I entered a dim and narrow side street, and, a little over fifty yards in front of me, about ten thugs huddled together, apparently plotting to attack me. I would have been a convenient victim, but not only was I not worried—I scornfully headed straight in their direction. When I was about ten yards away, they gathered together and came charging towards me with a mute ferocity. But I wasn't afraid for a moment. I smiled contemptuously and kept walking towards them at the same pace. Soon they had surrounded me, within touching distance—and they froze in their tracks. They no longer had the guts to fight, pulling back in terror. One of them said something derogatory in a threatening tone, but when I turned to look at him, he fell silent. With a light but authoritative shove, I made them stand aside and continued on my way.

Under normal conditions, these hoodlums would have pounced on me, beat me, thrown me to the ground, kicked and spat on me, and taken my money and passport. Such incidents were commonplace in this world of poverty and despair, and these men were no children. Their faces made it obvious that they were violent men who had committed such crimes in the past. Yet they had seen something in my face that terrified them and brought them to their knees. No doubt, they later would ask themselves about the eerie presence that surrounded me. All that I knew was that I had the guru's power, which I had received from the Dutch yogi when I left him.

Unbeknownst to me, I was soon to face the greatest temptation and the most important decision of my life.

The Temptation of Power

Continuing my walk into the dead of night, I entered a large park with a temple surrounded by colossal old buildings. I knew that thieves of all sorts were on the prowl but, with my newly found power, I no longer worried about them or took any precautions to prevent them from noticing me. Indeed, I had such enormous might that I could feel it in my veins. Various people approached me. Some would grovel. Others would pass by indifferently until I looked at them in the face—and that would be the last time they dared to approach me. I felt godlike and, in a powerful delusion, believed that I had unlimited potential and could acquire anything I wanted.

But, still, something troubled me, making me think long and hard. I sat down, lit a cigarette, looked at the stars in the Indian sky, and began to mull over everything. I felt an increasing desire for power that my mind and reason were not able to resist. I felt so at ease, psychologically and physically, that I wondered if I even wanted to resist that desire. And so, I began an inner dialogue with myself that lasted some time:

"What's so bad about having such tremendous strength?"

"So that's what you're looking for in life?"

"But what's wrong with walking around like a king, sovereign over all the world, with the ability to order everyone around? Why should I disdain not fearing anyone or anything?

What," I asked myself provocatively, "is so bad about every-thing being easy—about being able to have whatever I desire?"

"But supposedly you rejected such powers. Supposedly, you're no longer interested in having authority over others. Are you going back to the same old thing?"

"Yes, but this time the magnitude of power is astronomical. Nothing can resist me. Any woman I desire is mine for the tak-ing. I'll never be hard up for cash. There's no knowledge I won't be able to acquire."

"But where is love in all of this? Aren't you interested in the truth? What's the difference if you have or don't have every-thing else, if you don't have love and the truth?"

Suddenly, it all seemed empty, vain, senseless, and ridicu-lous. I made my decision: I wasn't interested. And, turning my back on it all, I went to the hotel and slept until the afternoon of the following day.

That day I spent many hours deep in thought, trying to come to some conclusion about what had taken place and about my original aim in coming to India. I carefully recalled the conversations I had had, the people I had met, and what I had seen and experienced, in order to determine whether the yogis were with God or with the devil. I asked myself again whether yoga was another path towards God or a trap of the devil. Was it a way to enlightenment—or a deception causing people to waste their time in a life without meaning or direc-tion? A decisive answer remained elusive.

On one of the nights that followed, I saw Babaji in my sleep. He took me by the hand and taught me how to fly. At the same time, he also taught me to sing a mantra that referred to the god *Shiva*, "*Om Namah Shivaya.*"[1] The mantra took

---

[1] The syllable *Om* is the most sacred syllable in Hinduism, with which most mantras begin. *Namah* refers to a bow or reverential salutation; it is the basis of the polite Indian greeting *namasté*. *Om Namah Shivaya* is translated as "I bow to *Shiva.*"

such root in my mind that when I woke in the night I found myself singing it. I felt a burning desire to go to the nearby train station, because I could feel that Babaji was getting ready to leave. I charged down the stairs, but the door of the hotel was already locked. I called for someone to open it for me, but not a soul was to be found. So I raced back up the stairs to the terrace, where I heard a sound rumbling in the distance: a multitude of voices were enthusiastically shouting, "Victorious holy father!" Babaji's followers were bidding him farewell. It lasted over an hour.

The whole time, the mantra *"Om Namah Shivaya"* was stuck in my mind, as it would be for days after. The melody was positively enchanting, but it still bothered me that it had been implanted there without my consent, and again I had cause to reflect on the opposite practice of the elder, who always asked my permission, respecting my person. At daybreak, I returned to my room for some sleep.

Mystical Experiences and Revelations at the Ashram of Satyananda

After my meeting with Babaji in Allahabad, I returned to Satyananda's ashram in Munger, where they welcomed me like an old friend. In accordance with my original decision to open up my soul completely to India, to experience her as a way of life rather than observe her as a tourist, I tried to live fully the life of the ashram. It was not enough just to think about the differences—I needed to live them, and I did so as a member of the ashram. I arose in the morning with the other residents, eating with them, working with them, talking with them, and practicing yoga with them. Nevertheless, I carried with me baggage from my Christian experiences, and this encouraged me to try to combine the techniques of yoga with Christianity. For example, when I would arise in the morning and start meditating, as soon as my mind reached a deep contemplative state, I would begin to say the prayer, "Lord Jesus Christ, have mercy on me," just as I had on the Holy Mountain.

After I refused to accept Niranjan's comment that Orthodox monks were at a lower spiritual level, I believe he started working on me in a spiritual manner. At the same time, on the Holy Mountain, the elder was praying for me with pain of heart on a nearly daily basis. Hence, I was attracted by two spiritual forces. Like a man on a tightrope, I felt the consequences of even the slightest leaning on my part. I gave my entire self over to a struggle in which my way of life—and ultimately my very being—was at stake. Even though I didn't exert myself physically, this was wearying on account of the intense spiritual effort involved. It would have been more than enough, simply going through the spiritual struggles and encounters that I did. But I also wanted to discern the nature and the origin of the spiritual experiences I was going through, something quite difficult for a person such as myself, who lacked a measure with which to judge.

I recall how my sleep changed. I didn't exactly sleep at night, having a dream or two. Certain changes were taking place. It was as though someone were moving things around, as though someone had entered my home and was not only rearranging the furniture but also tearing down walls and building new ones elsewhere. I felt as if someone had stolen the keys to my consciousness, hypnotizing me from a distance while I was asleep and breaking into the house of my soul.

Several times, I would wake up late in the morning, arising at seven o'clock instead of at five. Benoît would tease me for being lazy, but I still felt exhausted from the changes in my inner state that had taken place while I slept. I objected to his wisecracks: "But you just don't understand. So much was going on during the night. I wasn't sleeping, exactly." Even during the day, I was being influenced. Suddenly, I would enter an altered state in which another mind or spirit would come into contact with my soul. I would begin to draw strange and wonderful symbols pulsing with the occult. If I happened to be working in the gardens when this happened, I would use the soil. These strange states made up the permanent backdrop to my daily life, which was further colored by incidents of great intensity that I will describe shortly. I was deeply convinced that the president of the ashram was responsible for these states, but I didn't have the chance to question him: when I wanted to talk with him, he was always unavailable.

Other phenomena, however, were taking place as well. Once, when I was sitting in the printing house and doing some mindless task, I silently began to say the prayer, "Lord Jesus Christ, have mercy on me." I continued to say it for about a half-hour and, to my delight, I suddenly became aware of the presence of an invisible spiritual cloud enveloping me and flooding me with peace and joy. Although the Spirit came so gently and quietly, coming down, to use the words of Scripture, *like rain upon a fleece,*[1] His presence was quite palpable and obvious to me. I could feel the yogi in charge of the printing house glaring at me with a strange look. Nevertheless, I felt such divine assurance that his fixed stare didn't frighten me in the least. After this took place, they began to pay special attention to me. On the following day, while I was working in the garden, I caught an elderly yogi spying on me from the terrace of a building. Such incidents would become commonplace for a number of days. I believe that my invocation of the name of Christ and the support of the elder's prayers on my behalf were creating a certain resistance, which they could sense even if they couldn't pinpoint its cause.

[1] Psalm 71:6.

The Seizure

One day, around eleven o'clock in the morning, I had an eerie and abnormal experience. It was as though something had suddenly emptied my mind, causing my consciousness of self to nearly vanish. I was no longer in control of my mind or body: someone far off in the distance had seized control, leaving me with only the most tenuous sense of self. With utter indifference, I left my work and, like a robot, let something guide me unconsciously to my room. I went to my bed and lay down on my back, without moving, without sleeping, without thinking about anything, without hearing anything, and without having any sense of time. I could barely sense myself as a person, but I could feel something purring in my chest.

Gradually the force that put me in this state withdrew. I don't know precisely what it did within my soul, but I suspect that it was trying to make me change some of my views, by suggestion rather than persuasion. As I began to regain consciousness, I could hear Benoît yelling my name. Before I had time to get up, he burst into the room, agitated. "Hey, why did you bolt the door? I've been trying to get in here for an hour!" I was aghast, because the door was unlocked and I was still lying in bed, feeling rather stiff. Benoît was a very strong, muscular twenty-five-year-old who would have pushed on the door with all his strength. "I didn't shut the latch," I said, "the door was unlocked." My response irritated Benoît even more. "Five separate times I tried to get in and each time the door was locked tight. I was shouting for you to open up. Didn't you hear me?"

I looked at my watch. It was one o'clock in the afternoon: I had been in that state for two hours. My mind was drowsy and functioning slowly, as though I were half-drugged. I didn't know what to make of the door. I asked myself who had held it shut when Benoît was trying to get in—apparently, it was the same entity who had knocked me out and thrown me in bed. I found it astonishing that a spiritual power could have such a strikingly physical effect. My preliminary explanation for my state had been that someone had hypnotized me on the sly or at a distance, but a hypnotic state couldn't explain what held the door shut against Benoît—there was evidently some other power present.

The Light

Instruction in *nintra* yoga took place in the afternoon. One day a blond female swami from Australia led the class. We all lay down on the floor on our backs, closed our eyes, listened to the swami's voice, and carried out her instructions. After our bodies were relaxed, our imagination took over. We began to imagine beautiful images at her direction, such as late afternoons, flowers, and small streams. Gradually, our minds became detached from our senses and attended solely to the woman's voice. When I had entered deeply into this state, I suddenly saw the flash of a bright white light, even though I didn't try to imagine it, and even though the swami hadn't mentioned it in her instructions. It appeared on its own and lasted for but a moment. I didn't feel anything in particular upon seeing it, other than curiosity as to where it came from.

Gradually, the swami restored us to our normal conscious state. Some members of the class had fallen asleep during the lesson. The swami asked if any of us had seen a light. Although I liked her, I didn't say anything. The others would have viewed it as an achievement, and I didn't want to make them jealous or curious. I felt as though she sensed that I saw such a light and simply wanted confirmation. This fact inflated my already puffed-up ego with the idea that I had a special aptitude for yoga. I believe it was meant to entice me to continue; in any event, it did.

I didn't feel as though I had experienced something spiritual that served as a lesson, clarification, or revelation. Neither my mind nor my emotions were moved by what had taken place. It simply presented another question, and served as an encouragement to go deeper into yoga.

Ida, Pingala, Sushumna

One morning around ten o'clock, I decided to meditate for a while, so I crossed my legs in the lotus position, closed my eyes, and began. After only a few minutes, a power suddenly seized hold of me with the force of a fierce blow. It repositioned my body, tightening my muscles and making my spinal column perfectly straight. It literally forced me into a flawless lotus position. Simultaneously, I saw in my mind an image with lurid colors, portraying the three most important energy channels, or *nadis*. It resembled the staff of Asclepius, the symbol for the medical profession, but with two entwined serpents, as in Hermes' caduceus, instead of just one. The large central channel, called the *Sushumna nadi*, had a vivid yellow color, while the two thinner ones, the *Ida* and *Pingala nadis*, which intertwined around the central channel, were red and blue. This state lasted a few moments and then left me, like a strong hand releasing my mind and body. I had been daily having the experience of being seized by some power, but this experience had an intensity of a different order. It was quite literally overwhelming.

Naturally, I talked about this experience with the yogis, who viewed it as a sign of a special aptitude which I should make the most of by beginning to work on the energy channels. "They're almost open—you only need a little more work

to open them completely. *Kundalini* yoga is the path for you."
I was genuinely impressed and began to ask questions with
greater eagerness. The mysteries of the universe appeared to be
within my grasp. I was almost sold on this path, though I still
wondered what the power that I had experienced was.

The Spiritual Atmosphere

Still, I had my reservations. In general, I felt as though I were
in conflict with my environment. Also, as the members of the
ashram realized, I had a "weakness" for Christ. I mainly spoke
about this with Tony and Luke, both of whom had Christian
backgrounds. Tony believed that Christ was a yogi. I was
struck by the fact that they both believed that *Shiva* was alive.
They admired him and had posters of him in their rooms.
Christ, they told me, was a yogi, but *Shiva* was much higher
than Christ, since *Shiva* was the first yogi and had revealed
yoga. I was struck by how ready they were to deify *Shiva* and
demote Christ—especially Tony, who, oddly, claimed to be an
atheist, despite the contradiction.

When the residents of the ashram would chant *kirtana*,
they would worship, not only the gods of Hinduism, but also
their guru. There was a theory they advanced that the hymns
contained certain sounds or frequencies discovered by the spiritually advanced, which had an exceptionally positive effect on
the brain. Thus, to chant *kirtana* was considered beneficial. All
religious hymns, the yogis told us, use such sounds, but naturally those used for *kirtana* were the very best. This resembled
their explanation for the mantras, short phrases or prayers
which are repeated continuously, and which usually contain
the name of a Hindu god, such as *Shiva* or *Krishna*, and the
syllable *Om*. Mantras are invocations of or prayers to Hindu
gods, but the yogis claimed that the power of a mantra was not

derived from the invocation of the names of the gods, but from certain frequencies the sounds of the names contained. This apparently scientific explanation, as I observed, comforted Westerners who didn't believe in *Shiva* or *Krishna*, who would then be comfortable chanting the gods' names, or *Om,* hundreds of times a day. The yogis claimed that there were also Christian mantras, such as *Kyrie eleison* ("Lord, have mercy" in Greek) that had a beneficial effect on the brain, again on account of their sounds or frequencies—this view being a mark of their profound and broad-minded understanding of other faiths. I read about all this in contemporary Hindu texts and heard many yoga teachers speak about it.

I decided to put their teaching to the test. Instead of the Hindu mantra, I began to say, "Lord Jesus Christ, have mercy on me." Throughout the day, when I might have chanted *kirtana* to myself, I began to chant "To Thee, the Champion Leader," a hymn addressed to the Virgin Mary. Some mornings, I would also make some prostrations[1] in concert with my yoga exercises.

The results were evident. My roommate Benoît initially sneered at my doing my morning prostrations while he did half of his *kriya* yoga exercises. Then, in spite of the fact that he was considered advanced, he started to encounter difficulties in doing his exercises properly. Something had changed in the spiritual atmosphere and was blocking him, and he believed I was the culprit. He eventually requested another room and left. I was amazed to see such results from just silently saying the Jesus Prayer a few times and, now and then, making some prostrations.

Once in a while, I would sing my "Christian *kirtana*" while walking around the ashram. The displeasure on the faces of the yogis was obvious. When they would make an allusion to what

[1] A prostration is a reverential bow to the ground, accompanied by making the sign of the Cross.

I was doing, I would tease them, saying, "But these have beneficial frequencies too." Apparently, however, I couldn't convince them of that.

Being Seized and Being Visited

One afternoon, I was lying by myself in my room with my eyes shut and saying the Jesus Prayer with an Indian *mala,* or prayer rope. I was fully awake and my mind was perfectly clear. Then, something gently approached me and there was a palpable change in the region of my physical heart.[1] On this occasion, however, my mind, fully conscious, calmly followed this agreeable change, while my body remained completely relaxed. This experience was not a kind of hypnosis, accompanied by light-headedness and a lack of self-consciousness. On the contrary, my sense of self was very clear. There was a respect for my person in this experience.

Suddenly, my right hand, with which I had been using the prayer rope, stopped and shot up on its own accord, against my will. At the same time, I clearly heard the unlikely sound of fluttering wings, as though a great bird were flying away from me. I was unhappy about the interruption, but, even so, I felt calm and peaceful in the depths of my heart. In my mind I could see the elder, and in my heart I felt an abundance of sweetness and love which extended to the entire world, including Niranjan.

I left my room, and, taking five steps down the hall, ran straight into him. I had felt that he was responsible for some of the strange phenomena I was encountering, so I asked, "Niranjan, what's going on here? So many things are happening."

[1] *Author's note:* According to the Orthodox tradition taught by Athonite monks, the area of the physical heart is also the location of man's spiritual heart.

"Don't be afraid," he told me.

"I'm not afraid. Are you making these things happen?"

"This place has a lot of energy. The energy from the guru and the energy from the swamis adds up."

In other words, he was alleging that no one was responsible for what was taking place. That is, there was no volition or personal accountability on the part of himself or the other swamis—just an impersonal energy as incapable of moral decisions and responsibility as an electrical current. And if something bad were to happen, it would be this energy, and not him, that would be responsible.

The Library

The members of the ashram had access to a library with books about yoga and related topics. Most of its holdings consisted of translations of the guru's books into various languages. Indeed, it was his institutes that had introduced yoga—the science of yoga, in their words—to Greece. There were only a few books by writers outside of this guru's circle, authors whom the ashram considered part of the guru's pedigree or whose teachings they accepted.

In this library I saw a periodical published by the yoga institute with various stories from the life of the guru. In one article, the guru related how he used to roam about the villages of India. At one point, he helped a villager, who remunerated him by teaching him how to invoke spirits from the underworld. One evening, he went to a cemetery with some of his disciples in order to put into practice what he had learned. However, when the spirits came, he wasn't able to contend with them, so he turned them on a woman disciple, who was soon possessed by them. After being tortured a great deal, she finally died. In order to purify himself of this act, he remained continuously in the waters of the Ganges for three days and three nights.

The guru's actions—evening visits to a cemetery and the invocation of spirits—can be described with a variety of labels, such as spiritism, witchcraft, or even Satanism, but science is certainly not one of them. Perhaps those so-called spirits from the underworld were the demons warned of in the Gospels. In any event, it's worth noting the moral fiber of a guru who would sacrifice a disciple who had entrusted to him her entire life, body and soul, in order to save his own skin. It's also worth underlining that the guru deals with this moral crime by spending three days and nights in the waters of the Ganges. According to the text, there is neither sorrow, nor contrition, nor repentance for that appalling deed. Not a single tear is shed for the poor woman. Instead, the guru places himself in the waters of a river that supposedly has the capacity to clear a darkened and guilty conscience. (And, again, such a practice, part and parcel of the "science" of yoga, can hardly be characterized as something empirically proven. It's a purely religious act, peculiar to Hinduism alone among religions, and certainly unrecognized by science.)

The library also contained books by Swami Vivekananda (1863–1902), who had become famous in the West, especially in America and England, at the end of the nineteenth century for his lectures on Hinduism. He was the disciple of the great yogi and Hindu saint, Ramakrishna (1836–1886), who entrusted him with the mission of forming Hindu centers in America and throughout the world.

Since I had read some of Vivekananda's books, the last will and testament attributed to him, sitting on the shelf before me, caught my eye. I had never heard of this short book or seen it before, and since that time I have never seen it again. The contents of this book were startling and eye-opening. The author described a long-standing attempt or conspiracy to alter Western Christianity and replace it with Eastern beliefs. He claimed that this scheme for the destruction of Christianity was designed by certain higher spiritual beings (or spirits, from what I could gather), was set in motion several generations ago, and was now well in place. He considered himself to be but a humble servant of this plan, following in the footsteps of other earlier figures, whom he listed by name. He was satisfied that he had brought to completion that part of the plan that was entrusted to him and now he could leave this life with a sense of accomplishment.

What struck me was not only the admission of a "plan," but also the persons and means implicated. For example, the book mentioned the famous psychologist Carl Jung, who early in his career broke with the founder of psychoanalysis, Sigmund Freud, and went on to lay the foundations for much of contemporary personality theory. But some of what many no doubt consider to be his original discoveries were in fact beliefs taken from Hinduism regarding the structure and processes of the human soul, in which the original Sanskrit terms were replaced with his own simple and easily understandable ones. As these ideas became increasingly acceptable, his works became increasingly metaphysical, so that later in life Jung made no attempts to hide the connections with Hinduism, which he then acknowledged to have been his inspiration.[1]

---

[1] Jung (1875–1961) was fascinated with Eastern religions in general, embracing or adapting many of their concepts, and he owed a special debt to Hinduism. Scholar Harold Coward sees his concept of the archetype, which "came to be Jung's most significant psychological postulate, ... interacting constantly with the Indian notion of *karma*" as it developed. "Direct influence from Indian thought is evidenced in Jung's 1932 lectures on Kundalini Yoga," he notes. "By 1942, Jung ... admits to a deliberate extension of the archetype notion by means of karmic theory. *Karma,* he says, is essential to a deeper understanding of the nature of the archetype" (*Jung and Eastern Thought* [New York: State University of New York Press, 1985], pp. 97–98).

Satsang

On several occasions we would all meet in the afternoon in a large hall, with the president of the ashram seated in the center surrounded by the yogis, so that whoever had questions could pose them. This was called *Satsang*. I recall asking, "If someone reaches the point that he no longer believes in his own reasoning or in the explanations that his mind gives, how can he move forward? In other words, if he realizes that his explanations are just words without any substance, how can he advance beyond his present state? Since he doesn't trust the explanations offered by his mind, how will he find answers to his basic questions?"

Niranjan called upon an American swami to answer my question, who began by saying, "By faith, but there are two forms of faith." I would have liked to hear what else he was going to say, but at this point Niranjan motioned for him to stop. In any event, since the beginning of my involvement with their movement, I had been hearing from the yogis that our activities were not founded on religion or faith at all, but on science. For example, when Niranjan discussed the stories of the Hindu gods, he would not refer to "the Hindu faith," but to "the Hindu mythology"; and, to explain the effect of mantras, he, like the others, offered the apparently scientific theory of their "beneficial frequencies." So, when I heard the swami suddenly talk of faith, I thought to myself, "If it's all a matter of faith, I have my own faith"—namely, my faith in Christ.

Later on, I was pondering over what I had been told about Christ being a yogi who was a disciple of *Shiva*, about Christ founding and dying in a Himalayan ashram called "New Jerusalem," and about *Shiva*, the first yogi, being godlike and very great. The yogis didn't dismiss Christ, but they did relegate Christ to a second-tier status, claiming that Christianity and Hinduism were basically the same and not in conflict, that

Hinduism was simply at a higher level. I recalled a church hymn that I remembered from childhood, sung on Epiphany, when my grandmother would take me to see the cross being thrown into the river, as is traditional in Greece on that day. The words of the hymn were as follows: "When Thou, O Lord, wast baptized in the Jordan, the worship of the Trinity was made manifest. For the voice of the Father bore witness unto Thee, calling Thee the beloved Son, and the Spirit in the form of a dove confirmed His word as sure and steadfast. O Christ our God Who hast appeared and enlightened the world, glory to Thee."[1]

This memory was like a spark in my consciousness that lit a roaring flame. The Christian Church speaks about the Holy Trinity and the Holy Spirit, and states plainly that Christ is God incarnate. My hosts claimed that Christ was a disciple of *Shiva*. How could they claim that Hinduism and Christianity were the same, when their beliefs were so different?

A Final Attack

A few days later, while working with the German woman named Prakash, I told her that I had decided to go back and live on the Holy Mountain with the ascetic I had told her about earlier. She responded that it would be difficult, since that kind of life was for advanced souls. Out of the kindness of her heart, she wanted me to remain in the ashram, which she considered very spiritual. She both loved and admired the guru.

But I believe that the other yogis, and especially Niranjan, didn't take so kindly to my decision or look on it with such simplicity. Prakash would not have failed to relay to them my decision to leave the ashram and return to the Holy Mountain. And that afternoon, when I was alone in my room, I had a

---

[1] Troparion of the feast of Holy Theophany, in *The Festal Menaion*, Mother Mary and Archimandrite Kallistos Ware, trans. (London: Faber and Faber, 1969; reprint, South Canaan, Pa.: St. Tikhon's Seminary Press, 1990), p. 359.

terrifying experience of evil, that can only be described as a cold-blooded and brutal attempt to murder my soul.

While I was sitting by myself in my room and trying to think, I suddenly had the horrific feeling that, in an instant, my soul had collapsed in on itself. It was like a film clipping of a huge skyscraper collapsing into a heap of rubble within a few split seconds. All the columns and beams within my soul snapped, causing the whole edifice to come crashing down in a state of tremendous fear. I didn't have strength for even the slightest effort. Although a few moments earlier I had been planning my trip back to Greece, now it seemed extremely difficult to continue. I was not simply afraid of returning to Greece—in spite of the fact that I had wandered all over India, I was afraid of leaving my room. The mere thought of abandoning the ashram filled me with terror. I felt too feeble to deal with anything. I was wounded, shattered, and in a hideous state, like a frightened little dog who would gratefully be obedient to its master. I desperately wanted the protection of the ashram.

And then I whispered, "Elder, help me." Instantly, even before I could realize what was happening, I felt another force surge up within me and rebuild my soul, making it sturdier than it was before. My once-collapsed soul now stood tall, and I felt healthy and psychologically strong. I then heard in my mind the voice of the elder saying, "You need to struggle, my child." I was so stunned at the revelation of such forces acting on my soul that I shut myself up in my room for the entire remainder of the day. I then made a vow to the All Holy Virgin that, if she would help me escape the ashram, I would devote my entire mind to her as Christ's mother, leaving it in her hands. And, having made my promise, I began to chant, "To Thee, the Champion Leader," which I pledged to sing every day.

When I came out of my room the next morning, I noticed that there weren't as many people moving about as usual. Nevertheless, I went to the garden and began to work with

Prakash. Shortly thereafter, I heard the harsh voice of the yogi in charge of the printing house reprimanding me, "What are you doing out here? Don't you know that everyone is supposed to be inside today?" "No," I answered, "I just came outside." He angrily called Prakash to the side and spoke with her in private. She afterwards explained to me that by orders of the president we would have to work inside the printing house, where we would have spiritual protection. Indeed, everyone was inside the buildings in order to be protected. The president was quite disturbed by something that was wreaking havoc on the world of the ashram: it was as though they were fighting a spiritual war. This regime lasted for three days. "The elder's prayer," I thought to myself, "thwarted their schemes, just as it thwarted my Mind Control initiation."

In a few days, I gathered together my belongings in order to leave with Tony, the Englishman. He bid farewell to Niranjan before we left, as was the tradition at the ashram, and encouraged me to do so as well. I was willing to—after all, Niranjan had allowed me to stay for a reduced fee, almost for free in comparison with what the others paid—but unfortunately I got tied up somewhere, so that my parting was brief and poorly prepared. As I was walking outside, I spotted him inside a building standing by the window, and I called out, "Goodbye, Niranjan, I'm leaving." When he turned to see me, his large eyes grew narrow and he began to glare at me with a smoldering hatred. "What should I do?" I asked him. "Contact Sivamurti," was his response. I felt terrible and in shock from the way he scowled at me. It just wouldn't sink in that hatred was the source of his glare—I couldn't understand why he should hate me.

Years later, I received an explanation for what had occurred to me at the end of my stay at the ashram, when I came across a small article that Niranjan had written in one of the movement's journals. In the meantime, Satyananda had vanished from the scene and it was rumored that he had died.[1] After this, Niranjan had become the guru and leader of the movement, and went by the honorific title of *Paramahansa* Niranjanananda.[2] I was surprised to see him describe precisely what had happened to me many years before, when I had felt my soul painfully collapse into a heap of frailty. He writes: "The guru allows the *sannyasi* [that is, the yogi disciple] to continue to live in the ashram and to keep the mask of self in order to use it to face various circumstances. But, behind the scenes, the guru is carefully preparing for the ultimate collapse of his disciple's self. With the guru's slightest effort, the *sannyasi's* self vanishes in a flash."[3]

But Niranjanananda fails to disclose the unbearable spiritual pain and anguish involved in the "ultimate collapse." And he conceals the fact that the disciple reduced to a state of spiritual weakness becomes, not a *sannyasi*, but a totally obedient and dependent slave. Rather, he portrays it as a spiritual blessing: he claims that this removal of the barrier of self and the opening up of the spiritual pathway are what constitute the greatness of the gurus.

The Testimony of Eldress Gavrilia

Apparently, the sort of thing that happened to me was not an isolated incident. The Eldress Gavrilia (1897–1992) related similar

---

[1] It was eventually announced that Satyananda had retired from active involvement in yoga teaching in order to dedicate himself to solitary spiritual pursuits.

[2] *Paramahansa,* usually translated "Great Swan," is an honorific title given to Hindu ascetics who are judged as having reached an exceptional degree of spiritual attainment.

[3] *Nea tēs Yiogka Paianias* (Yoga News of Paiania), vol. 3, no. 1 (1999), p. 2 (in Greek). This journal is published by practitioners of Satyananda Yoga in Greece, who in 1984 established a residential ashram in Paiania, a suburb of Athens, under the leadership of Swami Sivamurti.

experiences she had when she was still a laywoman and stayed in the ashram of Guru Sivananda (1887–1963), volunteering in the ashram's clinic. Now Guru Sivananda, whom the eldress knew, was the teacher of Guru Satyananda, who was the teacher of Guru Niranjanananda, whom during my time in India I had known as Niranjan, the president of the ashram. In other words, my experiences were with the spiritual "grandson" of Sivananda.

I had the opportunity to meet the eldress at her apartment in Athens long after my trip to India. I had heard about how she had lived for years in India and now combined spirituality with a tender and simple way of relating to young people. Indeed, I was moved by the way this seventy-five-year-old lady received me, a twenty-eight-year-old at the time—by the way she treated me and spoke with me. We sat close together, *tête-à-tête,* and she spoke to me like an affectionate mother, filling my soul with her tenderness. I was struck by how much she respected Father Paisios, whom she knew only by word of mouth. Naturally, we spoke about India during her time there and about much that is now recorded in her biography, *The Ascetic of Love,* widely read after her death. She showed a genuine interest in me and sent me two letters, which, unfortunately, I have since lost.

It seems worthwhile at this point to relate one of her experiences with the spiritual "grandfather" of the guru I knew in India, excerpted from her biography:

Here [at the ashram of Guru Sivananda] occurred her important encounter with Alan [a twenty-six-year-old Australian visitor to the ashram], which was the beginning of their friendship and resulted in his Baptism. This incident certainly changed the stance of Sivananda towards her. It was probably the cause of peculiar circumstances that occurred at her expense, which she once described to us after much insistence on our part. Perhaps it is worth reading.

One night, while praying in her room, she opened her eyes and saw that the bed was in a different place! She closed her eyes again and continued with the Jesus Prayer. After a while she reopened her eyes and turned towards the window, but could no longer see the moon! "I had gone blind," she told Helen Virvou. "In agony, I continued to pray with great fervor. After some time I fell asleep. In the morning when I woke up, I could see! Then I understood that something had been done to me. When I met Sivananda in the main room, he asked me if I slept well. 'Yes,' I told him, 'very well!'"

He looked at me very carefully, went and spoke to a nun who was writing something on the typewriter, and again asked me the same question, while looking strangely at the monk who was standing behind me. I told him again, 'Yes, very well. Glory to God.' He looked at me thoughtfully, without saying anything more. *Months later, I learned that some persons do such tricks with the help of evil spirits, to frighten away un- welcome strangers or to lure others into staying.* I know a German lady who lost her mind with what they did to her. After a few days, Sivananda himself came and suggested that I move to the upper floor, because they had given me the wrong room by mistake! But I kept it. Since then, they started to look at me in a peculiar way. They sensed that Someone Mightier protected me, and I sensed that the hour of my departure was near.[1]

---

[1] Monachē Gavriēlia *(Nun Gavrilia), Ē askētikē tēs agapēs* (The ascetic of love), Seira Talanto, 16th ed. (Athens: Heptalophos Abee, 1998), p. 55 (in Greek). Emphasis added. (This book has been translated into English, as noted on p. 133 above. However, the full account appears only in the original, unabridged Greek text.)

Back at the Ashram of Sri Aurobindo

After my departure from the ashram of Guru Satyananda, I returned to the tranquil ashram of Sri Aurobindo in the suburbs of New Delhi. Although I hadn't formed any special relationship with the members of this ashram, they honored my request for a single room where I could be alone and think. The look of virulent hatred in Niranjan's eyes still haunted me. Being unable to understand the source of such hatred, I decided to write him a letter to tell him that I actually liked him, how upset I was about the way we parted, and how the hatred that I saw in his eyes frightened me.

Having dealt with that issue, I then started to review in my mind all the eerie things that had happened to me. I struggled to analyze everything and to comprehend the deeper meaning of what was going on, but I simply didn't have the criteria or the principles necessary to reach a conclusion. Weary with struggling to reason it all out, I tried to see what my instincts were and to let my heart show me the proper path, but my heart was as divided and wavering as my mind. I could also feel that I wasn't solely responsible for my vacillation: it felt as though Father Paisios and Niranjan were still spiritually intervening in my life daily.

One morning, I set out on three separate occasions in order to arrange my return ticket for Greece, only to change my mind each time along the way. When I returned to my room the last time, it was already noon and my eyes hurt from the blinding light of the sun. Exasperated with this feeling of being pulled in two directions, I locked myself in my room, sat down, and began to meditate. I recalled how one of Babaji's disciples told me that, if I would call Babaji, he would come immediately. So I decided to call him to help me.

While I was meditating, I mentally made the plea, "Come

to me, Babaji." Immediately, I felt as though my mind were engulfed by darkness. Alarmed, I opened my eyes, but to my horror the darkness had taken possession of my living quarters, transforming my room, formerly well-lit by the noonday sun, into a dark and gloomy cavern. I could perceive the shining of the sun, but only *outside* of my window. Within my room, the restless darkness nearly devoured me as it plunged me into a state of total fear and anguish.

Like someone drowning at sea, I cried out, "Elder, help me!" Immediately, my soul felt the touch of a refreshing breeze, and I could sense a change in the mood of the darkness. Like a person, the darkness started to express its emotions. It was not simply angry: it was frenzied with rage. Nevertheless, it quickly departed, leaving my room once more brightened by the light of the sun and my soul feeling strong and peaceful. I leapt up, put on my shoes, grabbed my wallet, and went to arrange my ticket for Greece. There was nothing left to analyze, compare, or ponder over.

Nevertheless, I still had to remain in the ashram nearly a week waiting for the day of my return flight. In the meantime, I ran into a woman who had been a disciple of Babaji for many years and whom I had first met at his ashram in the Himalayas. When I related my latest experience to her, she reacted as though it were perfectly normal and, in fact, began to tell me about her own similar experience. So I asked her, "How do you explain the darkness?" She replied, "Babaji wanted to show you the darkness in your mind." I didn't respond to her, because I knew full well that that darkness had not been my own. Admittedly, my mind was anything but illumined—but, even so, my mind didn't have the power to keep the sun's rays from passing through the window. I had also clearly felt as though the darkness hid someone, or, to be more precise, that the darkness was being generated by the person whom I had summoned, namely, Babaji. I had felt him rage when I called for the elder and saw his powerlessness in the elder's presence.

Later, she told me how she would mentally ask Babaji for different things such as employment in India, a pretty apartment, money, and other favors, and how all these desires would soon be fulfilled through the guru's power. Silva Mind Control, "white magic," yoga, and witchcraft had all offered me the same benefits in the past. Even Ares the hypnotist had held out similar promises. But I resisted the urge to accept the offer, deciding that it would be better to make do on my own, even if I grew tired in the process—for, ultimately, they were asking for my soul. Christ's question from two thousand years ago now resonated in my mind: *For what is a man profited, if he shall gain the whole world, and lose his own soul? Or what shall a man give in exchange for his soul?*[1] And so, I made my decision and set out on my voyage back to Greece—a solitary one, for my friends had already departed.

[1] Matthew 16:26.

CHAPTER FIVE

Home at Last

A Visit to the Holy Mountain after My Escapades in India

When I returned to Greece in March I found that, when I would speak to my friends, they were not able to really understand me. Most of them were materialists and, after all that I had been through, we were now coming from such different worlds that we had difficulty communicating. Nevertheless, they still loved and accepted me. When my mother saw me, she was very distressed over my new appearance—in India it had enabled me to blend in, but in Greece I stuck out like a sore thumb. So I changed my clothes and wore a hat over my shaved head.

I had the uncanny sensation of being more powerful than other men, even invulnerable. It was the same feeling I had begun to have in Allahabad, when something left the body of Babaji's Dutch disciple and entered into my own. And, despite my change in dress, a sensitive observer would still have been able to detect something strange about me, which even I found frightening: at times, the expression on my face would become strangely evil and crafty, showing the ferocity of a wild beast. This wasn't a permanent state. It would simply come over me from time to time, on its own and against my will. Once I was plunged into it, I couldn't get out if I tried. It would intrigue, intimidate, and even frighten those around me, who would

The cell of Elder Paisios.

then be careful about how they treated me—and this only flattered me in my vainglory and pride.

After spending a few days with family and friends, I went to the Holy Mountain, where my sensation of being powerful was gradually altered into a lack of sensation altogether. I felt odd merely approaching Mount Athos. The spiritual atmosphere surrounding the Holy Mountain disturbed me, making me feel afflicted and numb. My encounters with the monks I knew there were also strange. I was taken aback by their behavior, so perplexing and seemingly inexplicable: they would happily come to meet me when they saw me from a distance, but, as soon as they came near, they would appear ill at ease and not be so enthusiastically welcoming. It's not that they became cold-hearted, but they seemed cautious. They would speak briefly with me and quickly depart. Their behavior puzzled and distressed me, but in the end I wasn't very concerned about it, because I had really come to see Elder Paisios.

When I reached the elder's hut, he was by himself in the

yard. I approached his fence and called for him. He turned to me, gave me a stern look, and reproached me: "And what do you want here?" This unexpected response knocked the wind out of my sails. I thought, "Where will I go now, if he drives me away?" In fact, I had nowhere else to go, because there was no one who loved me more than Father Paisios. He had always welcomed me warmly, kissing me, embracing me, and speaking to me with kindness. I couldn't understand why he now gave me this kind of reception. I didn't say anything. I just bowed my head and waited in a dazed state to see whether he would drive me away or take me in.

In the end, he felt sorry for me and softened up. "All right," he said, "come on in for a moment and we'll see what we can do now." I felt great relief as I gladly entered his yard.

"So, why did you get a haircut?" he teased me. "Did you join the army?"

"No, elder," I smiled. "I went to India. Did you know?"

"Silly boy, do you think I wouldn't know that?"

"I wrote you a letter and I wanted to send it to you, but I lost it."

"It doesn't matter, I got it anyway."

The elder had again opened up his embrace to me. After about a half an hour of conversation, I got ready to leave. The elder asked me, "Where are you going to stay now?" "I'll go stay with Father Christos," I told him. "Okay," he replied, "come back again in three days." I started to get up when he told me to sit down, so that he could bring me a "gun." He returned smiling, with a thirty-three-knot prayer rope in his hand. "This shoots spiritual bullets that'll frighten away the devil so he won't come near you. Take it with you: you might need it." As I went out the gate, he grabbed the hat I was wearing, made the sign of the Cross over it, and put it back on me. He laughed, saying, "You'll need to have a helmet, so the evil one won't bother you with harmful thoughts."

Elder Paisios at his cell.

And then he gave me one of his gentle taps on the head, his way of trying to hide the spiritual gifts he imparted. As always, this blessing put me under the influence of the grace of the Holy Spirit, making me at the same time ecstatic and prudently modest. With this simple gesture, the elder would spiritually dress me like a prince—with a spiritual beauty that could be seen in my face, which, like that of an innocent child, became peaceful, guileless, and beautiful. Once, when I returned to the world after visiting the Holy Mountain, a friend of mine who didn't know Christ said, "Once again, you've changed and become like a little child." Of course, I knew it was a gift of the elder, who generously adorned me in this way even though I would then be dragged again by the passions into the pit of sin.

And so, having adorned me as much as possible under the circumstances, he sent me on my way. I went to Father Christos, with whom I had stayed before. He let me stay as a guest for several days, although he also seemed uneasy and reserved. One day I asked him, "Elder, will you keep me as a novice?" He answered, "My child, what am I to do with you, with all of those demons surrounding you?" I didn't understand what he was talking about. Of course I felt strange, but I attributed that to the powerful experiences I had gone through.

I was upset about being rejected by the ascetic, but Father Paisios had accepted me, and that was more than enough. He genuinely and unconditionally loved me, regardless of whether I was healthy or sick, handsome or ugly, strong or weak, intelligent or stupid. With such relief, comfort, and joy, what else could I desire?

A Demon, an Angel, and the Most Pure Virgin

And He [Jesus] said unto them ... In My name shall they cast out devils.
                                        —Mark 16:15, 17

Within a month after my return from India, I made a second trip to the Holy Mountain, intending to stay for a while. It was the time before the full arrival of spring. It had been raining continuously for days, and on this day it was cloudy and dreary with a chill in the air. When I arrived at the elder's cell, I didn't find any other visitors, on account of the rain and the time of year.[1]

Since it was chilly, the elder, though he usually received people in his yard, had me come inside. He led me to a rather large room which he used for receiving guests. The room had a stove in the middle which was lit just enough to cut the chill and dampness. Along the walls were makeshift benches covered by handmade woolen rugs. I don't recall what we talked about—in any event, even though time went by, the elder showed no signs of asking me to leave. I was huddled up on a little stool, on account of the cold and the state of my soul. It was comforting just to be in the elder's presence.

It seemed as though he were waiting for something—there was no good reason for me to stay for so long. In a short while, the bell rang, and the elder went to open the gate. He put the gate key on a wire and let it glide down to his visitor, who took the key, opened the lock, and came to the back of the house, where the elder awaited him. From the room I was staying in, I could hear their conversation. A loud and emotional voice called out, "My elder, my beloved elder," and I heard the visitor fall to his knees as he tried to kiss the elder's feet. Simultaneously, I heard the elder swiftly step back against the wall, trying to steer clear of him. "Don't do that, you silly goose, stop it," the elder begged. One could hear in the elder's voice,

---

[1] Towards the end of the winter season, the weather conditions often prevent the ferry from running to and from the Holy Mountain, placing those with jobs in danger of not being able to return on schedule. Hence, during this time of the year, nearly the only people visiting the Holy Mountain are students and those with special reasons for doing so.

in addition to his awkward and uneasy feelings, a certain sense of warmth towards the visitor.

I was amazed by the visitor's devout attitude towards the elder, and especially by the way he humbled himself at his feet. The entire scene conveyed a deep sense of reverence. I thought to myself, "He must be some young monk whom the elder has helped a great deal." To my great surprise, the visitor who then entered the room turned out to be a fifty-year-old man, serious-minded and old-fashioned, as his traditional mustache bore witness. I couldn't imagine what could ever make such an individual behave in that way.

With some visible embarrassment, the gentleman greeted me, and the three of us sat down in the room. The fact that I was in the elder's reception room must have made the man presume that I had a close relationship with the elder, because he seemed to have warm feelings towards me immediately, despite my odd appearance. I had warm feelings towards him as well, even though under other circumstances I would have had misgivings, not so much on account of his age as on account of our conflicting temperaments and ideologies. But the man's spontaneous behavior and his obvious love and unselfish respect for a poverty-stricken, lowly, unlettered old monk revealed that he was not obsessed with the status quo, but honored virtues that I also held in high regard.

I realized then in my heart how biased I was against certain people, and how unfair in my judgments. My relationship with the elder caused me at first to learn to accept people from the "other camp," and, eventually, to recognize my party mentality and to free myself from it, so that I could see in each person the image of God, regardless of whether he was dressed as a hippie, a right-winger, a leftist, a soldier, or a member of any other circle.

After the elder had treated the gentleman to the traditional Athonite welcome of a sweet and a glass of water, we exchanged some small talk, and then the elder asked me to go into the next room, where his chapel was located, in order to give the gentleman privacy to say whatever he had on his mind.[1] I entered, venerated the icons and sat down, saying the Jesus Prayer and, from time to time, looking out the chapel's small window and letting my eyes wander.

Then in the twinkling of an eye, everything in the chapel became radiant—it was as though light were emanating from everything in the chapel, even the walls. I could see the same powerful light shining outside of the window, even though it was a cloudy and dreary day. I had obtained another sense, like a blind man who suddenly acquires perfect sight. The light made everything I could see, both in the chapel and through the window, sharp and extremely clear. As I continued to look through the window, I saw a small white light, cloud-like, without any particular contour or shape, producing a radiance as brilliant as lightning and as clear as crystal. The light was immaterial yet personal, unrestricted by space, and it moved rapidly, circling around the cell.

This entity full of light made my soul feel calm and peaceful, full of assurance and free of every fear. It brought with it a tremendous festal joy, but a joy that was nevertheless quite sober. This experience, which would permanently affect the way I looked at the world, was of the same nature as my other experiences on the Holy Mountain, but, like the rest, it had its own personality. It made me feel especially peaceful. Although this change in my surroundings and sensitivity occurred suddenly, it would fade gradually: days later, my soul would still be able to feel the effects of these sensations of another order and nature than those experienced in everyday life.

I waited quietly, and after a short while the elder came in, having finished his conversation with the visitor. I turned to

[1] On the Holy Mountain, the cells of those who live outside of the monasteries are usually equipped with a small chapel.

The iconostasis of the chapel located in Elder Paisios's cell.
At right is the reading stand.

The *stasidie* (seats) in Elder Paisios's chapel.
The elder would pray in the third seat from the right.

him and calmly said, "Elder, I saw an angel." He carefully looked me in the face and peered into my eyes, as though he were searching for some kind of sign, and he calmly responded, "Oh, hmm, very well. Let's go inside." So we entered the adjoining room, where the visitor was waiting. By this time I had been in the elder's cell for nearly two hours, so I expected him to see us to the door, but he showed no sign of wanting to send us off. He began to tell us some yarn, embellished with humorous anecdotes. The visitor was sitting with the elder on a bench, while I was sitting across from them, on a tree stump. The elder's spontaneous and beautiful sense of humor often left his visitors in stitches, and we settled in to hear his tale.

So the elder began: "Once, a certain man went far away to hmm…." At this point, the elder seemed to struggle to recall the name of the country, and then, apparently pleased with himself, continued, "Let's say he went to Pakistan." At this point, he looked me straight in the eye. "He got into a real fix over there. They smudged some ashes on his forehead." I bit my lip as I recalled how the yogi disciple of Babaji had put a dot from the burnt sacrifice between my eyes. Although the elder appeared to be telling his story primarily to the visitor, he would give me a look at certain significant moments, and I soon realized that he was talking about me, though in such a way that the visitor wouldn't realize it.

By now, a strange feeling had come over me. Something within me was reacting negatively to what was being said, making me feel disturbed and upset. At this point, the elder turned to me and said, "Over there, the devil bothered this fellow, but he would say the Jesus Prayer and not give the devil any rest." I understood the elder's message, and began to say the prayer with my mind: "Lord Jesus Christ, have mercy on me." I no longer paid attention to the elder's account, but turned my mind towards the prayer. As the elder continued, he turned towards me, and, as though he were saying a line from his story, he said, "Come out of this man, thou unclean spirit!"[1] The elder then immediately continued the story while holding on to the visitor by the wrist. A short while later, he again looked at me, again as though he were relating a part of the story, and repeated, "Come out of this man, thou unclean spirit!"

The elder's face shone with a mystic radiance, hidden, but which I was nonetheless able to perceive. He was quite serious, and the look in his eyes betrayed the hidden glory of his soul. I rarely saw this particular look, and it revealed that I wasn't dealing with an average person, but someone qualitatively more magnificent. Indeed, the look in his eyes and the expression on his face revealed unknown dimensions of human nature. I continued to say the Jesus Prayer, now with greater earnest, though I didn't understand the significance of what was happening. Then the elder turned to me for a third time and said, "Come out of this man, thou unclean spirit!"

That is when I felt some immaterial thing being detached and separated from my soul, and coming out of me. I felt as though my mind and soul had been freed from the powerful influence of another spirit, and this made me quite aware of my soul as something concrete and tangible. Then I realized that I had been under a great deal of pressure. I could sense the onerous presence of the spirit that had come out of me, hovering at my left. Even at a distance, its dark power burdened my soul. I got up in order to get away from it, and took refuge at the elder's feet.

Within a few moments after the elder's last words and my liberation, the visitor surprised me again. He abruptly leapt to his feet and began to cry out, in an ecstatic state of wonder and amazement, "My Most Pure Lady, my Most Pure Lady! Elder, what is that fragrance? Elder," he cried with relish, "the Most

[1] Cf. Mark 5:8.

Pure Lady is in our midst!" Such immense joy had taken hold of him that he forgot about the elder's story, his own behavior, and everything else. With joy, he cried out and begged us to go to the chapel. I no longer felt the fearsome and powerful presence of that entity with which my soul had been burdened.

I knew then that these are not matters to be judged by the intellect, which can hardly comprehend them. Instead, they are the province of a divine knowledge born in the heart, which is much more certain and profound than what usually passes for knowledge. Truly, it is amazing that, although unworthy, I was accounted worthy to experience what until then I had only read about in the Lives of the Saints—which had seemed so simplistic!—or in the sober and profound discourses of the great ascetics of the Orthodox Church. Such experiences have an immeasurable existential depth, and they overwhelm the soul, filling it with the gladness and ineffable joy of experiencing God's infinite bounty. And we too experienced a festal gladness, savoring these mystical gifts, under the influence of which we put aside all earthly care. We felt joyful and humble.

We slowly made our way to the chapel. I felt that the elder's prayer, the fruit of his pure and guileless heart, was the cause of these divine visitations, and I wanted to thank him. So I went to make a prostration before him. But that obviously made him ill at ease, for he prevented me and said, "Make your prostration over there." And he pointed towards the iconostasis, at the icon of the Most Pure Virgin. Indeed, the elder had been timidly looking in that direction with deep reverence, and it was as though my behavior a moment before had been an interruption. I lifted up my head and looked towards the icon, expecting from the expression on the elder's face to see someone, but I didn't. I replied, "I already made a prostration there, earlier." "Oh, you poor thing," he tenderly answered me, "listen to me and go and make a prostration now." I could see that he wanted me to hurry, so I went. The elder was quite pleased for my sake, like a father seeing his son being accepted by a king.

The elder unhurriedly led us out into the yard, where we received his final blessing before leaving. He told me to shut the gate, lock it, and put the key on the pulley so that he could pull it up to his cell. And so, this fifty-year-old gentleman, and I, a twenty-five-year-old, set out together for Karyes along a rough uphill path under the cover of various trees and bushes.

When we were about one or two hundred yards from the elder's cell, the man said excitedly, "Do you realize that he's a saint? He's a saint, I tell you." "Yes, I know," I responded. He then took me by the hand and stopped me, looking directly into my eyes, and repeated, "Do you realize what I'm saying? He's a saint. Do you hear me?" He thought that I had only been politely agreeing with him, so I told him, "Yes, I believe it and I know it. I've known the elder for some time." He looked at me and was convinced that I was serious, so we continued on our way.

This gentleman was weighed down by a bulky old suitcase he had strapped to his shoulders. It was quite unnecessarily cumbersome, especially considering that the suitcase had a handle so that it could be carried by hand. I was at a loss as to why he didn't have a more manageable backpack. When the uphill path became steeper, he would stop, out of breath, and wipe the sweat off his brow every five paces. I offered several times to take his suitcase, but he always refused, and so we slowly continued our ascent and conversation.

I was curious about what made this traditional fifty-year-old gentleman so grateful and fervent as to fall to his knees, unashamedly attempting to kiss the elder's feet. His statement "he's a saint" must, I imagined, have been based upon something, so I tried to steer the conversation in such a way as to learn about it. It wasn't very difficult, since we already felt close because of the blessed experiences we had just

An aerial view of Elder Paisios's cell.

had with the elder (though he certainly had no idea that, a few minutes earlier, the elder had cast a demon out of me).

The suitcase was helpful in this conversation. He confessed to me that it was completely empty, and that he only carried it so that others wouldn't realize how weak he was. He told me, "I used to be a high-ranking officer in the Air Force. I was a lukewarm believer, who would go to church when I had to, when there was a feast or other event. I became ill because I smoked a great deal, about three packs a day, and I went to London, where the doctors removed three-quarters of my lungs. That's why I have trouble breathing. They left a quarter of my lungs intact, so I would have something to breathe with, and told me that I had, at most, about two weeks to live. So I returned to Greece in order to die. I was quite distressed, and decided to go to the Holy Mountain, which I had never visited before. When I arrived and heard about the elder, I set out to meet him. When I reached his cell, he opened the door before I could knock and said, 'It's good to see you, Demetrios. I've been waiting for you.' I was stunned to hear him call me by name the first time he laid eyes on me, and to see that he really did have something ready for me to eat. He had me sit down to rest a bit and told me, 'Don't worry and fret, everything is going to be all right.' And then he made the sign of the Cross three times over my chest, even though I still hadn't told him anything. Two and a half years have passed since that time, and I am still in good shape, without taking any medication. I didn't die within two weeks like I was supposed to and the cancer didn't spread. I just have some swelling and can't walk very well, because I only have a small portion of my lungs left intact. And so I come here to see the elder every so often."

And so the riddle of his behavior was solved, and I came to learn from one more person about the many gifts of the elder. As this incident reveals, he had the gift of healing people from illness, snatching them from the jaws of death, even at the last moment. Christ's words could be seen fulfilled in the elder: *And these signs shall follow them that believe: In My name shall they cast out devils; … they shall lay hands on the sick, and they shall recover.*[1]

(However, Father Paisios didn't heal everyone who was sick. To some, this was surprising and created doubt about the elder, who judged and acted differently from the way they would have. But what these people neglected to consider was that, with his discernment, the elder could see things whose existence they could hardly suspect, and so he knew how best to use the gift with which he had been entrusted.)

The Healing of a Brain Injury

Naturally, after the elder cast out the demon, I felt greatly relieved, as though a burden had been lifted off me. But, in spite of this significant change for the better, I still suffered from a continual low-grade headache. Some days later, during one of my conversations with the elder, I referred to this ongoing problem. We were together in his cell's chapel: he was standing up in a choir stall, and I was seated next to him. I told him, "Elder, I'm not well. They did something to my head." I explained to him that I felt as though the tissues in my brain had been damaged, right at the center of my skull. I could recall the very night that these symptoms began, in the ashram of Satyananda in Munger, India. While I was asleep, I was mysteriously visited, or rather attacked. When I awoke, I felt as though someone had scraped my brain with sandpaper.

The elder looked at me tenderly, with much loving-kindness. He didn't say a word. He simply stretched out his hand and stroked my head, holding his hand for a short while near my right ear. A gentle power passed through his hand to my

[1] Mark 16:17–18.

head, and it flooded my soul with a fearless calm and coura-
geous peace. Within a few seconds, I felt the joy of being completely well. In fact, it was as if the wear and tear of twenty-five
years had disappeared, and my brain felt as young and fresh as
it must have on the day I emerged from my mother's womb.

Of course, under normal circumstances, someone who had
been healed as I had would cry aloud, leap for joy, burst into
tears, praise God, or thank the elder. But I wasn't taken aback
by this indisputable miracle, because I already knew that
Christ had adorned the elder with divine glory and many gifts:
in his presence, supernatural phenomena became natural.
Moreover, his ways were so simple, natural, and easy-going
that I had come to look at such events as completely normal.
So I continued my conversation with the elder without com-
menting on what took place, received his blessing, and left.

A Shaking Tree on a Breezeless Day

I must stress how very differently I was affected by my spiritual
contact with the gurus and with the elder. In one instance, I
was wounded; in the other, I was healed. Now, the yogis gave
various interpretations and explanations that presented their
actions in a positive light, as great gifts and helps for spiritual
progress. A striking example is provided by my friend who was
suffering from hemorrhaging so severe that it left her bedridden. The yogis claimed that those hemorrhages were blessings
from the guru that were purifying her *karma.* The other girl
and I nearly swallowed such a wonderful, exotic-sounding explanation—though my friend who was actually suffering with
the ailment had trouble accepting it.

And yet, although I and they had suffered so much at the
hands of Hindu gurus, strangely enough, it still wouldn't sink
in. I had put myself in mortal danger and suffered assaults on
my person, body and soul, yet I still couldn't see. Perhaps by

the prayers of the elder, grace protected me for a season, lest I prematurely realize what I had gone through and be driven to despair. Perhaps I was simply foolish. In any event, I gradually came to an understanding of my spiritual injuries while I was in the protected environment of the Holy Mountain.

One day, some time after the elder had cast out the demon, I went to see him. After a visit between the two of us, I passed beyond his wire fence, and the elder prepared to lock it. We had been talking about yoga; and before leaving I said, "But elder, they're good people." Suddenly, a few feet away from me at my right, a seven-foot-tall bay tree began to quake violently, as though someone were venting hatred on it, shaking it hard enough to pull it out by its roots. And yet the day was breezeless—all the neighboring vegetation remained completely still. Terrified by this inexplicable phenomenon, I called out, "Elder, what's going on over there?" "It's your friend," he responded calmly.

I lowered my head in shame. This is when I really understood the nature of the yogis' kindness and became aware of the number of demons that my friends, the yogis, had sent my way. This is also when I was reminded that the elder was the one who was standing between the guru and me, as well as between the demons and me. I had put the elder through many trials and made him take up my spiritual burden: I would leave and he would have to confront the demons for my sake. I quickly and fearfully went my way. The yogis would have to get by the elder before they could reach me: he was on the front line in the spiritual battle, while I was still far behind, lying in the infirmary.

The elder used to say, "The devil isn't able to hide in a sack for long, since some horn will always show through the sack. But if you ask him, 'What's that sticking out?' he'll answer, 'Oh, that's not a horn; it's an eggplant.'" In other words, if evil showed itself for what it really was, everyone would flee from it for fear of being harmed. It has to be camouflaged and appear to be beautiful and good, so that people will accept it; and, in the same way, people engaged in evil have to act as though they are virtuous, so that they won't alienate others. This is why Christ openly rebuked the Pharisees, the supposedly virtuous men of biblical times, saying, *Ye are of your father the devil, and the lusts of your father ye will do. He was a murderer from the beginning, and abode not in the truth, because there is no truth in him. When he speaketh a lie, he speaketh of his own: for he is a liar, and the father of it.*[1]

I recall being overwhelmed with feelings of gratitude for the countless times the elder had taken up my spiritual burden on account of my own laziness and cowardice. I told him, "Elder, you've done so much for me, what can I ever do for you in return?" He answered, "What are you talking about, blessed child? Do you know how much good you've done for me? Do you know how many times you've put the prayer rope in my hands?" What he meant was that, because I was in danger, he had been forced to use his prayer rope for my sake even more than usual. I had made his strict spiritual regimen even more austere, and the elder considered this additional labor on top of his already great toils to be to his benefit. And from a spiritual perspective, in terms of eternity and Christ's ineffable Kingdom for which the elder yearned, it was indeed beneficial. *The Kingdom of Heaven suffereth violence, and the violent take it by force.*[2] The elder put these words of the Lord into practice by becoming a genuine monk, that is, one who strives constantly and mightily—even "violently"—to know God. The elder did this joyfully for the sake of Christ, Whom he had loved from early childhood—and in turn Christ gave him the Holy Spirit and the strength to continue along this path.

[1] John 8:44.
[2] Matthew 11:12.

The Choice between Light and Darkness

I profoundly felt that my mind was not sufficient to judge these experiences, which infinitely exceeded its bounds. Nevertheless, I had to take some steps towards sorting them out and deciding whom to follow and whom to leave behind. The elder, among others, was silently waiting for me to make this decision. Today, I realize that it wasn't my reason that was being called upon to make it. Rather, it was a decision for my heart, the deepest and most powerful part of my being: it wasn't a question of ideology created by the mind, but of faith being born in the heart.

One day, sometime after my experience with "my friend" in the elder's yard, I asked the elder about the yogis. By that time, I had become convinced that the yogis worked in cooperation with demons—but I couldn't understand how it was possible for anyone to make such a choice. "Elder, I just can't understand why they would want to be evil men. They are intelligent, educated people with many abilities. They don't have any reason to be evil." The elder looked at me and shook his head, but didn't say anything. Shortly afterwards, as planned, I left the Holy Mountain in order to be with my family for Pascha,[1] which we would spend in my childhood home of Florina, to which my parents had returned in their retirement.

One afternoon at the beginning of Holy Week, having made a stop in Thessaloniki, I was by myself in our home there, when, suddenly, my surroundings vanished. There were no images to be seen, sounds to be heard, or objects to be touched. My five senses had ceased functioning. It was as though the light switch had been flicked and the room plunged into total darkness.

---

[1] Pascha is the feast of the Resurrection of Christ.

My mind turned its full attention to a spiritual realm that it found utterly riveting and captivating. In one direction, I saw a soft but intense light—brilliant yet gentle. In the other direction, I saw a thick, cavernous darkness. Initially, I turned my attention towards the awesome, yet fearful, darkness. It made my flesh crawl, but I was overcome by curiosity, the desire to understand what it was. My mind advanced towards the darkness, and I began to sense the magnitude of its negation. The deeper I went, the greater this negation became, and the thicker the darkness. It had a vast power and, if I dare put it this way, a certain grandeur. It represented a negative perspective on reality, unhesitatingly extending into reality as depth, even as the light stretched infinitely into reality as height. On one side, there was immense love; on the other, immense hatred. The light was overflowing with unconditional altruism, while the darkness pulled away in utter self-centeredness.

Though I couldn't see into the darkness, I could feel the presence of souls in it, leaping about and shrieking with insane, wicked laughter as they were pulled deeper and deeper into the ocean of darkness, until the sound of their voices disappeared altogether. Frightened by this savage madness, I headed towards the light, seeking its protection. Just reaching its outskirts, I felt the relief of having been rescued from a grave danger.

Although I didn't advance very far at all into the darkness, I was able to feel the depths of its evil ocean. I could understand the very essence of the enticing power of sin to tempt, as well as its laughable powerlessness, utter dependence, and shadowy nonexistence. The darkness, I saw, is fearsome when it has won you over, but it is absurd and feeble when you reject it—it cannot defeat even a small child if he does not fall on his own. In the same way, I didn't advance far into the light—only, so to speak, skating its edge—but even there I felt confident and comforted by a fullness of life, peace, joy, and knowledge. The light loved me greatly in spite of my unworthiness and granted me its gifts, gifts I never dreamed existed.

At this point, I realized that the light created the world and every living being. The existential space in which each person dwells is itself a creation fashioned by the light, which also fills and permeates these spaces. One being decided to stay outside of the existential space created by the light, thus creating a sort of space for itself, though only by denying the light, turning from it, and driving it away. The darkness has no existence of its own, but only in that it denies the ever-existing and sovereign light. That is to say, the existence of the darkness would have been impossible without the existence of the light; though the light had no need of the darkness for existence, for its existence is self-sufficient. The light respected the free decision of its creation to reject it, and so kept its distance. In this way, a dark existential space made its appearance—the darkness, in this sense, became a reality.

The darkness resulted from the inclination of a conscious being, called Satan, who chose such a form of existence though he had no reason to. And this denial made the darkness a reality. Although this act of denial may have resembled God's act of creation, it was not creation, but an imitation of creation performed in reverse. That is, the devil tried to behave like God, but, since he did not have the ability to create on his own, he was only capable of denying God's creation, energies, light, and grace. He pulled away from the very borders of reality and made non-existence a way of being, thus "creating" death and darkness. For, until that time, there was neither death nor darkness, but all things were filled with light and life.

Just as the light's love wishes to unite all things, being the source of existence and creation, so the hatred of the darkness wants to divide all things, being the source of nonexistence and destruction. Just as the light extends out into the infinite beyond, so the darkness seems to extend into its infinite beyond. Just as there is a grandeur about the simple, yet infinite light of God, with all His attributes and energies, so there is a certain grandeur about the blunt, yet apparently infinite darkness of the devil, with all his deep-rooted and ferocious self-destructiveness, full of a stubborn and manic rage.

Having come to such realizations, I found myself, as with the flip of a switch, surrounded again by the familiar sights and sounds of my room. Within a matter of minutes, I had received a lesson of immeasurable depth. It was not only a revelation beyond words, of subtle differences of profound meaning and great importance, but also—and even more—a test and a trial of the deepest inclinations and intentions of my heart, to see whom I would follow and whom I would leave behind. Fortunately, although my heart initially moved towards the darkness, it ultimately found repose in the light—and, fortunately, the light still accepted me.

This experience taught me that, just as God surpasses the human mind, so do His works, His creations, and His gifts. On its own, the human mind can only acquire a relative idea about these realities, producing hypotheses, conjectures, opinions, and imaginary presuppositions to justify its views. However, aided by the grace of the Holy Spirit, it can begin to fathom these mysteries.[1]

I also received from this experience a deep appreciation of the mystery of human and angelic freedom, a divine gift beyond human understanding. My experience of light and darkness helped me to grasp the fact that God endowed angels and men with a free will so that they could move independently,

---

[1] *Author's note:* Here it seems appropriate to note one of Elder Paisios's teachings regarding faith. He used to say that God left various ambiguous and inscrutable passages in the Gospels on purpose, so that man would not be compelled to believe because of a host of proofs, but would have the opportunity to demonstrate the inclination of his heart.

freely and without compulsion in the moral sphere. The elder once told me, "God would forgive the devil if he would just say one 'Lord, have mercy.' There's a dear old monk near here who used to pray for the devil, because he felt compassion for him. After all, the devil was one of God's creatures—in fact, he was an archangel before he fell to such a sorry state. While the elder was praying for him, the evil one appeared in the corner and started to make fun of him, making rude gestures, like this." He showed me what he meant—the devil, sticking out his tongue, made a gesture that's used in Greece to call someone an idiot. "The devil," he concluded, "is unrepentant." As I would learn later, this elder was actually Father Paisios.

A Spiritual Operation

That Pascha, I received another gift. When I had returned from India, I was, like most people, profoundly ignorant of my true self and the contents of my own heart. Although my soul was covered with sores and laden with weaknesses, I pridefully believed that I was greater than I really was, overestimating my gifts and potentials and considering my faults to be merits. I claimed as my own doing the gifts God had given me, and blamed my failures on factors outside of myself. Pride and conceit, like a mental illness, prevented me from seeing the reality closest at hand: my own self. In my folly, I imagined that I had acquired exalted spiritual knowledge. In fact, I was being self-centered, living selfishly for my own gratification, ignoring my neighbor, and being oblivious to the call to sacrifice myself for the sake of others.

The elder had such humility that he was easily able to absorb all my immense pride. He handled me carefully, as though I were a dry and brittle leaf. He lovingly tended me as though I were an infant on its deathbed. And truly, I was on the verge of insanity and spiritual death.

Several weeks before Pascha, I had been in the elder's cell on the Holy Mountain. He was being funny, holding a small knife and pretending he wanted to cut my throat. Jokingly, he turned the knife around to the blunt side and put it to my neck. "Want me to operate on you?"

"Whatever you say, elder."

"Are you afraid?"

"No, elder, I'm not afraid."

And suddenly he became serious and said, "Okay, but not now. At Pascha." And he let me go.

Naturally, I was quite curious to see what Pascha would bring a few weeks later. I cheerfully and calmly waited for the day to arrive. The eve of Pascha came, but nothing happened. The night of the Resurrection service came; still, nothing happened. Then, Sunday evening, I was alone at home and my parents had gone out. I watched a moving television program about Christ and then turned off the television and went to the adjoining room. From my window, I could see an illuminated cross that had been erected on a nearby mountaintop.

I got on my knees and began to pray. I gradually felt the gentle blessing of the elder come over me. It was as though he were standing behind me and blessing me. Both my body and soul were immersed in a sweet, yet all-powerful presence whose pure influence was like warm, living, and life-bearing waters, penetrating the very marrow of my bones and recharging them as though they were drained batteries. It was as though my entire parched being had gratefully begun to imbibe life in all its dimensions. Gratitude towards God welled up in my soul for that Person Who is so strong that He conquered death, and so good that He granted me life, happiness, and joy by putting death to flight, defeating sin, and freely expunging my debts.

In a mysterious way, my spiritual vision became clearer, so that my mind, which had formerly been entirely drunk with pleasures, could now vividly perceive the enormity of my spiritual blindness, of my utterly warped vision of reality, of my terribly negative attitude towards God. Then I realized that my soul was nearly dead, at the threshold of nonexistence. It was as though my soul, weakened, were imprisoned in a narrow tomb sealed with a huge stone too heavy to lift. In that miserable tomb, there was no room to move, not even an inch, and no air to breathe. Incapable of action, my subjected, miserable soul had admitted defeat, and I beheld my own death approaching in a place where even the thought of salvation was impossible. In despair, I asked myself how I had come to such a state, who had locked me up in that ghastly spiritual prison, and what demon had become my perverse prison guard.

And then a good and all-powerful Deliverer came, overcoming with mercy and divine love the terrible self-destructive power of the devil and sin. I felt the tombstone removed and my soul being set free, so that it could slowly and hesitatingly begin to move its numb limbs and feel itself warmed and vivified by the blessing. At last, with the loosing of my Gordian knot,[1] by virtue of the great condescension of God I began to understand the world and myself, an unworthy sinner. New horizons were opened to me in this revelation, bringing tears to my dry eyes, which were unable until this time to weep because of the coldness of my heart. Now the floodgates were opened, and I wept with tears of joy, relief, and gratitude for the resurrection of my soul, knowing that I had been refreshed with Life from the life of my Deliverer, the Bearer for my sake of the burden of my sins and death.

My references to a tomb and to a stone sealing it, to life and death, are not idle metaphors. My soul was quite literally dead. With my own free will, I had gouged out my spiritual eyes and murdered my soul, becoming drunk with hedonism

---

[1] The phrase "Gordian knot" refers to a legend associated with Alexander the Great. Used generally, it refers to a problem of great difficulty.

and choosing to become and remain self-centered. It is truly folly for a creature to deny his Creator, for a beneficiary to hate his Benefactor, for a sick man to strive to slay his Doctor, for a weakling to insult the Almighty, for a fool to scoff at the Fount of Wisdom, or for a mortal to boast in the presence of Immortality. How had I dared to, and why? For the first time in my life, I could clearly see into the depths of my soul, and what I saw was utterly repugnant. I condemned myself. And yet I had been resurrected.

God's long-suffering with my wretched, dark existence was beyond my understanding. He had saved me, though so foul did I see myself to be—a burden even to creation—that I wanted to vanish from existence. As I wondered in astonishment at God's willingness to put up with this filthiness and to tolerate my wretched existence, prayer, like a mighty torrent welling up from the depths, burst through the gateway of my heart. "My God, my God, why should I exist? How can You endure me? Blot me out, end my cursed existence! I don't want to continue my evil life, without reason or purpose, full of passions—pride, selfishness, anger, jealousy, injustice! O God, put an end to me! I don't want to breathe the air anymore, filling it with the stench of my vice, hatred, and resentment. Long-suffering and forgiving God, incomprehensible!" I felt God's simple goodness and sweet patience, His loving-kindness and humility, and I loved Him—calmly, deeply, peacefully, powerfully. And yet, in the face of His generosity, my love was so small, so cheap!

The comparison between God and myself was too much for my mind to take. I soon grew weary from my continuous sobs. But even at a time such as this, my arrogance was still alive. I had the great temerity to decide to turn and look at the one who had been standing behind me all this time and blessing me—to dare to observe him. But as soon as I accepted the thought, the presence vanished. "O elder, forgive me." Indeed, although I didn't see that it was the elder, I had no doubts. It was surely him, present there even physically, a spiritual surgeon excising a great portion of my pride. But unlike human operations, the elder's operation left no residual pain, but only joy, peace, and the yearning for another such blessing. His scalpel went deep, but instead of wounding, it only healed. In truth, the Lord gives *light to them that sit in darkness and in the shadow of death;*[1] for *where sin abounded, grace did much more abound.*[2] And so, in peace, I fell asleep.

Alas, however, I still hadn't become wise, as my folly only a few days later would bear witness.

Uncle Elijah

There was an old man we called Uncle Elijah, who used to live at the foot of the hill close to the last homes on the outskirts of Florina. He didn't have his own home or any possessions other than the same old rags that he wore regardless of the season. In the winter, he would wrap himself up with plastic to keep from getting wet. Even though many people would offer him their storage sheds to stay in, he would always come up with some excuse, so that he could continue to sleep outdoors near a chapel that he had built. For food, he ate whatever people would give him. Most of the time, he kept to himself. Everyone knew him, and most people thought he was crazy, although there was always some room for doubt. His quick-witted answers impressed everyone, and in fact it was said that he was very learned and went mad on account of all his studies. There were plenty of strange tales about Uncle Elijah that made people curious, including the rumor, or rather suspicion, that he was a saint. Children enjoyed talking with "Dante," as they called

[1] Luke 1:79.
[2] Romans 5:20.

Uncle Elijah.

him, and they genuinely loved him for his carefree and uninhibited way of life.

From childhood, I remember him as a stooping old man who slowly dragged his feet as he walked. When I was in elementary school, I remember meeting him on the road as he was walking backwards, as he often did. I asked him, "Uncle Elijah, why are you walking backwards?" "Because the devil is bothering me," he answered, "and I don't want to look at him. He's standing over there. Don't you see him?" And he pointed to a certain spot. I looked there and felt a spine-chilling fear, but I didn't see anything. He asked again, "Don't you see him?" I responded negatively and, full of apprehension, ran away.

Some years later, during an exam period in junior high, I recall some of my fellow students who were rather shaky in physics cheerfully coming out of the room where they had taken their physics examinations. They had passed the tests that they were in danger of failing, and with raised voices they happily recounted how Uncle Elijah had told them the very questions that would appear on two of their exams. At first, we didn't believe them, but when they swore emphatically and related all the details of their conversation, a large number of other children began to go and ask Uncle Elijah about the questions on their exams. Uncle Elijah, however, told these children to study and, if they still insisted, he would send them to an icon of the Holy Virgin to pray for her to help them.

Although Uncle Elijah would make many absurd and un-intelligible statements when speaking, many sensible and educated people went to speak with him. I knew several cases of people who in all seriousness maintained that, in spite of all his gibberish, Uncle Elijah had helped them with counsels that had referred to situations and problems that had not yet arisen.

The way of life to which he adhered for so many years reminded me of the form of Christian spiritual asceticism followed by those known as "fools-for-Christ." Few people attempt such a difficult path, because it is an arduous struggle that requires a very firm spiritual foundation.

In old age, Uncle Elijah finally agreed to move into a shed during the winter months, where I spoke with him before I set off for India. When I told him about my plans, he invited me into the shed and spoke to me at length about his life, in order to teach me about Christianity. Before 1940, he intended to be a village clerk. He loved the Most Pure Virgin very much. Once, he told me, when he was walking through a field going to another village, some wild dogs started to chase him. He was forced to climb up a tree, where he remained throughout the entire night, praying and singing to the All-Holy Virgin. In fact, he composed a beautiful hymn to her in the tree, which he recited to me.

He was in Florina during the German occupation, and,

one day, as he traveled to his job walking along the road on the outskirts of the city, the Most Pure Virgin appeared to him. Dazed, he stayed rooted at the spot for some time before continuing on his way. In the meantime, the British were bombing the city in order to destroy its railroad station, where many Germans had gathered. When Uncle Elijah reached the building where he worked, he found nothing but a large crater where it had once stood. If the Most Pure Virgin hadn't delayed him, he would surely have been killed. So he returned to the place where the Virgin appeared to him, built a small chapel he called "The Merciful Pure Virgin," and lived next to it for the rest of his life.

He told me that he said the prayer, "Lord Jesus Christ, have mercy on me," and that he had visited the Holy Mountain long ago. When I spoke to him about Father Paisios, he seemed to know him very well, even though he hadn't left Florina for years. "Oh, he has surpassed us all. Tell him to pray for me and send me a prayer rope." He then grew silent and prayed. I told him about the techniques I had learned at the Silva Mind Control seminar several months earlier. I tried to use some of them in his presence, but, to my surprise, absolutely nothing happened. He then told me, "Don't go to India. They'll eat you alive over there." I didn't listen to him, of course, and went anyway.

The Radiance of Uncle Elijah

The next time I saw him was after my return, the day after the elder's "operation" on me. I awoke a changed man. I could still palpably sense the elder's blessing, which made me feel wonderful, peaceful, and full of affection for my surroundings. That morning, I was taking a walk when I ran into Uncle Elijah—"the least of those in the city," as he referred to himself.

This stooped old man with long, dirty hair and an unkempt beard was sitting on the edge of the sidewalk, where he had lit a fire in a trash can. The children had stopped playing in order to encircle him. With his head bent over, he would speak to them, looking up at them every once in a while.

As I watched him, I noticed that he was enveloped in an immaterial, transparent, colorless light. This radiant, gladsome light was very sweet and was similar to the white light I had seen around the elder, although it was less intense. It was the grace welling up within him, and this, like a magnet, was attracting the children. I had long considered him to be a spiritual person, who hid his great ascetic struggle under the cover of foolishness, in order to avoid vainglory and the praise of men—since his love was God, and not the world with its barren comforts. Now, I could see with my own eyes that my belief had been justified. With the familiarity granted me by the grace I had just received, I cheerfully approached him and said, "Hello, Uncle Elijah." Startled, he lifted up his head and at once recognized the presence of the elder's blessing. Astonished, he looked at me carefully, as though he were trying to discover the cause of this change in me. "Last night," I told him, "Father Paisios put me in this state." "Ah, yes," he responded, "He has surpassed us all." He then began to ask me various questions. At one point, I told him, "Elder, I can see a radiance about you, coming from a light shining within you." He didn't respond, but with some embarrassment bent his head.

"Thou Shalt Not Tempt the Lord Thy God"

Then was Jesus led up of the Spirit into the wilderness to be tempted of the devil.... Then the devil taketh Him up into the holy city, and setteth Him on a pinnacle of the temple, and saith unto Him, If Thou be the Son of God, cast Thyself down: for it is written, He shall give His angels charge concerning thee: and in their hands they shall bear thee up, lest at any time thou dash thy foot against a stone. Jesus said unto him, It is written again, Thou shalt not tempt the Lord thy God.

—Matthew 4:1, 5–7

According to the Gospels, on one of the occasions that the devil tried to cause Christ to sin and break God's commandments, the Lord silenced him by referring to the commandment *Thou shalt not tempt the Lord thy God.*[1] In the Old Testament it is recorded that it was by the mouth of the Holy Prophet Moses that God gave man this commandment, which forbids man to test his Maker, acting deviously towards God and so bringing on himself many woes. Unfortunately, I didn't have this commandment in mind in the days after my "operation." My ignorance and insolence were the cause of my falling to a great temptation after the great blessing I had received.

A few days after Pascha, I decided to take an afternoon walk in the forest outside Florina. As I have already mentioned, I had become a changed man. Suddenly, with my calm and clear mind, the world seemed more vivid, and my relationship with God's creatures deepened, becoming more sensitive and sincere. It was a joy to be with the animals, the birds, the trees, and even the smallest blade of grass bursting with life. I understood their way of life directly, by experience and not by abstract reflection. I cheerfully spoke to them and they listened to me. I tenderly caressed them and understood their intentions and the movements of their inner beings. I loved them all. This extraordinarily beautiful, peaceful, and loving relationship between man and the world must have characterized

---

[1] *Ye shall not tempt the Lord your God, as ye tempted Him in Massah* (Deuteronomy 6:16).

the genuine life of Paradise. "The elder must be in such a state every day," I thought.

Indeed, he once said, "When I was in Stomio at the little monastery near Konitsa, there were two bears who would come to the place where I would dispose of the garbage. The poor things were hungry, so I would go and give them some bread. The animals can recognize your disposition when you approach them, if you intend to kill them or if you approach them with love. Even the wildest beast won't bother you if you approach it with genuine love." At this point, the elder opened up his hand and called to a red robin that was resting in the branches of a tree, and the little bird came and happily perched on the elder's finger. "The animals enjoy being with man and look at him as their king," he continued. "In Paradise, Adam called the animals one by one and gave them each a name according to its kind. Animals recognized man's superiority and were happy in his presence. After the fall, however, this relationship was destroyed. Man looked at the beasts with the intention of killing them, and the animals became wild. Nevertheless, the wild animals are still more sincere than man is. If you approach them with love, they return to that pristine state. Man has ruined the animals. Even the dog that lives continually by man's side has changed, acquiring a police mentality and a distrustful character. I used to feed a little kitten around here that would come and rub itself up against my leg and purr. Although it was very tame, when one day I tossed a piece of bread to it, the animal pulled back in fear. What had happened to it? Someone had thrown stones at it and ruined the animal's attitude towards people. So you see, this evil state of affairs begins with man." When I again asked the elder if it were really true that the fiercest of wild beasts won't bother someone if he approaches it with love, he insisted that it was. And now I understood by experience what the elder had said at that time.

Despite the fact that I was in this blessed state, the thought came to me, "I wonder what would happen if I sang some hymn from the Hindu *kirtana* or said a mantra?" I was overcome by senseless curiosity to find out if I would enter another state, or if nothing in particular would happen: first man falls in his mind, and later in deed. So I began to chant something from *kirtana* and to say the mantra that Babaji had given me in my sleep, "*Om Namah Shivaya.*" I scarcely managed to say this mantra, and immediately I felt both an internal and external change. A weirdly icy breeze passed through the tree branches and gripped my soul with fear. The grace of Christ that kept my soul calm vanished, and with it my peaceful and tender relationship with the world vanished as well. In its place, there was another, strained power smothering me and altering the spiritual atmosphere, so that everything seemed alien and unnatural. Simultaneously, I felt frightened and callous. I was no longer able to let myself be relaxed and free. The trust and love that filled my soul when I was with Christ were gone.

I realized then that I should have been careful. I tried to escape from this foreign influence and become as I had been before, but all attempts were in vain. The blessing that had rested upon me had obviously departed. I was at a loss as to how this change took place so rapidly—it was like something one runs across in books about witchcraft. In my distress, I fervently began to say the Jesus Prayer aloud: "Lord Jesus Christ, have mercy on me." I was no longer interested in exploring differences or becoming an adept judge of spiritual states. I simply wanted to reacquire what I had lost: the sense of being a small child in Christ's arms and the sweetness of His presence. I realized then that nothing else in life other than that is really worth knowing.

The Jesus Prayer warded off that suffocating power and my inner fear, but my soul still felt the absence of His presence. I no longer felt fully alive and wide awake. Instead, I felt alone and deprived. Even now, I still sorrow on account of being guilty of betraying, wounding, and turning my back on Him Who loved me so greatly, compelling Him to depart in sadness. I foolishly despised and squandered the great gift that my father had given me, and rightly suffered the consequences. Not having acquired that gift with my own personal toil, I didn't appreciate its value and struggle to preserve it as I should have. Notwithstanding, the elder felt pity for me and guarded a trace of that experience deep within my soul, unscathed by my folly. I learned from my mistake—I pray that others might have the humility to learn from it as well.

Consolation from Elder Porphyrios

After Pascha, I returned to Mount Athos and to the cell of Father Christos. At one point, I learned that an elder named Father Porphyrios had recently come to the Holy Mountain to stay for a while in the skete of Kavsokalyvia.[1] I had heard so much about this highly respected elder that, as soon as I learned that he was on Athos, I immediately decided that I would visit him. I knew that he would resemble my own elder, but I wanted to see what holiness would be like in another person—that is, I was interested in discovering the traits of another God-bearer. I also had real needs at that time, since I was still open to spiritual attacks by the gurus and evil spirits. Various elders would give me spiritual gifts in order to heal me, to support me, to bring me to understanding, and to enable me to know firsthand the difference between the experiences of mystical Christian Faith and Hinduism. They taught me the

---

[1] A *skete* is a monastic community combining aspects of the life of a hermitage and a coenobium (that is, a community of several monks in which all aspects of life are in common). At a skete, several small monastic dwellings, housing one or a few monks, are located around a central church. These smaller dwellings function independently of each other, with the entire skete gathering in the central church together for prayer on Sundays, and in some cases more frequently.

Elder Porphyrios.

The cell of Elder Porphyrios at Kavsokalyvia, Mount Athos.

difference between divine and demonic energy. I subconsciously hoped that Father Porphyrios would have a "gift" for me as well.

So I set out on a two-day journey within Mount Athos, which left blisters on my feet by the time I reached Kavsokalyvia. Kavsokalyvia is a skete consisting of about thirty cells situated on a steep rocky slope of Athos, where a few impressive trees grow through cracks in the granite and where the danger of an avalanche is always present. The cells are at a considerable distance from each other and each cell has its own little garden. There is a steep and rugged path that leads to the shore, where boats can dock if the sea is perfectly calm. It's not possible to have many possessions, since even bare necessities have to be hauled up an arduous path, carried on one's back or with a mule if they are too heavy. The monks there are consequently frugal and used to hardship.

Along the way, I would run into monks or laymen who would tell me that Father Porphyrios was seriously ill and wouldn't receive anyone. I continued on my journey, praying as much as I could until I eventually reached the cell where the elder was staying. When I announced myself at the door, a dark-complexioned monk around thirty years old came out and told me, "The dear father isn't able to receive you, because he's very sick." Almost immediately thereafter, another, older monk came out and sadly told me the same story. I told them that I would just like to receive his blessing, but the monks politely yet firmly held their ground. Then I heard Father Porphyrios calling from within for them to help him come out. And, in a short while, they carried out a little old monk wearing a woolen cap on his large head, who could not stand up and whose face revealed much pain with every faltering movement. Nevertheless, he was graced with a tranquil spiritual nobility and a magnificent simplicity that revealed him as a king in the spiritual realm.

The mere sight of the little elder filled my heart with yearning, joy, and a deep calm. I wasn't interested in the chair they offered me: I felt such joy and unworthiness in his presence that it was comforting just to be seated on the ground at his feet. The monks, however, didn't want to see me humbled like this and insisted on honoring me by having me sit facing the elder in the same kind of chair he was using. The thought of impudently sitting across from the elder as an equal made me very uncomfortable, but they kept insisting. The elder, however, understood me completely and rescued me from my predicament, saying, "He's just fine where he is—let him be." And so I sat there peacefully, feeling the secure joy of being in the very embrace of God by the prayers of the elder.

I could feel the elder's great love for me, and I felt as though I were in his spiritual embrace. I could sense an enormous spiritual strength in that decrepit old body, which, in spite of being on the verge of physical death, was an inexhaustible well of life rejuvenating my dying soul. It was indeed a paradox that an old man with one foot in the grave could grant life in every sense of the word to a twenty-five- year-old youth. Nevertheless, whereas he was about to leave his battered body and begin true and everlasting life, I was spiritually at death's door, despite the fact that I was a physically strong young man. And so I gratefully and joyfully partook of the life-giving waters that he silently offered me, and I felt life enter my soul.

We spoke a bit about India, and he told me to be careful not to let the devil trick me again, because what I had gone through was very dangerous. He didn't need to say very much, because I understood his meanings from what I experienced in his presence. His very person revealed the real depth of the world in its spiritual dimension, which lies beyond the decay of ephemeral matter. There was no need for ideological discussion or rational analysis. There was no need to try to discover, conjecture, or conclude anything. I didn't speak about the grace of the Holy Spirit or hear about the grace of Christ—I experienced it, and I rejoiced in that experience. He said, "I will be praying for you, so come and see me again."

So I took his blessing with a feeling of joyful sadness, bid him farewell, and left. When I began my ascent up the path, however, my sense of joy intensified. Not only did my soul feel rejuvenated: my body had acquired such strength that I nearly ran up the steep and rugged trail. I realized that I wasn't alone: the elder was with me, for I felt him at my side. I could feel his presence in my soul, although, in fact, I was no doubt in his. On the days that followed, I felt the elder keeping me company and making every moment peaceful, profound, sweet, and beautiful, through the power of the Holy Spirit. When I saw him several days later, he said, "I've been with you every day—could you tell?" In awe, I responded, "How could I not tell, elder?" It would have been easier to ignore the shining sun than to ignore such an intense experience. And yet, although everything that took place was so clearly supernatural, it all happened in a natural way, while I was living my daily life.

Elder Paisios in the Light of the Transfiguration

One day some time later, when I was leaving Elder Paisios's cell, I recalled something that was troubling me and I mentioned it to him: "Elder, that yogi, Niranjan, was able to produce a light." "What kind of light?" he asked. "Once, when we were all sitting around him, his body suddenly started to give off a golden-yellowish light in the form of a continually expanding sphere, which eventually engulfed us all. I wasn't the same afterwards—it altered my way of thinking. What was that light?"

Without saying a word, the elder gently lifted up his hand and placed it on my head. Suddenly, the entire yard was flooded with a light that welled forth from the elder and could be seen in all directions. It was as powerful as a flash of lightning, but it was continuous, showing no sign of passing away. Although it was intense, it didn't hurt my eyes. On the contrary, I couldn't get my fill of looking at this sweet, immaterial, noetic light. And, although the light was supernatural and rare—not like a white light, but more like glass, or water—there was still something so very natural about it that it didn't startle me, but instead granted me a profound sense of joy. This light was all-embracing and intoxicating, yet it left my movements peaceful and my mind extremely lucid. Although I was absorbed by the vision of this light, I continued to see my natural surroundings. My five senses continued to function normally, while alongside of them another sense, a spiritual kind of vision, had begun to function as well. Although it was around noon and the sun was shining brightly, when the immaterial light began to emanate from Father Paisios, the sun's light seemed weak by comparison, like that of the late-afternoon sun.

I didn't say a word, but I understood many things. Afterwards, when I reached the Monastery of Koutloumousiou, the monks could see that I was deeply changed and asked me, "You're coming from Father Paisios, aren't you?" I nodded my head. This experience left a mark on my soul that I can still feel twenty years later, even though the intensity of my feelings waned within a few days. It left my soul with a sweet peace, which deeply changed me in a mystical, hidden way.

Truly, if I had remained ignorant of the light that came forth from the elder, I would have remained impressed by the enchanting light of the yogi—which was, in fact, truly remarkable. But after my experience, I naturally made the comparison between the light of Niranjan and the light of the elder. These two lights were as vastly different as an old piece of tin differs from a bar of solid gold, as falsehood differs from truth, and as man differs from God. The elder's invincible light not only surpassed the light of the yogi, but it utterly prevailed over it. I had already heard so much from the elder about the light of the yogis, but words just weren't sufficient to grant me true understanding, so he had granted me this spiritual gift so that I could understand the difference by experience.

Once, when I was speaking with the elder about the lights that one sees during meditation, he told me, "We don't want to see those kinds of lights, so we turn away from them. When I was at the hermitage of Saint Epistimi in the Sinai desert, I would leave my cave at night and go to pray at a neighboring peak, from which I could see the monastery. I would hold a lighter in my hand that I would light every so often so that I could see where I was walking on the rocks. One night, when I had walked a few steps from the cave, there appeared a light as bright as a spotlight that illumined the whole region as though it were day. I realized that it was from the evil one and said to myself, 'I don't want to see that kind of light,' and I returned back to the cave."

As powerful as my experiences with the elder were, his words were of great value as well. Of course, I can do no more than express what I understood of his words, along with the writings and spoken teachings of other spiritual strugglers. From these, I gathered that the spiritual phenomena I had experienced were a result of the natural receptivity of the human soul to both divine grace and demonic influence. On this plane, all depends upon a person's free will, in accordance with which he opens the gateway of his soul to Christ or to the devil. When people trample on their conscience, *the law written in their hearts*[1] by God in order to guide them towards the good, they alienate themselves from Him, the source of

---

[1] Romans 2:15.

goodness and light. Their minds grow dark and they commit sins that give the devil the "right" to linger around them—and this is how people find themselves under demonic influence.

If they continue further along this path, the evil spirits will enter them and they will become demonically possessed. But the elders on Mount Athos had also known people, such as sorcerers and Satanists, whose minds were so perverse that they wanted the demons to enter them and actually invoked the demons so that the devil would come and seize their souls. Some were motivated to do this because they lusted for power over others—so that others would admire them and be obedient to them. And, often, they desired worldly goods and sinful pleasures in order to satisfy whatever other passions might dominate them.

In any event, when a person has become open to demonic influence, the devil can indeed grant him, or rather exercise through him, the considerable power the devil naturally possesses as a spirit. Thus, such a man might gain great physical capabilities, such as were possessed by the man who had an unclean spirit in the country of the Gadarenes, who was able to break his chains into pieces.[1] He might be able to alter his appearance, to speak with peculiar voices, to cause himself to levitate, or to make lights or different objects appear. He may seem to be able to foretell events, and he may be able to reveal a person's hidden sins, amazing and frightening his hearers with his knowledge of the past. Moreover, acting through the demons, such a man can exploit others' imaginations in order to form images and sounds in their minds, and can also bring about striking physical effects, such as cracking a mammoth tree or shattering a large boulder. I knew these phenomena well.

Nevertheless, the elder told me, Christ has bound the

[1] Cf. Mark 5:1–13.

devil, so that he cannot wreak all the havoc that he desires. "The most insignificant demon has such power that he could make the entire earth collapse with a stroke of his tail, but God does not allow it." On another occasion he said, "Suppose the president were speaking on the balcony before a crowd of thousands watching him from below. If God permitted the devil to appear on that balcony for just one moment, they would all drop dead from fear."

And yet, despite the terrifying visage of the devil in his true form, a person who has opened his soul to the devil's power may appear to be quite virtuous. The elder referred to a passage from the New Testament: *For such are false apostles, deceitful workers, transforming themselves into the apostles of Christ. And no marvel; for Satan himself is transformed into an angel of light. Therefore it is no great thing if his ministers also be transformed as the ministers of righteousness; whose end shall be according to their works.*[1]

On the other hand, when someone approaches God by keeping His commandments and participating in the Mysteries of Christ, God comes to abide in that person's soul. With the keeping of Christ's commandments, man shows his love for God, and when a man loves Christ, he will keep His words, and His Father will love him, and They will come unto him, and make Their abode with him.[2] Then man's soul is so closely united with God that he and God become one: *He that is joined unto the Lord is one spirit.*[3] Thus, man's soul experiences *theosis* and acquires by grace those traits that are God's by nature: immortality, light, glory, knowledge of the future and the past, dominion over matter, authority over illness, and much more.[4]

[1] 2 Corinthians 11:13–15.
[2] Cf. John 14:23.
[3] 1 Corinthians 6:17.
[4] In Orthodox theology, *theosis* (deification) is a process in which man truly participates in the life of God, is united with Him in a communion of

*But we all, with open face beholding as in a glass the glory of the
Lord, are changed into the same image from glory to glory.*[1] In such
a person, the light of Christ that is present in his soul is so intense that it also illumines his body, so that when that person so
wills for reasons he knows best, he can reveal his soul's glory to
others. He does so even as Christ revealed His divinity to His
three disciples on Mount Tabor: *Jesus taketh Peter, James, and
John his brother, and bringeth them up into an high mountain
apart, and was transfigured before them: and His face did shine as
the sun, and His raiment was white as the light.*[2]

In time I realized that Father Paisios could also be numbered
in the company of these God-bearers. By his words, deeds, and
life, he manifested the light of Christ—and, when there was a
need, he also manifested it in a special, supernatural way.

Spiritual Warfare in the Army

I had stayed on Mount Athos for about six months, from
March until September, after my return from India. But, at the
beginning of October I left, because I had to report for the military service required of all men in Greece.

I left only about ten days before I had to report for duty,
because I was afraid that I would get mixed up with my old
friends on my old stomping grounds, and return to my former
ways. And yet, although I avoided going out, the telephone
rang off the hook with old friends, especially some former

love, and becomes Godlike. The path to *theosis,* which was closed at the fall,
has been opened again to man through Christ's incarnation, death and
resurrection. The classic exposition of this doctrine was provided by the
fourth-century theologian Saint Athanasius the Great: "God became man
so that man might become god." The Orthodox Church emphasizes that
the believer does not become God by nature, as is Jesus Christ; rather, he
becomes one with God through God's grace or energies working in him.

[1] 2 Corinthians 3:18.

[2] Matthew 17:1–2.

female acquaintances who were relentlessly looking for me. I turned out to be easy prey to the evil one's slightest temptation, because I still found sin irresistible, and so I was gradually seduced into taking up old habits after all. Naturally, my self-destructive ways caused me much pain and distress. This time, however, I knew about repentance and confession, so I went to my spiritual father in order to be able to stand on my own two feet and fight the good fight. Of course, the elder's prayers supported me greatly in my struggle to overcome, with the power of God, those temptations that I found so powerful.

Unfortunately, my previous dissolute life had given the devil power over me and had terribly weakened my will-power which, in the face of sin, was now nearly nonexistent. It was as though an invisible power were dragging me into sin by force. Certainly, the devil, who strives to bind the human soul with the various passions, had my soul very tightly bound. My particular struggle, however, was more than a fight against sinful inclinations: I often felt the tangible presence of the demons around me. Sometimes, I could sense them paving the way to make sin easy and feasible. At other times, I could feel them making my flesh burn with passion, and predisposing others towards sin in the same way. From my life in the army I could provide many examples of what were nearly daily occurrences, but I will confine myself to three representative ones.

The first instance involved my struggle to live chastely. There was a girl who had fallen in love with me, and, during the few days between the time that I left the Holy Mountain and when I reported for military service, she was constantly on my heels. Although I turned her away, she persisted, until finally she became disappointed and returned to Canada, where she had been studying. It had now been months since we had been in the same vicinity, and I thought that I could relax from that particular trial, but I was mistaken.

While still fulfilling my military service, I received a three-day furlough in order to go to Thessaloniki to see my relatives. When I learned that the elder was visiting nearby, I joyfully went to see him as well. We talked, he gave me the traditional kiss of peace, and I got ready to leave. But, when I had walked a few feet away, he called me back and looked at me intently. I thought he wanted to tell me something else, but instead he kissed me again, but on the neck—once on the right side and once on the left side. And then he sent me away with the blessing of the Most Pure Virgin. I assumed this to be a demonstration of his love, which I was, as always, perfectly happy to receive—but it did seem odd of him to kiss me on the neck.

When I got home that afternoon, the telephone rang, and to my surprise the girl was on the line, and calling from Thessaloniki. "What are you doing here?" I asked. "I thought you were in Canada."

"I realized that you'd be here this week," she answered, "so I got on a plane yesterday and came to see you."

What could I tell her, now that she had traveled all the way from Canada for the sole purpose of seeing me? When she came over, she explained that she had come to Thessaloniki because she had had a strong feeling that she would be able to find me, although she didn't know why.

We drove to a scenic spot, where, though we started out just talking and joking around, gradually the mood grew sexual. I tried to resist, but felt myself caving in. She, meanwhile, had become drunk with desire and was throwing herself into my arms. I would push her away, but she would come back with a vengeance. At a certain point, I felt as though we weren't alone: there was an evil spirit keeping us company and completely overpowering the girl with a degree of lewdness that I had never seen before. But, although I realized there was a demonic presence, I wasn't intimidated; I even felt indifferent. I was at the limit of my self-control and felt myself being conquered by lust.

Nevertheless, I made an effort and tore away from her in order to clear my mind. I walked around the car, so that we were separated by about twenty feet. Suddenly, I felt what seemed like a giant hand fondling me, making me light-headed with a rush of pleasure. The girl again drew near and pressed into my arms. When she began to kiss me, I felt too paralyzed to fight, even though I realized that the evil spirit was at our side and increasing our cravings. Inwardly, I had already given in.

Then, she kissed me on the neck, once on the right and once on the left—precisely where the elder had kissed me earlier. I pushed her away from me, suddenly angry at what we were doing. I felt as though we had committed a sacrilege, with a sensual kiss defiling the holy kiss of the elder, and the temptation was over.

My anger and indignation came from a sense I had that that kiss was deeply disrespectful of the elder, a sort of assault against his dignity—almost as though it harmed him. It was impure, while his love had been utterly pure. Now I understand that, had I been more mature spiritually, I would have seen that it was not for the sake of the elder that I should have had the reaction that I did. I should instead have been indignant at the insult to Christ, the source of the elder's holiness and purity (and, indeed, of purity itself). And I should have been angry at a situation that insulted—rather, that harmed—*me,* by taking me further from Christ, the Source of that divine life and love into which I had just begun to enter.

And yet this was a true beginning for me, a crucial moment—for it was the first time in my life that I had been able to overcome evil spirits. Before that day I did not know that I was capable of this, and so I lived in fear of them. But the elder had greater confidence in me and, rather than warning me to avoid the battle, he armed me and left the fight in my hands. And so it was that, with my decision against the enemy, I saw that his great power is far less than the power that comes from one's resistance to him.

(As for the girl, though she obviously was not a believer at that time, she later had some extraordinary experiences that made her question her lifestyle and, with the power of Christ, begin a new life as a conscientious member of the Church.)

When I later told the elder about the girl knowing that I was to be in Thessaloniki, he told me, "When someone has a close relationship with another person and a lot of love, the soul can know things like that from far away. But many times the devil gets involved and makes a mess out of everything. He'll whisper to a boy and a girl about going someplace, and they go there and run into each other. Then he does the same thing with another place, and he keeps it up until they say, 'Hey, there's something special about what's happening to us,' so he can throw them into sin in the end. The tempter's a great movie director. That's why you shouldn't pay attention to coincidences like that, because otherwise you might get tricked. If it's from God, He'll find another way to let you know, one that's even more clear."[1]

The second incident from my time in the army involved my struggle at the time of prayer. After curfew when the soldiers would go to sleep, I would sometimes go to some isolated place

[1] *Author's note:* When the elder spoke of "sin" in the context of sexual love, I initially found it perplexing. My friends and I viewed this love as something quite precious, giving beauty to human life in a dreary world, and I wondered why the Church put such limitations on it. And so I once asked the elder about this. He spoke to me at length, and then concluded, "If you cut a bunch of grapes from the vine, they won't mature—they'll go bad and rot. It's the same way with this love: if you cut it off from the Mystery of Marriage, where it would be nourished by the grace of God, sooner or later it'll turn sour and end up warped in one way or another."

in order to pray. I would use my prayer rope and say the prayer, "Lord Jesus Christ, have mercy on me." One night, after I had started praying, I suddenly felt a spine-chilling presence that left my body covered with goose bumps. Although I realized that some demon was approaching me, I wasn't frightened, but simply continued to pray. The evil presence, however, became increasingly fierce, and suddenly I felt two clammy yet powerful hands take hold of my heart and my throat, and begin to strangle me. In terror, I cried out, "Saint Arsenios, help me!" It immediately stopped and moved away from me. I felt calm, reassured, and happily continued my prayers.

The third incident took place at my army camp in Evros. I had found an isolated open hangar, where I would go to pray after nightfall when no one else would see me. On one such evening, I had trouble concentrating while saying the Jesus Prayer. I remained standing and continued to try, but my mind would just wander hither and yon. Since I wasn't able to pray with my mind, I decided to pray with my body by making some prostrations—after all, I reasoned, prostrations are a kind of physical prayer.

I had barely managed to make ten prostrations when I was engulfed in a light like a golden, reddish fog. I could see it and could feel its chilling and spine-tingling presence: an evil spirit was making an open attack. Immobilized by fear and in a quandary as to what I should do, I chose to leave rather than to get myself into trouble. At the time it seemed like a good idea—I was at a disadvantage then because I had lately committed some serious sins, which had given the devil power over my soul, and I felt my weakness. But I later repented for my cowardice in fighting him.

I went to bed and fell asleep, naïvely believing that the storm had passed. In the days that followed, however, I didn't feel well. I was dizzy, drowsy, and weak. Suspecting that I was running a slight fever, but uncertain just what my ailment was, I went to see a friend, the army doctor, for an examination. Although he examined me carefully, he couldn't find anything wrong. My condition continued for some time, making it difficult for me to fulfill my military duties. Between the dizziness and drowsiness, I wasn't able to pay attention to my work. In the meantime, the doctors were beginning to attribute my condition to psychological factors. But this was hardly a satisfactory explanation, because I wasn't upset about anything at the time. On the contrary, I was otherwise quite content.

After the passage of two to three months in such a state, I had stopped praying, because I found it too difficult. In fact, I even had difficulty reading the newspaper. One day, I decided to open an Old Testament that I had in my desk drawer and read a few pages, since I wasn't able to pray. To my astonishment, I wasn't able to distinguish the letters, and I suddenly felt so nauseous that I had to lay my head on the desk so that I wouldn't fall from my chair. At this point, I realized that I was under a demonic influence. I put the Old Testament on my head and asked the Lord for some divine consolation. When I finally came to, I decided that, now that I knew what was wrong with me, I had to find a way to see the elder.

I eventually saw him while on furlough. I asked him, "Elder, would you make the sign of the Cross over me? I don't feel well. It's as though someone has thrown a net over my head and is pulling it towards the ground. I'm dizzy and drowsy all day long." The elder lovingly embraced me and held my head against his chest, making the sign of the Cross over my head three times. That was all it took—at once, I felt entirely better.

I told the elder all about the red light and my ensuing condition. In fear, I asked him, "Elder, does the devil really have such power?" And he answered, "We are the ones who give him that power, by our sins." Indeed, most Christians never have—or are even aware of—such experiences with the powers of evil, because they have not given the devil authority over them by immoral living or witchcraft, yoga, and related activities. In shame, I recalled my many and grievous sins of late, and afterwards I went to confession.

At the Athonite monastery of Stavronikita, I once chanced upon a layman who used to hold an important administrative position in the Hare Krishna movement. When I met this young man, who was only a few years older than I was, he had returned to Christianity. He told me how much he suffered, for years, at the hands of the devil when he tried to escape from his tyranny. My own fears and illnesses were minor in comparison with what he had gone through: all the faculties of his soul had been under the devil's dominion. Fortunately, the older monks helped him immensely. "If it had not been for Father Paisios," he once confided in me, "I wouldn't have been able to escape."

A Blessing from Elder Porphyrios

During part of my mandatory service, I was stationed in Athens, and I often made the one-hour trip to see Elder Porphyrios at the monastery he had built outside the city, where he lived the last years of his life. Each day, a crowd of people would go to see him. In fact, the central bus agency had created a special stop on their route known as "the elder's stop," on account of the number of pilgrims who daily requested to get off at the monastery. When I would go to see him, even before I reached the monastery I could often feel the sweetness of grace that came from being encircled by his prayers. When he would make the sign of the Cross over me, I would feel *the peace of God, which passeth all understanding.*[1] In his presence, all my needs, even my physical needs, were met mysteriously, miraculously, and effortlessly.

[1] Philippians 4:7.

For example, there was public transportation available for going to the monastery, but not for returning from it. This was a problem that constantly put me in danger of being thrown into the detention center. However, in spite of the fact that there were usually no vehicles on the road after dark when I would have to return, I would always find some car that would pick me up, and often the driver would take me right to the army camp. I put my trust in the prayers of the sick elder lying nearly motionless in his bed, and he took care of me.

After I told my Athonite spiritual father about the many wonderful things that happened to me around Elder Porphyrios, he asked, "Since you love Father Porphyrios so much, why don't you ask him to make your knee better?" My right knee had been injured years before, when I used to train in Kung Fu and was kicked in a match. This had damaged my cartilage, causing my knee to swell and retain fluid under the kneecap, which resulted in a sharp pain that made movement difficult. Since this injury had been seriously aggravated by army exercises and marches, I had gone to the military infirmary for an examination, and the doctors had determined that I should take one month's sick-leave so that I could have a knee operation.

In the meantime, however, I went to see Elder Porphyrios, and recalled my spiritual father's suggestion. So I said, "Elder, my spiritual father says that you should make my knee better." "Well," he said, "all right, since your spiritual father says so." Although he was lying in bed, he raised his weak hand in the form of the priestly blessing and made the sign of the Cross over my knee. I felt a sweet, gladsome power tenderly touching my knee and penetrating to the very marrow of the bone. Then, I started to wonder what would happen to the water molecules—if they would disappear by the action of God's grace. This scientific question, or presumptuous curiosity, made me continually follow the progress of my knee after I left the elder, whether I was walking around or having a conversation. I wanted to perceive the moment when God would act. Three days went by, but my knee wasn't any better. I was still in pain when I moved, and I began to be troubled by thoughts and doubts about whether anything would happen. At a certain point, however, I got fed up with my doubts and told myself, "You loser, all you're interested in is miracles—as if miracles were for the likes of you." And so I forgot about the whole matter and stopped paying attention to my knee.

One morning, about a week later, I awoke in the military dorm and was stretching in bed, when I realized that my knee hadn't been bothering me for some time. I moved it and felt no irritation. I got up and began jumping up and down. Normally, in its damaged state, my knee would have bothered me after two or three jumps, but this time I felt no soreness whatsoever. I went out in the yard of the camp and ran about a hundred meters without any pain. Tears of joy and gratitude came to my eyes. God had healed me when I stopped believing that I would get well, so that I would realize that it was a gift from God and not the product of my own faith. The next few days I paid attention to my knee and noticed no irritation. Without noticing anything strange happen, I had become completely well without any fanfare, secretly, in a sacred mystic way, as divine grace is wont to act.

Years have passed since then. The scheduled operation never took place, and my knee has never bothered me again. On my very body I carry around living evidence that Father Porphyrios was a charismatic elder, and at times of faltering faith I stroke my knee and remember the all-powerful and most-sweet compassion of God and His saints. This bodily benefit thus became a source of spiritual strength and a sacred reminder of a contemporary saint.

Indeed, I have known many people who have told me about miraculous interventions that took place by the prayers of Elder Porphyrios. One acquaintance of mine, for example, had a brain tumor and went to get the elder's blessing two days before he was to fly to England for the scheduled operation. The elder made the sign of the Cross over the man and told him to chant the supplicatory canon to the Most Pure Virgin, that she might remove the tumor. Two days later, the English doctors and my acquaintance were shocked when they were not able to locate the tumor after repeated examinations. So, the man returned without having the operation and continues to lead a normal life. On account of this miracle, he stopped dabbling with Hindu philosophy and magic, becoming a genuine and conscientious Christian.

Another man I met had been suffering from a sort of thoracic cancer, which disappeared when the dear old elder made the sign of the Cross over his chest. Since he was unmarried and had no other obligations, this man stepped down from his job and devoted the rest of his life to the service of Christ.

A third person, a close friend of mine, broke her neck in an automobile accident. The X-rays indicated that the bones in her neck were fractured and the doctors said that she would never be perfectly well. Several months later, when she had recovered well enough to stop running back and forth to the hospital, a few people told her that she should visit the elder and get his blessing. The elder made the sign of the Cross over her and told her to take off her supportive neck collar. She did, and she had new X-rays taken, which showed that everything was normal—to the great astonishment of her doctors, who stood gaping at the old and the new X-rays. Twenty years have gone by, and she remains completely well, glorifying God, Who is wonderful in His saints.[1]

The elder had other gifts as well. For example, he told another friend of mine that there used to be a monastery near my

[1] See Psalm 67:35.

friend's native village. Although the elder had never been to the region, he gave my friend precise directions to the area outside of the village, so that he could go and find the ancient monastery, which by then had been hidden beneath the earth and forgotten even by the villagers. The elder described it to my friend as though he were looking directly at the landscape, describing the rock formations and the trees. My friend went to the place and found everything exactly as the elder had described.

Another Encounter with Demetrios

Demetrios[1] and I met again shortly after I completed my military service, while I was visiting the island of Aegina to venerate the relics of Saint Nectarios. On that day, as I knelt in a small chapel, venerating his holy skull, the saint bestowed on me a gift that completely filled me. Grace from his presence enveloped me and intoxicated me. I walked around the courtyard and in the room where he had lived, and I felt much spiritual joy. I felt that my soul had come into contact with the saint, and I felt a sense of familiarity, even intimacy, as if I knew him. On that day our relationship became fast and firm. I was in a state of spiritual bliss, joy, and peace. I could feel Saint Nectarios's presence, along with the joy and absence of fear that arise when we are certain that the saints are with us.

I was in this condition when I boarded the hydrofoil to go back to Athens, pondering this gift I had received. What could it mean? It was then that I saw Demetrios on the deck, sitting off on his own, reading in a chair. I thought that I should speak to him. The saint's gift to me became associated in my mind with the person of Demetrios.

So I walked over to him, and we took up our conversation

---

[1] That is, the Freemason mentioned in chapter 1 above.

where we had left off five years earlier. Three points from this conversation remain in my memory, because of the deep impression they made on me at the time. Like me, Demetrios had also gone to Aegina to pay homage, but at an ancient pagan temple.

I told him about my trip to India, emphasizing this aspect of my life. "How are you doing?" I asked. "Are you still just studying, like you used to, or have you started practicing the things you're reading?"

"Of course I'm not just studying. We get together regularly to practice witchcraft techniques."

Naturally, I already knew this, but his open declaration, not typical of Greeks involved in the occult, struck me. Of course, he was under the impression that he was speaking with someone like himself. He had left his old job and found a new one using his connections with Masonry, around which his interests and hence his life revolved.

I told him, "I visited the Monastery of Saint Nectarios. That place is filled with energy. You should go and check it out for yourself."

"No way. I'm not going there. It's not my style. It's the opposite of where my soul leans. I just don't like that place—I find it repulsive."

I was both surprised and deeply saddened. How could there be people who felt like that? How could they dislike the grace of God so bluntly and categorically? I had felt such joy and peace in the saint's presence. He must, I thought, speak this way out of ignorance.

I told him about my experiences and described in detail what I was still feeling. I admitted that I had changed and become a Christian.

"Okay," he replied, "Christianity is a very exalted philosophy, but as a religion it doesn't have anything to offer."

Although I always had wanted to believe that such

THE GURUS, THE YOUNG MAN, AND ELDER PAISIOS

arguments were used exclusively out of ignorance, our lengthy conversation, in which I had the opportunity to explain the Christian Faith to him, convinced me otherwise. We disagreed many times, although I no longer recall over what points. But one of his comments stands out in my mind. It was said with such an insane obstinacy that I gave up trying to persuade him. He told me, "If what you are saying is true, then I would rather be in hell with the devil." It's true what they say about the effects of one's inner choices in this life. The doors of hell are closed from the inside.

The Jesus Prayer and the Hindu Mantra

Prayer, by reason of its nature, is the converse and union of man with God, and by reason of its action upholds the world.

— Saint John of the Ladder[1]

One of the greatest spiritual gifts that Elder Paisios gave me was his guidance along the mystical path of the Jesus Prayer. This started at the beginning of our acquaintance and continued until his repose twelve years later. The Jesus Prayer consists of the repetition of the phrase "Lord Jesus Christ, have mercy on me."[2] The Jesus Prayer is not recited as a mantra, but as a prayer to the Person of Christ.

Prayer, as I learned, is a relationship between two persons, God and man, who move towards each other. Thus, the swiftness or slowness with which a person advances in prayer depends on both the human and divine wills. Neither the freedom of God in His sovereignty nor the freedom of man in

[1] *The Ladder of Divine Ascent,* step 28.1 (Brookline, Mass.: Holy Transfiguration Monastery, 1979), p. 212.

[2] The Jesus Prayer is also said with the words "Lord Jesus Christ, have mercy on me, a sinner," or "Lord Jesus Christ, Son of God, have mercy on me, a sinner."

his free choice are ever violated. For his part, man offers his good intention, his labors, and his desire to draw near to God. God, in turn, offers His grace.

No matter how great a man's ascetic labors may appear before the eyes of men, his offerings are infinitesimal in contrast with what God offers. Man takes one step, and God responds with a thousand in order to bridge the gap. Nevertheless, man's small and insignificant step in God's direction is absolutely crucial, because it reveals man's intention and good disposition, giving God the "right" to approach him, without infringing his spiritual freedom. Unlike the hate-filled, tyrannical devil, God deeply respects human freedom and never violates it, because He loves man. He desires a relationship of love with man, and love can exist only when people are free.

In the beginning, when I would say the Jesus Prayer I would often feel bored, tired, and drowsy. Then, by the prayers of the elder, God would give me some "sweets" from His "pastry shop." He would approach me like a gentle spiritual mist, immediately changing the disposition of my soul. An ineffable peace would make me feel as light as a feather, so that I would cheerfully desire to say the prayer, and I would pray with relish. This happened relatively frequently. Once it was so intense that, for two days, I literally hungered and thirsted for God. I wanted to pray, to say the Jesus Prayer, to delight in ruminating on God, and to have my fill of Him. The more I would say the Jesus Prayer, the greater my hunger and yearning for God would grow. Thus, by the elder's prayers, the uphill climb became a downhill stroll; the difficult was made easy, and the arduous pleasant. This is how I began to pick up momentum and to continue to work at this blessed labor of prayer.

Occasionally, when I would venerate the wonder-working icons on the Holy Mountain, I would feel a sweet soreness in my heart as though it were pierced. I felt something similar at the end of a vigil in honor of a certain saint. These phenomena always had a beneficial spiritual impact on me. The elder told me, "The saint gave you a treat for his feast day." At other times when I would pray, I felt as though my heart opened up like a flower. Once when I was alone and felt inexplicably oppressed, I went to my room, knelt down and told God, "Dear Lord, please comfort me a little." I hardly managed to finish saying that, when God made His presence tangibly felt with His grace comforting me deeply. That is when I realized what a tenderly compassionate Father we have—a Father Who would hear the prayer of someone so insignificant, who had so many times embittered Him. On yet another occasion, the prayer "Lord Jesus Christ, have mercy on me" started to repeat itself in my heart on its own without any effort on my part. The elder said that the motor of my heart had been set in motion and that such phenomena are gifts of God's grace. At such moments, he advised that one quietly and attentively listen to the inner self-acting prayer.

The elder would often give me various spiritual gifts that would open my mind to understand the Gospel and give me a nudge towards a higher quality of prayer. Once, when I was in the yard behind his cell, he took me by the hand and with a smile joked, "Wouldn't you like a gift?" I timidly lowered my head and answered, "I don't know, elder—you know what's best." With much joy and love, he looked at me, and I quite literally felt a fire inflaming my heart and making it warm. This burning sensation is mentioned by the Holy Fathers[1] when they speak about the variety of manifestations of Divine grace: a purifying or burning grace for beginners, an illumining grace for those in an intermediate state, and a deifying grace for the perfect. The Gospel also refers to this in the passage about Christ's appearance after His Resurrection to two of His disciples on the road to

[1] The term Holy Fathers (or Holy Mothers) refers to Christians now departed whose life and teachings exemplified the Christian Faith.

Emmaus: *And beginning at Moses and all the prophets, He ex-pounded unto them in all the Scriptures the things concerning Him-self.* And when *He vanished out of their sight ... they said one to another, did not our heart burn within us, while He talked with us by the way, and while He opened to us the Scriptures?*[1]

I had been praying the Jesus Prayer for several years when suddenly something unforeseen took place—it was as though I had a mental block that completely prevented me from saying the prayer. In contrast, when I would pray "Most Holy Theotokos, save me," that prayer flowed smoothly and nearly on its own. This change raised questions in my mind, making me recall the vow I had made to the Most Pure Virgin when I was in the ashram of Satyananda at Munger and frightened by the spiritual attacks I was suffering: "O All Holy Virgin, deliver me from this place and I will devote my entire mind to thee, leaving it in thy hands, and daily chanting 'To Thee, the Champion Leader.'"

So I thought that this mental block was a sign that now, at an appropriate time, the Most Pure Virgin was seeking from me the fulfillment of my vow. I related the story of my vow to Father Paisios and he agreed. Naturally, I followed the elder's advice and continued in prayer to the Virgin Mother of God.

In a short while, the Most Pure Virgin rewarded me abun-dantly. One night while I was standing under an olive tree and saying the prayer, my *nous*[2] was suddenly seized, leaving me speechless and motionless, in a passive state of wonder. It was as though I were taken up on high into a spiritual heaven where I beheld gray-colored images that resembled

[1] Luke 24:27, 31–32.
[2] As noted above, *nous* is a Greek word usually translated as "mind" or "intellect." In Orthodox Christian tradition, it refers not to man's rational faculty, but to his highest faculty, by which he directly perceives spiritual realities.

black-and-white photographs. These images portrayed an immense and sweet light, bright from the light of a greater Light within it, the fount of Light, which I could not see. Around this immense light there were also smaller lights resembling sparks, moving serenely. I gradually came to an inward certainty that the immense light was the Most Pure Virgin, radiant with the Light of the Holy Trinity shining forth from within her. She was so much more exalted, pure, and magnificent than all of God's other creatures, that the holy angels and archangels appeared as mere sparks or as lowly burning candles in the presence of the summer's noonday sun. She had advanced so far in the likeness of God that there was a vast spiritual gap between her and the rest of creation. This is when I understood why Saint Andrew of Crete referred to her as "god subsequent to God, having the second place after the Trinity."[1] All of this took place within a few moments, but moments immersed in eternity.

When I returned to my normal consciousness, I was standing under the olive tree in the midst of the night. Later, I happily went to tell the elder, even though I knew it was hardly necessary. He was quite pleased for my sake. When we talked about what I had realized regarding the sacred figure of the Theotokos, he confirmed all my thoughts.

The elder had seen the Most Pure Virgin many times and had spoken with her. He told me, "When I was at Saint Epistimi on Sinai,[2] I wanted to travel to Greece at one point, but I couldn't put my papers in order no matter how hard I

---

[1] Nikodēmos Hagioreitēs (St. Nikodemos of the Holy Mountain), *Theotokarion* (Thessaloniki: Ekdotikos Oikos Vas. Rogopoulou, 2007), p. 177 (in Greek). The quoted text appears in the third verse of the Prosomia (Stichera) in the Plagal of the First Tone for Sunday evening.

[2] *Author's note:* Saint Epistimi is the name of a hermitage where the elder lived for about a year and a half in a cave. It is located on Mount Sinai and is about an hour's walk northeast from Saint Catherine's Monastery.

tried. I was in terrible distress, and I prayed, 'Most Pure Virgin, I have helped so many people in this life—now isn't there anyone to help me?' As soon I said that, the Most Pure Virgin appeared before me and said, 'Don't be troubled. I'll take care of you myself.' She then took my papers in her hands and put them in her bosom."

"Elder, were you able to leave afterwards?"

"In a few days, everything worked out smoothly and I returned to Greece."

"And how did the Most Pure Virgin look, Elder?"

"Radiant and robed in golden garments."

When yogis claim that the Jesus Prayer resembles their own mantras, they are in fact trying to fit the Jesus Prayer into their own Procrustean bed. Of course, there are similarities, but there are also enormous differences—both a table and a horse have four legs, but to conclude that they are consequently the same would be an error of the crudest sort. But this is just the kind of error the yogis make when they claim that the Jesus Prayer is a kind of mantra. A brief examination of the essential differences between the Jesus Prayer and a mantra should provide those with an open mind the wherewithal to draw the proper conclusions.

First, consider how the Orthodox tradition understands the meaning of the Jesus Prayer: "Lord Jesus Christ, have mercy on me." The word "Lord" is the name for God most frequently encountered in the Old Testament in the oft-repeated formula "Thus saith the Lord ..." or in the commandments: *I am the Lord thy God.* When Orthodox Christians call Jesus Christ, "Lord," they are confessing that He is the God of the Old Testament Who spoke to the patriarchs—Abraham, Isaac, and Jacob. The Word is the Person who gave the law to Moses. In other words, the One who spoke to the prophets was none other than the second Person of the Holy Trinity, Who later took flesh and was united with human nature in the Person of Jesus Christ. Furthermore, when we say "Lord Jesus Christ"—with faith, with all our heart's strength—we come under the influence of the Holy Spirit, as Saint Paul says: *No man can say that Jesus is the Lord but by the Holy Spirit.*[1]

Having recognized the existence of the true personal God outside and beyond his own self, from this God a Christian asks "mercy." The elder once told me, "Mercy contains all things. Love, forgiveness, healing, restoration, and repentance all fit within the word 'mercy.'" It is the mercy of God that brings about repentance, purification from the passions, the illumination of the *nous,* and, in the end, *theosis.* From my journey I have learned that salvation comes from the mercy of Christ, the unique Savior of mankind, rather than from my intelligence, my prideful endeavors, or the techniques of yoga. Salvation and *theosis* are so very precious that it is impossible for anyone to make any effort or do any ascetic labor that would be equivalent to even the smallest fraction of their value.

Indeed, from my conversations with other fathers who were laborers in the Jesus Prayer and from my own experience, I know full well that prayer is a gift from God. Nothing is accomplished by human labor alone, for Christ said, *Without Me ye can do nothing,*[2] and as the Apostle James bears witness, *Every good gift and every perfect gift is from above, and cometh down from the Father of lights.*[3] Even as God granted us existence, in the same way He gradually grants us to know Him and be united with Him through prayer, leading us ultimately to life eternal.

Now, consider how the yogis view a mantra. First of all, there are many mantras, and each refers to one of the many

[1] 1 Corinthians 12:3.
[2] John 15:5.
[3] James 1:17.

gods of the Hindu pantheon such as *Krishna, Rama, Vishnu,* or the goddess *Kali.* There is not one standard explanation given by yogis for the mantras; rather, their explanations are tailored to the receptivity of each listener. For beginners who are not disposed to worship idols, yogis give a pseudo-scientific, mechanistic explanation: they claim that the benefit accrued by repeating the mantra is due to certain frequencies produced by its pronunciation, which cause spiritual vibrations that activate spiritual centers within man. (However, the existence of such centers in man can only be taken on faith—if someone willingly *chooses* to believe such a claim.) For those who are inclined towards psychological interpretations, the yogis present the repetition of a mantra as a type of auto-suggestion that enables the practitioner to program his inner world according to positive models. When addressing those who have become more involved with Hinduism and now believe in many gods, the yogis claim that the worshipper receives the blessing of whatever god is being invoked.

What constitutes the infinite distance separating the Christian Jesus Prayer from the Hindu mantra, however, is that which lurks behind the name of the god being invoked in a mantra and invited into the soul. Through the mouth of the Holy Prophet David, God declares, *All the gods of the nations are demons*[1]—in other words, behind the names *Krishna, Rama,* or *Shiva* are demons lying in wait. Once they are invoked by the use of the mantra, the door is open for the devil to begin his theatrical productions, using sounds, images, dreams, and the imagination in general in order to drag the practitioner deeper into deception.

Another significant difference between the Christian Jesus Prayer and the Hindu mantra is the diametrically opposed viewpoints of the two faiths regarding techniques and the

---

[1] Psalm 95:5.

human subject. I recall a conversation I had with Niranjan after he had given me permission to begin to practice some supposedly powerful yoga techniques. I said to him, "It's fine practicing the techniques, but what happens to the human passions of greed, lust for power, vainglory, and selfishness? Aren't we concerned about them?" "They disappear," he replied, "through the practice of the techniques." "Do they just disappear like that, on their own?" I asked. "Yes, they disappear automatically, while you are practicing the techniques."

What an astonishing assertion: physical exercises can wipe out the inclinations that a person's soul acquired in life through conscious choices. But, in reality, man, as a self-determining and free moral agent, can change the conscious aspect of his personality and his moral sense only by the use of his own free will to make conscious decisions in real-life situations. Any external means to automatically induce such a change in a person's consciousness without his consent circumvent man's free will, obliterate his volition, and destroy his freedom, reducing man to a spineless puppet manipulated by a marionettist's strings. Hinduism's relentless insistence on properly performed techniques with automatic results degrades man by depriving him of his most precious quality: the self-governing free will. It restricts the boundless human spirit within a framework of mechanical methods and reflexes.

Orthodox Christian Faith, on the contrary, recognizes and honors the gift of human freedom as a divine trait. This recognition and approach help man to be actualized as a free being. Precisely on account of the human freedom to choose, man's often-unpredictable responses can't be limited to the mechanical reflexes of a closed system, but can innovatively turn in any spiritual direction that he, as a free subject, wills. This is why Orthodoxy is not adamant about techniques and methods. In freedom and with respect, Orthodoxy seeks the human heart, encouraging the individual to do what is good for the sake of the good, and pointing out the appropriate moral stance of the soul before God, which an individual can then freely choose to embrace.

Genuine spiritual development entails a deepening familiarity with God and with one's own self, acquired through moral choices that a person *freely* makes in the depths of his heart. Spiritual progress is a product of man's way of relating to himself, to his fellow man, and to God by the good use of his innate moral freedom. This is why Christ calls out, *If any man wills to come after Me, let him* freely *deny himself* [1]—that is, without being deceived, without being psychologically compelled, and without being forced, all of which are inappropriate to the spiritual nobility of Christian life.

Father Porphyrios had a small parrot that he taught to pray in order to illustrate the absurdity of some Christians' empty repetition of the words of prayer, as well as the ridiculousness of the opinion commonly presented in Eastern religions that someone can make moral advances by physical exercises or breathing techniques. Every so often, the parrot would mechanically say, "Lord, have mercy." The elder would respond, "Look, the parrot can say the prayer, but does that mean that it is praying? Can prayer exist without the conscious and free participation of the person who prays?"

Spiritual War

Even before I met the elder, I instinctively knew that a tremendous and terrible war is being waged on the earth, in every corner of the planet. The battlefield on which this war takes place is the human mind and the human heart. Either our decisions, our choices, and the way in which we deal with events in our lives point us towards life, knowledge, and joy, or else we proceed in error towards death, ignorance, pain, and grief.

[1] Matthew 16:24, Luke 9:23.

Our enemies' hatred for us is fierce. Their desire is to utterly destroy us, and so, with cold calculation, they devise treacherous plots in order to lead us to ruin, misery, and ultimately death. They attempt to capture the human mind, blocking any window capable of admitting the light of real knowledge—which would let a person appreciate his own greatness and worth. They would persuade the mind to sell itself cheap, for a glittering bauble, so to speak. These enemies are not impersonal entities. They have faces and names, belonging to the same genus and species. They are cunning, unscrupulous, and work unceasingly to achieve their aim. They do battle with the human race as a whole and with each person individually. We have just about been conquered by them: humanity is under their subjugation, if not completely, then to a great extent.

Over the centuries a considerable number of people have gone over to the side of these enemies of ours, either voluntarily or because they were deceived by them. Some of these now find themselves under these enemies' direct power, serving them, doing their work, and expediting their schemes. In exchange they are often helped by them materially in this life. For example, they might find jobs easily, or acquire power over others or wealth. But, though they have material things, they do not have peace, so in the end they cannot really take joy in what they have and find satisfaction. Indeed, they live in danger, in a deep and permanent state of fear. For their masters have a hatred for them as humans, and to these masters they exist to be used—and discarded, as they often are, once they have served their purpose.

There have been, however, individuals who have discovered and unmasked these hidden enemies of ours, people who saw the extent of their cunning as well as the degree to which they dominate the world. These individuals have chosen to resist them, not intimidated by their power or afraid of the effort or danger involved—for all such people are sure to find

HOME AT LAST

themselves objects of special coercion. In this fearsome battle they prefer to die on their feet, resisting rather than surrendering. Such people, as far as I am concerned, are true heroes, who endure the hardship of the front lines in order to make things somewhat easier for those of us at the rear. A good number of them have put our enemies to shame, defeating them in individual combat—and making them tremble with fear. For what our enemies dread most is that the rest of humanity might come to know about these victories, and that other people might follow this example.

Thus, our enemies do not just hate us but also fear us—not because of who we are, but because of who we might become. That is, they hate and fear us because of our potential, which so greatly exceeds their own. Every one of us wages war on the field of battle, and victory and defeat occur on an individual basis. And, although a victorious warrior, who has freed himself from the enemy's influence, is able to advise us, the desire to move forward depends on us. We have to provide the willingness, as warriors, to struggle. Once that is present, help is there, powerful help. Father Paisios was indeed a warrior of this sort.

Holy Communion and the Centrality of Christ

And Jesus came and spake unto them, saying, ... Lo, I am with you alway, even unto the end of the world.
—Matthew 28:18, 20

Elder Paisios always stressed that Christ God is everything, and that he himself was merely His disciple. This is why he always tried to remain inconspicuous, seeking neither personal glory nor followers. The elder truly had many capabilities, but his sole concern was to guide those who approached him away from his own person and towards Christ alone.

287

Because I was under the influence of a Hindu way of thinking, in which every guru tries to portray himself as god incarnate, I was initially confused in my understanding; but, through the prayers of the elder, I came to realize that the Person of Jesus Christ is at the center of all things. Christ was the source of Father Paisios's life and strength. I once asked him about this. He answered me, "My child, I'm just a human being. I pray to Christ and He replies. If His grace abandoned me, I'd be just another bum on the streets of Omonia."[1] And this is precisely what Christ proclaimed in the Gospel: *Verily, verily, I say unto you, He that believeth on Me, the works that I do shall he do also; and greater works than these shall he do.*[2] And, elsewhere, *Without Me ye can do nothing.*[3]

Initially, I would look at the priests of the Church with doubts and suspicion. "Father Paisios is a saint and has many spiritual gifts," I would tell myself, "but what kind of spiritual power does an average, overweight parish priest have? Can he really grant spiritual gifts like the elder, or is he in fact an entirely lesser person?" The answers to these questions were given to me in time, when I once received Holy Communion amidst a large crowd in an average parish church.

I had fasted, gone to Confession, and said my prayers before Communion as usual, but this time, when the priest placed Holy Communion in my mouth, I felt Christ Himself flooding my entire being, body and soul. Christ the Creator united Himself more intimately and more deeply with me, the work of His hands, than is possible for two people in this world to be united. People are physically separated by the boundaries of their own skin. Even an embryo is separated from its mother by the wall of its newly forming skin. Christ,

---

[1] Omonia Square in Athens, known at that time for being populated by drug addicts, prostitutes, and thieves.

[2] John 14:12.

[3] John 15:5.

however, became one with me on a deeper level, in a unique union. His Blood literally merged with my blood; His Body literally was fused to my body, so that my hands, my feet, my eyes, and all the other parts of my body had become members of the Body of Christ.

His heartwarming peace pervaded my entire soul, making it leap for joy in a state of wonder. After the passage of so many centuries—and after I had committed so many sins—Christ God ineffably condescended to come and palpably dwell within me, making me for a short while a God-bearer. I was in awe at His manifest presence in my mind, soul, and body. It was beyond my comprehension how this took place, but I knew then that such a union with Christ was possible and always would be.

I was so moved that I was no longer able to remain standing. So, I went to my place, where I tried to hold back the sweet tears of joy at being one with Christ, Whose great love had bridged the ontological gap separating divine and human nature. Nearly two thousand years ago, our sweetest Lord Jesus declared, *He that eateth My Flesh, and drinketh My Blood, dwelleth in Me, and I in him.*[1] And lo, on this day, my union with God was the personal, yet unfathomable, fulfillment of those words. And once more, Christ tells us for all time why He condescends to be united with us in this Mystery: *Whoso eateth My Flesh, and drinketh My Blood, hath eternal life; and I will raise him up at the last day.*[2] Looking towards the last day and eternal life, Christ loves us so much that He gave us this great offering, because He desires for us to become like Him even in His divinity, living with Him for all eternity.

An all-consuming love for all of us, in every generation, led God the Word to become man, to call us His friends and

[1] John 6:56.
[2] John 6:54.

brethren,[1] to open the way towards *theosis* with His Resurrection, and to freely and bountifully offer Himself to us at every Divine Liturgy. *Jesus Christ, the same yesterday, and today, and forever,*[2] as perfect God wrought all things in perfection. That is, Christ brought to completion the work of man's salvation once and for all, so that there would be no need for supplements, corrections, or adjustments with the passage of time. The life-giving and effective Mysteries that Christ instituted have been present in the Church for two thousand years, granting eternal life to the faithful. And, *at the last day,* those who recognized this life-giving path but neglected to follow it will be without defense.

This experience made me realize the truth of the Church's teachings: Christ is the Head of the Church, the Fountain of her life, and the Center of her sacramental worship. With the descent of the Holy Spirit, the Church was gathered under the auspices of the Apostles whom Christ had sanctified to be the ministers of His Mysteries. Through ordination to the priesthood, this special blessing to celebrate the Mysteries of Christ was passed down to the priests of the Church from generation to generation without break or interruption.

A priest can celebrate the Mystery of the Divine Liturgy without being a saint, but a saint who is not a priest cannot do so. Elder Paisios, for example, who was not a priest, could not celebrate the Mysteries of Christ, even if he could work a thousand miracles. He would bend his holy neck under the priest's stole for the Mystery of Confession, and would wait with yearning for the priest to celebrate the Divine Liturgy so that he could commune. Like a nursing child receiving life from his mother's milk, so the elder received life from the divine grace of the Mysteries of the Church, the mother of all Christians. He also was a product of the Orthodox Church, one of her

---

[1] Cf. Matthew 12:49, John 15:15.
[2] Hebrews 13:8.

most radiant children, in whose person shone forth the virtues and the might of Christ Who sanctified him. Truly, *Wondrous is God in His saints.*[1]

The Christian Mysteries and Magic

Having personally experienced both the Christian Mysteries and magic, I can affirm that there is nothing magical about Holy Communion or the other Mysteries of the Christian Faith. The Mysteries are performed with the power of Christ and require conscious and voluntary participation. In order for Christ to act within the divine Mysteries, the communicant has to will to participate in the Mystery consciously: he must yearn for it, and he is required to prepare for it with personal struggle. This is why those who nonchalantly approach the Mysteries out of habit experience very little change, if they experience anything at all. When, however, a person manifests his desire for God and his assent to being united with Him by taking pains to repent sincerely, God in turn will approach the genuinely repentant one to the extent and degree that He knows will be beneficial for that person's soul.

The importance of conscious participation in the Mysteries of Christ can be seen in the elder's response to a man who foolishly boasted about communing frequently. The deluded fellow pridefully thought that he had become holy, because he would commune two to three times a week. The elder told him, "Look here, it's not so important how often you commune. What's most important is how you prepare yourself and then, afterwards, how much you tend to Christ Who's living inside you. If people were sanctified just by frequent Communion, then all the priests who commune every Sunday and during the week would be saints."

[1] Psalm 67:35.

An Experience of God, "Who is Everywhere Present and Fills All Things"

Once I had the great blessing of driving Elder Paisios somewhere in my car. Sometimes, in the presence of his unaffected simplicity, natural kindness, sense of humor, and great humility, I would forget myself and get carried away in a familiarity that bordered on audacity. I would view the elder simply as my father, momentarily forgetting that God dwelt constantly within him, and that, as a God-bearer, he had attained to the furthest reaches of human existence. I would forget how with a word he could cast out demons and make incurable diseases vanish, how his face would shine like the sun before me, and all the rest of the endless string of gifts with which the Holy Spirit had adorned him. So on that day, in my bold forgetfulness, I asked, "Elder, tell me about God. What is He like? Speak to me."

The elder didn't say a word, so I simply continued to drive up the curving mountain road in silence. Suddenly, I began to feel God's presence everywhere: in the car, out in the hills, and to the reaches of the farthest galaxies. He was "everywhere present and filling all things," without being identified with any of them. He permeated everything, without being mixed or confused with anything. Being Spirit, the ever-existent God permeated the material cosmos, without ever being identified with changeable matter. Being Spirit, God dwelt in the eternity of an infinite present containing past, present, and future. This reminded me of what I had once read in the works of Saint John of Damascus: "We believe, then, in One God, one beginning, having no beginning, uncreated, unbegotten, imperishable and immortal, everlasting, infinite, uncircumscribed, boundless, of infinite power, simple, uncompound, incorporeal, without flux, passionless, unchangeable, unalterable, unseen, the fountain of goodness and justice, the light of the mind."[1]

Indeed, His power is everywhere present, yet beyond all perception and beyond the reach of arrogant human attempts to discover it, able to be known only when it reveals itself. This power is what brought the trees, the mountains, the stars, and man himself into existence and what sustains them. In a moment, this power could make them all vanish without any uproar, any tumult, or any resistance, as easily as the flick of a light switch can plunge a well-lit room into total darkness.

Simultaneously, I felt in my heart that God's almighty power is also infinitely noble, with a refinement that could never allow His power or His presence to pressure anyone. Although He is so very near us, He remains unseen, so that we feel neither weighed down nor obligated even by His presence—for He in no way wishes to restrict us, but instead desires us to be completely free to do as we wish. He not only avoids compelling us through fear, power, and might, but He even avoids swaying us with His beauty, His love, and the irresistible sweetness of His presence. He does this out of an unfathomable respect for human freedom. Of course, He loves us with a fiery love and desires to draw us towards Himself, resorting to manifold other ways that reveal His boundless wisdom, personal attention, and tender loving care for each one of us. Indeed, the vastness of the universe which He watches over in no way lessens His love and concern for us. In turn, He seeks, but does not demand, our love, which can be found only with complete freedom.

My soul felt such joy, contentment, and repose in the presence of God, Who is so simple, yet so mysterious. I now understood what one of the Church Fathers meant when he wrote about how God becomes all things for those who love Him:

---

[1] *An Exact Exposition of the Orthodox Faith* 1.8 ("Concerning the Holy Trinity"). *Nicene and Post-Nicene Fathers*, 2nd series, vol. 9, p. 6.

nourishment, clothing, rest, comfort, knowledge, strength, and all the rest. The hope that, when I would die, I would live near Him brought me such joy that I yearned for death if death would mean being with Him. At the same time, I feared that my sin and vices might separate me from Him forever.

How could I not be moved by God's fervent love, which persists in spite of the fact that our virtues are as naught in the presence of His myriad gifts? He tenderly loves us in spite of the fact that we have so many foul vices that should inspire only loathing. Even though we have become stingy in the presence of His generosity, crafty in the presence of His wisdom, greedy in the presence of His kindness, and prideful in the presence of His dominion, He endures our vices and our folly, loving us and desiring to grant us beauty, wisdom, and strength. Unfortunately, we deny the gifts of God, for, in the end, we don't want these gifts as much as we want to follow the passions—even knowing the destruction to which they lead.

In God's embrace, I was filled with a deep calm that cast out all fear. Resting in the palm of His almighty hand, I had nothing to fear, for He knows all things in perfect wisdom and love. I felt a certainty about the origin of this world, its path through time, and its ultimate destination. And I rejoiced, for I knew that in the end He would be victorious and that His kindness and holiness would prevail.

I wasn't in this state very long—perhaps for about two or three miles along the winding mountain road—but it was a very distinctive state, set apart from other altered states one experiences under the influence of alcohol, drugs, pleasure, pain, distress, or fear. It was as though someone lifted a veil from my mind, enabling my soul to live, not in a different world, but in the same world—the same world in its entirety. Like a deaf man who suddenly begins to hear the sounds of the world surrounding him, like a blind man who suddenly begins to see the images and colors of this world, hitherto invisible, in like manner I suddenly began to sense God in the world, with all the immeasurable wealth, beauty, and significance that this sensation contained. For a moment, I was taken out of the tomb of my passions and lived as man was meant to live. I imagine that in an earlier age such a sensation was more common among the sons of men. In Paradise, before man's spiritual senses were damaged by the fall, Adam and Eve no doubt had an even more vivid sense of God's presence than I did at that time, since Holy Scripture relates how they saw, heard, and spoke with God. Alas, the thick scales of vice have now coated my spiritual eyes and the muck of sin has stopped up my spiritual ears.

It is certainly worth noting that the elder responded to my request to hear a few words from him with fervent prayer that moved God to grant even a wretch like me such an inestimably rich and bountiful experience. How greatly the elder must have loved me in order for him to have prayed so ardently for me! In truth, the elder's generosity was in emulation of the generosity of our Lord, God, and Savior Jesus Christ.

At a certain point, I began to tell the elder what I felt, but he wouldn't speak and didn't want me to speak either. Like a fool, I kept on talking—showing him, as it were, his own backyard.

My sensitivity gradually diminished and eventually disappeared, but this gift made me immensely grateful to our Lord Jesus Christ. As paradoxical as it may seem, I simultaneously felt deeply satisfied by and unquenchably thirsty for the One Who enabled us to call Him Father; immensely joyful at knowing the true God and heartrendingly sorrowful at losing the One Who calls us His children.

Epilogue

After all that had happened, there had been born in my soul a wish to live only for Christ, in the most spiritual and focused way possible; and so I had a desire for the monastic life. However, I wasn't sure that I had the strength for it. When I asked Father Paisios about this, he said, "Some people are meant for monasticism, other people are meant for marriage, and others can take either road. As for you, you could become a monk or get married. You have to choose on your own what gives you peace."

Thus, these two paths remained before me, and for a number of years I was unable to choose between them. I tried four times to become a monastic—that is, I became a novice monk on four separate occasions—but each time I encountered problems. The final time I became a novice, it was with a very spiritual community located a short distance from Elder Paisios. It was an ideal situation, and I was full of gratitude. Indeed, it was the best period of my life, and I made great spiritual progress, such as I never had before. But at long last it seemed that I had passions which prevented me from entering upon this high and spiritual manner of living. And so I changed course and decided to marry.

The elder always loved me, no matter what. When he saw my sorrow because of my inability to embrace the monastic life, he said to me, "I will always love you, and so will your wife, and so will your children; and I will pray for them."

And so I married and had children, and I chose a career. I live in the world as an Orthodox Christian, trying, as much as

Elder Paisios leaving Mount Athos to visit spiritual children,
November 5, 1993.

possible, to live a life pleasing to Christ and to participate in
the Holy Mysteries.

I was blessed by God to be regularly in the company of the
elder until his departure from this life. And until the present
time not even a day has passed without my thinking of him,
and often. His assistance has been ever with me, directing me
to the Lord, and he has helped me with many difficulties, both
practical and spiritual, as I have struggled to follow Christ.
Our relationship is living and, I believe, unto the ages, just as
he promised it would be.

Once, when I was filled with joy upon seeing him after a
long separation, the elder, who was also very joyful, said to me,
"This joy is nothing compared with what we'll experience
when we meet in heaven." When the elder spoke of heaven, he
spoke from experience. This heavenly man, this earthly angel,

was a gift of God to our age. As one who emulated Christ, and in whose soul Christ was formed, he revealed Christ to us.

May we all have his blessing.

A Final Word

Having spoken so strongly regarding the events that I experienced in India, I would like to make it clear that I have acquired a great love for the Indian people, whom I only wish I could aid in their great poverty and pain. I met many good Indian people who were caring and altruistic. Elder Paisios used to say, "The Indian people have spiritual depth, and they're spiritually restless. They don't fill their heart with nuts and bolts. They yearn for God, but they're in a deception—the devil deceives them and cripples them. If the Indians came to know Christ, with the heart they've got, they'd make great spiritual progress." My experiences make me object to their spiritual tradition, but not to the people. My objection is ultimately an objection to the devil, who hides behind the gurus' supernatural activities. I pray that Christ will deliver the people of India from an evil tyranny and lead them into Paradise. My heartfelt prayer is that they come to know Orthodoxy, that they come to know Christ, and that they be released from the stranglehold of the caste system in which the Brahmanic tradition has placed them, in order to make spiritual progress and to know joy.

APPENDIX ONE

Testimonies from Greek Orthodox Spiritual Fathers

The following testimonies about the present book and its author were written by respected spiritual fathers in Greece and Cyprus who were in close spiritual contact with Elder Paisios of Mount Athos.

From Metropolitan Athanasios of Limassol, Cyprus

GREETINGS

This book, written by a man dear to my heart, describes events he has personally experienced. Therefore, one could even say he was obliged to record his recollections, in order to help those who are seeking the true light, who search for the Truth and for authenticity in their lives, so they might not be lost.

I too can testify to what he has written, because I was an eyewitness to many of the events that he describes: since I lived on the Holy Mountain at that time, I played a part in the development of his relationship with the righteous Elder Paisios. I already knew much of what is written here, but I nevertheless encouraged him to record it, so that it would not be lost.

Seeing the benefit that so many have received from this book, I truly rejoice and bless the name of God, Who made us worthy to see firsthand this saint of our days, Elder Paisios; and

I call down his prayers upon us all, that we may ever live in the light of Christ's presence and of His love.

With my blessings,
✠ Athanasios of Limassol[1]
Holy Metropolis of Limassol
March 23, 2005

From Archimandrite Theoklitos of the Holy Monastery of Saint Arsenios, Northern Greece

It gives me great satisfaction to see the worthy volume *The Gurus, the Young Man, and Elder Paisios* published in the English language. The success it has had in other countries—in Greece, Russia, Romania, and elsewhere—promises success also in the English-speaking world. Many souls have benefited from it, and many more will benefit from it.

The author's dozen-year-long relationship with the holy Elder Paisios, his apprenticeship under the elder and his close disciples, and his lengthy stay on Mount Athos, in the holy ascetic home of this charismatic brotherhood, helped him to understand subtle, yet crucial, spiritual matters. For a quarter-century, he has been a conscious member of the Orthodox Church, living within its bosom and being nourished by the

[1] Metropolitan Athanasios lived for many years as a monk on Mount Athos, where he received spiritual guidance from Elder Paisios. At that time known as Father Athanasios, he is the priest-monk of Koutloumousiou Monastery mentioned in chapter 2 of the present book, who first told the author about Elder Paisios and encouraged him to meet the elder.

In 1993, a year before the Elder Paisios's repose, Father Athanasios returned to his native Cyprus to found monasteries. In 1999 he was consecrated to the episcopate and appointed as Metropolitan of Limassol in Cyprus. He features prominently in the popular books by Kyriacos C. Markides, *The Mountain of Silence* (2001) and *Gifts of the Desert* (2005), where he is referred to pseudonymously as "Father Maximos" (about these books, see pp. 306–7 below).

Holy Mysteries, seeking ever-closer union with God. I know and love him.

Because this book is a record of genuine personal experience, I believe it can speak directly to truth-loving readers and help them understand the spiritual wealth, the depth and breadth, and the spiritual nobility of the Orthodox Faith. This Faith is not a human ideology or philosophy, but a divine gift to those who seek the truth.

Since the author has had personal experiences of Eastern spiritualities, and—through the prayers of the blessed Elder Paisios—of the grace of the Holy Spirit, he is in a position to illustrate clearly and distinctly the differences between them.

I hope that the equally valuable second part of the book, more theoretical than biographical, will in time be published as well.

Archimandrite Theoklitos
Abbot of the Holy Monastery of Saint Arsenios[1]
Vatopedi, Halkidiki, Greece

From Hieromonk Euthymios of Mount Athos

The author of *The Gurus, the Young Man, and Elder Paisios* traveled a difficult road in his quest for a spiritual relationship with the personal God, finding himself disappointed by the false promises of Eastern religions. His search was sincere, and so God did not abandon him, making provision for him to come to know the Holy Mountain and to meet Elder Paisios. He found in the elder a man cast in the mold of Christ. He felt his love and was helped through his prayer and by his counsel.

---

[1] Archimandrite Theoklitos, as abbot of the above-mentioned Monastery of Saint Arsenios (see p. 13 above), not far from Mount Athos, had close spiritual ties with Elder Paisios, from whom he received guidance for himself and his brotherhood.

His ideological confusion was put to rest, and he realized that the only true God and savior is Christ Who became man, and that the Orthodox Church is the steward of revealed truth and of saving grace.

As he sought to live the Orthodox spiritual life, he also gave thought to the hazards and lack of knowledge that endanger young people. Moved by sympathy for them, he recorded his experiences in book form with the blessing of Elder Paisios. The work, written in a lively style, attracts the reader's interest.

Elder Isaac[1] read the manuscript along with his brotherhood, and they contributed their observations. They found it to be a beneficial work, worthy of being published in order to help young people especially. In fact, many people of different ages have been helped by it to avoid the sufferings that the author underwent. It is my hope that the readers of the English translation will receive benefit from it and will find the sure road that leads to eternal life. Amen.

Hieromonk Euthymios
of the brotherhood of Elder Isaac[2]
The Hermitage of the Resurrection
Kapsala, Mount Athos

---

[1] Elder Isaac of Mount Athos (1936–1998) was a close spiritual son of Elder Paisios, and directed his monastic brotherhood according to Elder Paisios's guidance. He is the author of the definitive biography of Elder Paisios, first published in Greece in 2004 (see p. 303 below).

[2] As a member of Elder Isaac's brotherhood, Hieromonk Euthymios knew Elder Paisios well. He helped Elder Isaac write the biography of Elder Paisios, and was instrumental in completing the work after Elder Isaac's repose.

Appendix Two

Suggestions for Further Reading

Elder Paisios of the Holy Mountain

While Elder Paisios is well known in Greece, and much has been published by and about him in the Greek language, he is only just becoming known to the English-speaking world. Some works by and about him have been published in English, and others still await English translation. The definitive biography of the elder, *The Life of Elder Paisios the Athonite* by Hieromonk Isaac (Mount Athos, 2004), consisting of over seven hundred pages in the original Greek, is expected to be published in English translation in the near future. The following books are available in English at the current time:

Christodoulos (Ageloglou), Priest-monk. *Elder Paisios of the Holy Mountain.* Mount Athos, Greece, 1998. A short biography of Elder Paisios, together with a soul-profiting collection of his teachings and some anecdotes from his life.

Middleton, H. *Precious Vessels of the Holy Spirit: The Lives and Counsels of Contemporary Elders of Greece.* Thessaloniki, Greece: Protecting Veil Press, 2003. A collection of lives and teachings of twentieth-century Greek elders, including a chapter on Elder Paisios and a valuable introduction to the whole phenomenon of eldership in the Orthodox

Church by a respected theologian of Aristotle University in
Thessaloniki.

Paisios, Elder. *Athonite Fathers and Athonite Matters*. Souroti,
Greece: Holy Monastery of the Evangelist John the Theologian, 1999. A treasury of stories from the life of the Holy
Mountain, many concerning persons and events with
which Elder Paisios was personally familiar.

———. *Elder Hadji-Georgis the Athonite, 1809–1886*. Souroti,
Greece: Holy Monastery of the Evangelist John the Theologian, 1996. Elder Paisios's biography of a renowned nineteenth-century elder of the Holy Mountain.

———. *Epistles*. Souroti, Greece: Holy Monastery of the Evangelist John the Theologian, 2002. A collection of letters of
Elder Paisios to his spiritual daughters, the abbess and
nuns of the St. John the Theologian Monastery in Souroti,
Greece.

———. *Saint Arsenios the Cappadocian*. Souroti, Greece: Holy
Monastery of the Evangelist John the Theologian, 1996.
The elder's intimate portrayal of the life of a priest-monk
recently glorified as a saint, who lived and served in Elder
Paisios's native village in Asia Minor. Saint Arsenios bap-
tized the elder and prophesied his future calling.

———. *With Pain and Love for Contemporary Man*. Souroti,
Greece: Holy Monastery of the Evangelist John the Theologian, 2006. The first volume to be translated from the elder's collected spiritual discourses.

Rakovalis, Athanasios. *Talks with Father Paisios*. Thessaloniki,
2000. Teachings of Elder Paisios on a wide variety of top-

ics related to contemporary life, recorded by one of his spiritual children.

Vigopoulou, Mersine. *From I-ville to You-ville.* Thessaloniki: Uncut Mountain Press, 2006. A children's book based on the teachings of Elder Paisios. Young and old alike can benefit from the simple yet profound lessons on spiritual life contained in this book, set within a captivating story.

Orthodoxy and Orthodox Spirituality

There is today much that can be recommended to the English reader by way of an introduction to the Orthodox Church, her spirituality, saints, and elders generally. Here is a partial list of books the inquirer may find helpful and enlightening:

Anonymous Russian pilgrim. *The Way of a Pilgrim.* R. M. French, trans. San Francisco: Harper San Francisco, 1991. A spiritual classic, *The Way of a Pilgrim* is an autobiographical account of a simple Russian pilgrim who sets out to learn how to "pray without ceasing." This book was made famous in the West by J. D. Salinger in his novel, *Franny and Zooey.* It is available in a number of different editions and translations—the above English translation, originally published in 1930, is the first.

Cleopa, Elder. *The Truth of Our Faith: Discourses from Holy Scripture on the Tenets of Christian Orthodoxy.* Thessaloniki, Greece & London, Ontario: Uncut Mountain Press, 2000. A renowned elder of twentieth-century Romania replies to a Lutheran's questions about Orthodox Faith and practice, citing extensively from his prodigious knowledge of Holy Scripture.

Damascene, Hieromonk. *Father Seraphim Rose: His Life and Works*. Platina, Calif.: St. Herman of Alaska Brotherhood, 2003. The biography of an American convert to the Orthodox Faith and his struggle to live out the "desert ideal" of Orthodox monasticism in northern California in the twentieth century. As a young man, Father Seraphim studied East Asian philosophy, immersing himself primarily in the Chinese philosophical tradition, before encountering Christ in the Orthodox Church.

Lossky, Vladimir. *The Mystical Theology of the Eastern Church*. Cambridge & London: James Clarke & Co., Ltd., 1957. Reprint. Crestwood, N.Y.: St. Vladimir's Seminary Press, 1976. Originally published in French in 1944, this classic work faithfully presents the Orthodox Patristic tradition in a manner that is both concise and remarkably deep. The theological language it employs may be rather dense for those just embarking on a study of Orthodox theology, who are therefore recommended to begin with *Orthodox Dogmatic Theology* by Fr. Michael Pomazansky (see below).

Markides, Kyriacos C. *The Mountain of Silence: A Search for Orthodox Spirituality*. New York: Doubleday, 2001. Markides, a Cypriot émigré to the United States, professor of sociology, and researcher of spirituality, records his conversations with an Athonite elder, "Father Maximos," who had been a disciple of Elder Paisios before returning to his native Cyprus to found monasteries. "Father Maximos" is a pseudonym for Father Athanasios, who in 1999 was elected to the episcopate and appointed as Metropolitan of Limassol in Cyprus (see the letter of Metropolitan Athanasios on pp. 299–300 above). Although *The Mountain of Silence* is marred by the interjection of the often confused opinions of Markides, the book is valuable for its faithful rendering of the words of Metropolitan Athanasios of Limassol, who hands down the teachings of Elder Paisios and offers profound teachings of his own based on what he acquired spiritually from the elder.

———. *Gifts of the Desert: The Forgotten Path of Christian Spirituality.* New York: Doubleday, 2005. A sequel to *The Mountain of Silence,* this book has the strengths and weaknesses of its predecessor. The highlight of the book is chapter 14, "Synaxis," which contains a transcription of an inspiring talk by Metropolitan Athanasios to the monks of the Panagia Monastery on Cyprus.

Pomazansky, Protopresbyter Michael. *Orthodox Dogmatic Theology.* 3rd ed. Platina, Calif.: St. Herman of Alaska Brotherhood, 2005. Originally written as a theology textbook for Orthodox seminarians, this book is more accessible than Vladimir Lossky's *Mystical Theology of the Eastern Church* (see above), and covers a broader range of topics, but it is not as in-depth in its treatment of certain areas of theology. Fr. Michael quotes abundantly from the Holy Scriptures and the writings of the Holy Fathers in presenting the unchanging teaching of the Orthodox Church.

Porphyrios, Elder. *Wounded by Love: The Life and the Wisdom of Elder Porphyrios.* Limni, Evia, Greece: Denise Harvey (Publisher), 2005. A book about Elder Porphyrios of Kavsokalyvia, who is featured in chapter 5 of the present book. Elder Porphyrios began his monastic life on the Holy Mountain but for health reasons lived most of it in Athens. A holy and grace-bearing elder like his contemporary, Elder Paisios, Elder Porphyrios was granted many spiritual gifts by God.

THE GURUS, THE YOUNG MAN, AND ELDER PAISIOS

Seraphim (Rose), Father. *God's Revelation to the Human Heart.* Platina, Calif.: St. Herman of Alaska Brotherhood, 1987. The transcription of a talk on spirituality given by this well-known American convert to Orthodoxy on the campus of the University of California at Santa Cruz shortly before his death.

Sophrony (Sakharov), Archimandrite. *His Life Is Mine.* Crestwood, N.Y.: St. Vladimir's Seminary Press, 1977. An in-depth treatment of Orthodox spiritual life by Elder Sophrony, the famous disciple of Saint Silouan the Athonite who founded the Monastery of St. John the Baptist in England. Like the author of the present book, as a young man Elder Sophrony delved into the practices of Eastern religions before returning to the Orthodox Christian Faith of his childhood. From his own experience, Elder Sophrony offers an extremely insightful comparison of the experience of the Personal God in Orthodox Christianity and the experience of a "Transpersonal Absolute" in Eastern religions. (See Part II, chapter 2, "The Jesus Prayer: Method," which also includes a comparative analysis of the Jesus Prayer and Hindu mantras.)

———. *Saint Silouan the Athonite.* Crestwood, N.Y.: St. Vladimir's Seminary Press, 1999. The life and teachings of one of the twentieth century's most renowned monks of the Holy Mountain, the Russian peasant Saint Silouan, as told by his disciple, Elder Sophrony.

———. *We Shall See Him as He Is.* Platina, Calif.: St. Herman of Alaska Brotherhood, 2006. The spiritual autobiography of Elder Sophrony, describing his experience of union with God (*theosis*) through grace, and the path of spiritual struggle and repentance leading to that union.

Theophan the Recluse, St. *The Spiritual Life and How to Be Attuned to It*. Safford, Ariz.: St. Paisius Serbian Orthodox Monastery, 2003. A series of letters written by one of the spiritual masters of nineteenth-century Russia to a young woman asking for his advice on how to live a spiritual life.

Ward, Benedicta, trans. *The Sayings of the Desert Fathers: The Alphabetical Collection*. Revised ed. Kalamazoo, Mich.: Cistercian Publications, 1984. One of the earliest sources of Orthodox monastic spirituality, *The Sayings of the Desert Fathers* is a collection of short stories and teachings by various monks and hermits of the fourth- and fifth-century Egyptian desert arranged in alphabetical order by their names.

Ware, Timothy. *The Orthodox Church*. 2nd ed. New York: Penguin Books, 1993. Although some Orthodox may quibble with certain of the author's statements, this book is still the standard introduction to all aspects of Orthodox history, life and teaching. Ware is an English convert to the Faith who was consecrated to the episcopate and is today known as Metropolitan Kallistos of Diokleia.

The Holy Mountain of Athos

Finally, there is a growing bibliography for those interested in the Holy Mountain of Athos itself, both for a scholarly and non-scholarly audience. Interestingly, much of the material produced before the 1970s has now been rendered somewhat obsolete by the torrent of renewal and fresh monastics the Holy Mountain has seen since that decade. Here are a few recommended works:

Alexander (Golitzin), Hieromonk, ed. and trans. *The Living Witness of the Holy Mountain: Contemporary Voices from*

Mount Athos. South Canaan, Pa.: St. Tikhon's Seminary Press, 1996. A wonderful introduction to the Holy Mountain, featuring a history of Athos, a description of Athonite life, and stories, teachings, and lectures by and about Athonite elders and monks.

Cavarnos, Constantine. *Anchored in God: Life, Art, and Thought on the Holy Mountain of Athos.* Athens: "Astir" Publishing Co., 1959. Reprint. Belmont, Mass.: Institute for Byzantine and Modern Greek Studies, 1991. Although this book was written long before the many changes in Athonite life over the last thirty years, it remains a fascinating look at many aspects of the Holy Mountain by a pious and learned pilgrim.

Cherubim (Karambelas), Archimandrite. *Contemporary Ascetics of Mount Athos.* 2 vols. Platina, Calif.: St. Herman of Alaska Brotherhood, 1992. A collection of the lives of nineteenth- and twentieth-century Athonite elders.

Hierotheos (Vlachos), Metropolitan. *A Night in the Desert of the Holy Mountain.* 2nd ed. Levadia, Greece: Birth of the Theotokos Monastery, 1995. Conversations with an Athonite hermit on the Jesus Prayer.

Joseph of Vatopaidi, Elder. *Elder Joseph the Hesychast: Struggles—Experiences—Teachings.* Mount Athos, Greece: The Great and Holy Monastery of Vatopaidi, 1999. An extensive and intimate life together with an account of the teachings of one of the greatest figures of twentieth-century Athonite life, by one of his last surviving direct disciples.

Speake, Graham. *Mount Athos: Renewal in Paradise.* New Haven, Conn.: Yale University Press, 2002. Perhaps the most comprehensive and informative introduction to the Holy Mountain, this book features a lengthy history of Athos, an account of its recent renewal, an analysis of its present-day achievements as well as problems, personal accounts of pilgrimages to the Mountain, and extensive, full-color photographs throughout. Graham Speake is an English convert to Orthodoxy and the founder of the Friends of Mount Athos Society.

ST. HERMAN OF ALASKA BROTHERHOOD

Since 1965, the St. Herman Brotherhood has been publishing Orthodox Christian books and magazines.

Write for our free catalogue, featuring over fifty titles.

St. Herman of Alaska Brotherhood
P. O. Box 70, Platina, CA 96076 USA

You can also view our catalogue and order online, at
www.sainthermanpress.com